AN ARAMAIC APPROACH TO Q

This is the first book to examine the Aramaic dimension of Q since the Aramaic Dead Sea scrolls made such work more feasible. Maurice Casey gives a detailed examination of Matthew 23.23–36 and Luke 11.39–51 and demonstrates that the evangelists used two different Greek translations of an Aramaic source, which can be reconstructed. He overturns the conventional model of Q as a single Greek document, and shows that Jesus said everything in the original Aramaic source. His further analysis of Matthew 11.2–19 and Luke 7.18–35 shows the evangelists editing one Greek translation of an Aramaic source. The same is true of Matthew 12.22–32//Luke 11.14–23, for which Mark (3.20–31) utilised a different Aramaic source. A complex model of Q is thus proposed. Casey offers a compelling argument that Aramaic sources behind part of Q are of extremely early date, and should make a significant contribution to the quest of the historical Jesus.

MAURICE CASEY is Professor of New Testament Languages and Literature at the Department of Theology of the University of Nottingham. He is a member of the *Studiorum Novi Testamenti Societas* and the author of *Aramaic Sources of Mark's Gospel* (Cambridge University Press, 1998).

SOCIETY FOR NEW TESTAMENT STUDIES

MONOGRAPH SERIES

General Editor: Richard Bauckham

122

AN ARAMAIC APPROACH TO Q

An Aramaic Approach to Q

Sources for the Gospels of Matthew and Luke

MAURICE CASEY

University of Nottingham

CAMBRIDGE
UNIVERSITY PRESS

PUBLISHED BY THE PRESS SYNDICATE OF THE UNIVERSITY OF CAMBRIDGE
The Pitt Building, Trumpington Street, Cambridge, United Kingdom

CAMBRIDGE UNIVERSITY PRESS
The Edinburgh Building, Cambridge CB2 2RU, UK
40 West 20th Street, New York, NY 10011-4211, USA
477 Williamstown Road, Port Melbourne, VIC 3207, Australia
Ruiz de Alarcón 13, 28014 Madrid, Spain
Dock House, The Waterfront, Cape Town 8001, South Africa

http://www.cambridge.org

© Maurice Casey 2002

First published 2002

Printed in the United Kingdom at the University Press, Cambridge

Typeface Times 10/12 pt.   *System* LATEX 2$_\varepsilon$ [TB]

A catalogue record for this book is available from the British Library

Library of Congress cataloguing in publication data

Casey, Maurice.
An Aramaic approach to Q: sources for the Gospels of Matthew and Luke / Maurice Casey.
   p. cm. (Society for New Testament Studies monograph series; 122)
Includes bibliographical references and index.
ISBN 0 521 81723 4 (hardback)
1. Q hypothesis (Synoptics criticism)   2. Aramaic literature – Relation to the New Testament.   I. Title. II. Monograph series (Society for New Testament Studies); 122.
BS2555.52.C37   2002
226′.066–dc21

2002024648 CIP

ISBN 0 521 81723 4 hardback

CONTENTS

Preface   *page* ix
List of abbreviations   x

1   **The state of play**   1

2   **Method**   51

3   **Scribes and Pharisees: Matthew 23.23–36//
     Luke 11.39–51**   64

4   **John the Baptist: Matthew 11.2–19//Luke 7.18–35**   105

5   **Exorcism and overlapping sources: Mark 3.20–30;
     Matthew 12.22–32; Luke 11.14–23; 12.10**   146

6   **Conclusions**   185

Select bibliography   191
Index of passages discussed   206
Index of names and subjects   209

PREFACE

This book was written in 1994–99. In 1994–96, I held a British Academy Research Readership awarded for me to write *Aramaic Sources of Mark's Gospel* (SNTS.MS 102. Cambridge, 1998), as well as this book. The publication of the rest of the Aramaic Dead Sea scrolls in 1994 enabled more fruitful work to be done than I had planned, but at the same time it ruined the proposed timetable for completing the two books. I am extremely grateful to the Academy for this award, which enabled me to complete a major piece of research, including all the Aramaic for this book as well as the previous one. Other duties and engagements have contributed to the subsequent delay.

I am also grateful to all those who have discussed with me the problems of method and of detail which this work has entailed. I effectively began this research while reading for a doctorate at Durham University under Professor C. K. Barrett, whose extraordinary combination of learning and helpfulness with lack of bureaucracy or interference remains a model to which one can only aspire. I would particularly like to thank also the late Professor M. Black, Professor G. J. Brooke, Professor B. D. Chilton, Professor J. A. Fitzmyer, Professor M. D. Goulder, Professor R. Kearns, the late Professor B. Lindars, Professor M. Müller, Professor C. M. Tuckett and Professor M. Wilcox. I would also like to thank members of the Aramaic Background and Historical Jesus seminars at SNTS, the Jesus seminar at meetings of British New Testament scholars, and an annual seminar on the Use of the Old Testament in the New now generally held at Hawarden, for what I have learnt from them. I alone am responsible for what I have said.

I would also like to thank Professor A. C. Thiselton, Head of the Department of Theology at the University of Nottingham 1992–2000, for his impartial and unfailing support of work; my Nottingham colleagues Dr R. H. Bell and Rabbi Dr S. D. Kunin for many hours spent sorting out problems with the word processors on which these books were written; and the libraries of Durham University, St Andrews University, SOAS and the British Library for the facilities necessary for advanced scholarly work.

ABBREVIATIONS

Most abbreviations are standard. Those for biblical books follow the recommendations of CUP; those for periodicals and series of monographs follow S. Schwertner, *International Glossary of Abbreviations for Theology and Related Subjects* (Berlin and New York, 1974); most others follow the recommendations for contributors to the *Journal of Biblical Literature* 117 (1998). Others are as follows:

ABRL	Anchor Bible Reference Library
ANRW	H. Temporini and W. Haase (eds.), *Aufstieg und Niedergang der römischen Welt* (many vols., Berlin, 1972–).
cur	Curetonian
DSD	*Dead Sea Discoveries*
ET	English Translation
hark	Harklean
JSP	*Journal for the Study of the Pseudepigrapha*
JSP.S	Journal for the Study of the Pseudepigrapha Supplement Series
MPIL	Monographs of the Peshitta Institute, Leiden
palsyrlec	Palestinian Syriac Lectionary
sin	Sinaitic Syriac

1

THE STATE OF PLAY

The present state of research into 'Q' varies from the chaotic to the bureaucratic. At the chaotic end of the spectrum, there is no agreement as to whether Q existed, nor as to what it was, if it did. At the bureaucratic end of the spectrum, an amorphous group of scholars have agreed that it was a Greek document. It was produced by a Q community, whose concerns can be worked out from it. Some of these scholars suppose that we can work out what this Q community did *not* believe from what was not in Q, to the point that the Q community did not have an atonement theology because Q has no passion narrative. Most scholars who believe this also believe that Q was the first Gospel, and that its picture of Jesus was that of some kind of Cynic philosopher. As we narrow down the group of scholars to more detailed agreements, so we see an increase in the number of common judgements made in the interests of a consensus of the group, with quite inadequate attention to evidence or argument. We also see the large-scale omission of Aramaic, the language in which Jesus taught.

The purpose of this book is to suggest that the use of Aramaic has something to contribute to the study of Q. In a previous book, I suggested that the Gospel of Mark consists partly of Aramaic sources which have been literally translated into Greek. Consequently, they can be partly reconstructed. In the light of recent research, including that stemming from the discovery of the Dead Sea scrolls, I sought to lay down the most fruitful way of doing this, and I exemplified this with reconstructions of Mark 9.11–13, 2.23–3.6, 10.35–45 and 14.12–26.[1] In this book, I propose to see what we can do for Q. After discussing the history of research, I consider again the most appropriate methodology for this kind of work. I then reconstruct and discuss the sources of Matt. 23.23–36//Luke 11.39–51 and Matt. 11.2–19//Luke 7.18–35. I turn finally to one of the 'overlaps' between Mark and Q, and discuss the recoverable Aramaic sources of Mark 3.20–30, Matt. 12.22–32, and Luke 11.14–23; 12.10. Throughout

---

[1] P. M. Casey, *Aramaic Sources of Mark's Gospel* (SNTS.MS 102. Cambridge, 1998).

these discussions, I continue the work of my previous book in that I seek to contribute not only to our understanding of Q, but also to the recovery of the Jesus of history.

We must begin with a critical history of scholarship. Here I do not seek to catalogue all previous work, but to select from the history of scholarship significant advances and mistakes, so that we can see more clearly how to proceed, and what pitfalls to avoid. One of the pitfalls lies in different definitions of what Q was, or is. For clarity's sake, I therefore anticipate one outcome of this book by giving the definition which I use when I conduct my own discussion of Q: Q is a convenient label for the sources of passages which are found in both the Gospel of Matthew and the Gospel of Luke, and which have not been taken from Mark's Gospel. It will be clear that this entails some controversial conclusions, and that we must be careful to note that it does not entail others. It implies that Q was not a single document, and that Luke did not take all his Q material from Matthew; I shall argue for both of these hypotheses in detail. It means that we can meaningfully discuss whether a passage such as Matt. 11.28–30 is to be described as part of Q; it is not found in Luke, but we could discuss whether it was in the same documentary source as Matt. 11.25–27//Luke 10.21–2, whether Matthew added it, whether Luke knew it or whether Luke left it out. It also means that our evidence for Q is found in Greek; it does not specify that this is, or is not, how it reached the evangelists. I shall argue that some parts of Q reached both evangelists in the same Greek translation, and that other parts are due to two different translations being made, whether by the evangelists, their assistants or by more distant sources.

From Holtzmann to Tödt

Serious modern research into Q effectively began with Holtzmann, though this is not what he called it. In a book published in 1863, he suggested that there was one source A behind the Triple Tradition of the synoptic Gospels, and a second major source behind the Double Tradition. This source he called Λ, which stood for λόγια.[2] At this stage, however, the priority of Mark had still not been established, nor had anyone shown

---

[2] H. J. Holtzmann, *Die synoptischen Evangelien: Ihr Ursprung und geschichtlicher Charakter* (Leipzig, 1863). For predecessors, cf. J. G. Eichhorn, 'Über die drey ersten Evangelien. Einige Beyträge zu ihrer künftigen kritischen Behandlung', in *Allgemeine Bibliothek der biblischen Literatur* 5 (Leipzig, 1794), pp. 761–996; F. D. E. Schleiermacher, 'Über die Zeugnisse des Papias von unseren beiden ersten Evangelien', *Theologische Studien und Kritiken* 5, 1832, 735–68; C. H. Weiße, *Die evangelische Geschichte kritisch und philosophisch bearbeitet* (2 vols., Leipzig, 1838), vol. I, ch. 1, esp. pp. 83–6.

what could be done with Aramaic. Meyer made the first major advance in our understanding of the Aramaic background to the synoptic Gospels in 1896. For example, he offered this reconstruction of Matt. 12.32:[3]

כל דיימר מלא על ברנש ישתביק לה וכל דיימר על רוחא דקודשא לא ישתביק
לה.

It is a great advantage that the complete sentence has been reconstructed, for this ensures that ברנש emerges as a normal term for man. It is also good that, even in an era long before the discovery of the Dead Sea scrolls, there are no problems with the late date of the Aramaic used. Moreover, the proposed reconstruction permits the understanding of Luke 12.10 as an alternative version of the same Aramaic. This might have led to important advances in our understanding of Q. Also helpful was Meyer's reference to Mark 3.28. This was, however, as far as Meyer went, even in the best book then written on the Aramaic background of the Gospels, and the best for another fifty years.[4] The important advances which might have flowed from this work were simply not made.

The massive variety of other comments from the same period of scholarship included some brief but useful points. It was at about this time that this source was called Q. This has been noted in the works of Simons in 1880 and Weiß in 1890, and became popular partly because of the work of Wernle in a notable book published in 1899.[5] Thus Wellhausen could describe it simply as a 'zusammenhangenden Quelle, die man mit Q bezeichnet'.[6] Among Wellhausen's own more enduring suggestions was that at Matt. 23.26 καθάρισον correctly represents the Aramaic *dakkau* (reinigt), whereas at Luke 11.41 τὰ ἐνόντα δότε ἐλεημοσύνην represents a misreading of the same word as *zakkau* (gebt Almosen).[7] This is plausible, and a useful contribution to the whole question of the relationship between

---

[3] A. Meyer, *Jesu Muttersprache. Das galiläische Aramäisch in seiner Bedeutung für die Erklärung der Reden Jesu und der Evangelien überhaupt* (Freiburg i.B. and Leipzig, 1896), p. 94.

[4] For further discussion of Meyer, and a critical *Forschungsberichte* of the whole Aramaic question, see Casey, *Aramaic Sources of Mark's Gospel*, ch. 1.

[5] E. Simons, *Hat der dritte Evangelist den kanonischen Matthäus benuzt?* (Bonn, 1880); J. Weiß, 'Die Verteidigung Jesu gegen den Vorwurf des Bündnisses mit Beelzebul', *Theologische Studien und Kritiken* 63, 1890, 555–69; P. Wernle, *Die synoptische Frage* (Freiburg i.B., Leipzig and Tübingen, 1899). Simons uses 'der apostolischen Quelle' in reference to the work of B. Weiss, abbreviates it to 'Q.', defined carefully as 'Die apostolische Quelle nach W.' (p. 22), and proceeds to use 'Q.', almost always with a full stop, as an abbreviation of this. Weiß uses 'Quelle' in its normal sense, meaning 'source', introduces Q in brackets for the Redenquelle (p. 557), and then simply proceeds to use Q as a symbol for the sayings source lying behind Matthew and Luke.

[6] J. Wellhausen, *Einleitung in die drei ersten Evangelien* (2nd edn, Berlin, 1911), p. 58.

[7] *Ibid.*, p. 27.

4 An Aramaic Approach to Q

the different forms of Q material.[8] At the same time, however, the fact that Wellhausen normally confined himself to single words meant that this was a very conjectural process, which could never lead either to a complete understanding of Gospel sources or to a proper understanding of translators. Wellhausen also commented on the possible language of Q. He noted that verbal agreement is sometimes so high as to require a Greek Q, whereas in other passages there are variants which may be explained as resulting from two translations of an Aramaic source.[9] It is the problems posed by this facet of the evidence that still require resolution.

A comprehensive attempt to reconstruct Q in Greek was made by Harnack.[10] Harnack began with those passages of Matthew and Luke which have the highest level of verbal agreement. This enabled him to argue that Q was a Greek document, and the argument from this first set of passages is very strong indeed. The similar argument for the next set of passages, in which the level of verbal agreement is lower, is more of a *tour de force*. Harnack argues that a single Greek translation was used by both of the evangelists, and that this was translated from Aramaic. He did not, however, supply the detailed argumentation which would be necessary to establish this position; indeed he has no detailed argumentation on the Aramaic question at all. This has been a constant defect of Q research ever since.

A major contribution to the study of Q was made by B. H. Streeter, most notably in *The Four Gospels* (1924).[11] One reason why this became a standard work is that it offered a complete solution to the synoptic problem, including decisive arguments for the priority of Mark. Streeter said very little about Aramaic, however. He treated Q as a document written in Greek, and discussed whether passages where there was considerable variation in wording between the Matthean and Lucan versions belonged to it. A most inadequate treatment of Aramaic is just squeezed into the discussion of the 'minor agreements'.[12] Here the changes which Matthew and Luke made to Mark's excessive use of καί, and to his equally excessive use of the historic present, are correctly seen as the reactions of

---

[8] See further pp. 23–4, 82 below.   [9] Wellhausen, *Einleitung*, pp. 59–60.

[10] A. von Harnack, *Sprüche und Reden Jesu. Die zweite Quelle des Matthäus und Lukas* (Leipzig, 1907); ET *New Testament Studies*, vol. II: *The Sayings of Jesus. The Second Source of St Matthew and St Luke* (London, 1908).

[11] B. H. Streeter, *The Four Gospels. A Study of Origins* (London, 1924). See earlier B. H. Streeter, 'On the Original Order of Q', in W. Sanday (ed.), *Studies in the Synoptic Problem by Members of the University of Oxford* (Oxford, 1911), pp. 141–64: 'St Mark's Knowledge and Use of Q', in Sanday (ed.), *Studies*, pp. 165–83: 'The Original Extent of Q', in Sanday (ed.), *Studies*, pp. 185–208.

[12] Streeter, *Four Gospels*, pp. 296–8.

two Greek writers to one whose Greek has been influenced by Aramaic. Moreover, this is correctly seen as the reason for those minor agreements which consist of them both doing so in the same passages. Streeter did not, however, offer any reasonable demonstration that Aramaic was really the cause of unusual features in Mark's Greek, still less of his bald assertion that 'Mark's Greek is that of a person who had been brought up to think in Aramaic.'[13] More centrally, he offered no proper discussion of the possibility of Aramaic sources of Q at all. He did not even consider the possibility that some passages might be the result of two translations of Aramaic source material.

Streeter also stored up future trouble by arguing that very little was omitted from Q by Matthew and Luke.[14] His arguments for this position carry no weight at all. His first is that Matthew omitted very little from Mark. This, however, demonstrates nothing, since Matthew might have preferred Mark because it gave a coherent outline for the ministry, but felt that it needed expanding with some more of Jesus' teaching. He could have selected from a massive Q what he needed for this purpose, making a somewhat longer Gospel, and leaving most of Q out. The mere fact that he edits most of Mark does not tell us the size of his Q nor how much of it he used.

Moreover, Luke did leave out a lot of Mark. Streeter's second argument is that Luke used a mutilated copy of Mark.[15] This omitted most of the 'great omission', going straight from Mark 6.47 αὐτὸς μόνος to Mark 8.27 καὶ ἐν τῇ ὁδῷ. Streeter's arguments for this view are absolutely arbitrary. For example, he suggests that it would explain Luke's omission of the place-name Caesarea Philippi as the scene of Peter's confession (Luke 9.18). But this is the only mention of Caesarea Philippi in the Gospels, and it is a long way north of Galilee in an area which Jesus is not otherwise known to have visited. Luke may therefore have omitted it because he thought it must be a mistake. In short, Streeter's argument assumes his result: he regards this view as probable only because he thinks sources are more likely causes of changes than editorial alterations. It is, however, most unlikely that a copy of Mark would be mutilated in this way, and that so assiduous a collector of information as Luke would be unable to obtain an unmutilated copy. We would therefore require strong evidence to believe this, and we have none at all. Streeter adds special explanations of Luke's omission of other pieces of Mark, such as that the pith of the long discussion of divorce (Mark 10.1–12) is given in the last two verses,

13 *Ibid.*, p. 297.   14 *Ibid.*, pp. 289–91.
15 *Ibid.*, p. 290, picking up on pp. 175–8.

for which Luke has an equivalent in another context (Luke 16.18).[16] This is quite misleading, for it still shows that Luke left out pieces of Mark. He is equally liable to have left out pieces of Q.

Most of Streeter's arguments that very little was omitted from Q by Matthew and Luke are of no weight for reasons of this kind. They also *presuppose*, rather than demonstrate, that Q was a single document. If it were several documents, Matthew and Luke might have included material from some documents and not from others because they either knew only some of them, or knew only Greek and not Aramaic, or because they selected some rather than others until they had sufficient material, or because they found some documents which fitted their purposes and others which did not. It follows that the treatment of Q in this standard and influential work is seriously defective. It omits any serious discussion of possible source material in Aramaic, and puts forward entirely spurious reasons both for considering it one unified document, and for imagining it as source material from which Matthew and Luke did not omit anything very much.

Burney included Q in his attempts to uncover Jesus' poetry.[17] For example, he devoted a whole chapter to 'The Use of Parallelism by Our Lord'.[18] Having first noted this as a formal characteristic of Hebrew poetry,[19] he set out many Gospel sayings in such a way as to draw attention to this feature of them. Burney also offered complete Aramaic reconstructions of several passages, including for example Matt. 8.20//Luke 9.58.[20]

Burney's work was, however, vitiated by errors of method. Even the chapter on parallelism sets out Gospel passages in English, which underlines the fact that Burney never demonstrated the existence of Aramaic sources of Q. He has no detailed discussion of passages where the Matthean and Lucan versions are seriously different, so he never tackles the implications of Aramaic phenomena for our model of Q. For example, he notes that Luke 11.47 is different from Matt. 23.29. Having set out most of the Matthean version in parallel lines in *English*, all he does about the differences is to set out the Lucan version, also in parallelism in English too, and he simply declares that 'the second stichos' summarizes Matt. 23.30–1.[21] This is not sufficient to demonstrate anything. Some of the chapter on rhythm conducts the discussion in English too, which

---

[16] *Ibid.*, p. 178.

[17] C. F. Burney, *The Poetry of Our Lord* (Oxford, 1925). For a more general assessment of Burney's work on the Aramaic background to the Gospels, see Casey, *Aramaic Sources of Mark's Gospel*, pp. 19–22.

[18] Burney, *Poetry*, ch. II.   [19] *Ibid.*, pp. 15–22.

[20] *Ibid.*, pp. 132, 169.   [21] *Ibid.*, p. 68, with n. 3.

is methodologically quite inadequate. The brief discussion of rhythm in Aramaic poetry includes for example Dan. 4.24, but apart from the rather arbitrary way in which Burney set it out in lines,[22] there is nothing to suggest that this is really poetry at all.

Burney uses the Matthean version of the Lord's prayer for a reconstruction which is supposed to consist of two four-beat tristichs; the formula may be said to be two (stanzas) × three (stichoi) × four (beats). This is said to have been an aid to memory. Burney then declares the Lucan version mutilated, and suggests that we can hardly hesitate as to which is the more original. Finally, he suggests that it has features of rhyme.[23] This hypothesis, which never receives properly detailed discussion, runs from the improbable to the impossible. It is surely improbable that we have two stanzas, in an orally transmitted poem with no break in the sense, from a culture not known to have had poems in two four-beat tristichs. Luke's opening πάτερ must surely go back to Jesus' rather distinctive אבא, whereas the Matthean version is more conventional. It is surely at least as probable that Luke's version is original, which upsets Burney's formula drastically, and underlines the fact that it is *Burney's* formula, not something which has arisen naturally from the culture under study. Consequently, the arrangement of the supposed reconstruction of the Matthean version is not a satisfactory criterion for determining authenticity.

Burney's discussion of rhyme is entirely spurious. Rhyme should not be regarded as a feature of ancient Semitic verse at all. Burney brought forward no evidence that rhyme was a feature of Aramaic verse. He discussed Hebrew poetry instead, and commented that 'the few occurrences which can be collected seem for the most part to be rather accidental than designed'.[24] His examples are indeed all produced at random by the fact that Hebrew words have a limited number of endings, with the result that similar ones occasionally occur together in groups. Burney produced the same effect with Aramaic versions of selected sayings of Jesus. His first example from the Lord's prayer[25] is supposed to have the ending -ā set in strophe 1a, with *d^ebišmayyā* for ὁ ἐν τοῖς οὐρανοῖς, rhyming at his strophe 3a with exactly the same form *d^ebišmayyā* for ὡς ἐν οὐρανῷ, and rhyming in strophe 3b with *b^ear'ā*. But the first example of דבשמיא is probably a Matthean addition. Burney does not explain the behaviour of the translator in putting two different Greek expressions for the same Aramaic one, and the whole notion of these words rhyming really only reflects the ending of the Aramaic definite state. Finally, some of the words

---

[22] *Ibid.*, p. 110.   [23] *Ibid.*, pp. 112–13, 161–2.
[24] *Ibid.*, p. 147.   [25] *Ibid.*, pp. 112–13, 161–2.

used by Burney are not correct. So, for example, *dᵉyōmā́* for ἐπιούσιον, supposedly giving the same rhyme with *ā́* in the second stanza, is surely wrong. It is not, however, *randomly* wrong: it is the translation of a late traditional understanding of ἐπιούσιον *into* Aramaic, which illuminates the nature of Burney's supposed reconstructions – they are translations *into* Aramaic, not genuine reconstructions at all.

For these reasons, Burney's work is faulty from beginning to end – he made many mistakes, and demonstrated nothing beyond the already obvious fact that some of Jesus' sayings show signs of parallelism.

The next piece of work on Q to have been considered important was that of Bussmann.[26] Bussmann argued that R, his abbreviation for *Redenquelle*, should be regarded as a composite of two collections. Those passages in which there is close verbal agreement between Matthew and Luke are dependent on a Greek source, which he sometimes labels T for *Täuferquelle*, passages which may have derived from circles close to John the Baptist. Those passages in which there is considerable verbal varia-tion between Matthew and Luke were derived from an Aramaic source, 'nur Reden enthaltende, also wohl das eigentliche R'.[27]

The important point made by Bussmann is his clear recognition of the two different types of source material, and his guess at the cause of this, that Matthew and Luke used one Greek translation for some Q passages, and used or made two Greek translations of Aramaic source material in others. He did not, however, discuss a single Aramaic word. It follows that Bussmann could not possibly *demonstrate* that the variations between Matthew and Luke were due to two translations. While his hypothesis was basically plausible, it could not be defended in this inadequate form against the argument that the variations are due to heavy editing, and that what really happened was that Matthew and/or Luke edited much more vigorously in some passages than in others. Nor did Bussmann offer a sufficient argument for believing that the supposed Aramaic source was a single document.

If Q was a document, it deserves a commentary. The first real attempt to supply one was made by T. W. Manson, who also offered a commen-tary on the teaching peculiar to each of Matthew and Luke.[28] Manson's Q does not include all the material in which Matthew and Luke overlap. He asserts that translation and even mistranslation account for some vari-ants, but he gives very few examples, at least the majority of which are

---

[26] W. Bussmann, *Synoptische Studien*, vol. II: *Zur Redenquelle* (Halle, 1929).

[27] *Ibid.*, p. 137.

[28] T. W. Manson, *The Sayings of Jesus* (1937, as part II of *The Mission and Message of Jesus*, ed. H. D. A. Major et al. Reprinted separately, London, 1949).

taken from earlier scholarship.[29] For example, he repeats from Burney the view that Matt. 6.22–3 is rhythmically superior to the version of Luke, and refers back to Burney for a 'retranslation into Aramaic'.[30] It is not, however, clear that the original saying was verse in any meaningful sense, and Burney's work on rhythm is largely spurious.[31] For reasons of this kind, most of Manson's scattered comments on Aramaic are unhelpful. Manson's Q also includes passages such as Luke 3.7–9, which is almost verbally identical with Matt. 3.7–9 in Greek. This is difficult to reconcile with positing translation variants in other passages. We must conclude that, like Harnack and Streeter, Manson failed to investigate the Aramaic dimension of Q.

A brief article by Barrett is worthy of mention at this point, even though it was too short to deal with Aramaic reconstructions.[32] Barrett pointed out clearly and forcefully that the Q material does *not* have common order in the two Gospels as a whole. The common order at the beginning is partly explained by common use of Mark which has, for example, the temptation of Jesus after his baptism, and this was sufficient to cause Matthew and Luke to put Q material about John the Baptist, and then the temptations of Jesus, in the same order. Barrett also noted that whereas some passages are verbally identical in Greek others were explicable as resulting from two translations of Aramaic source material. The evidence so clearly summarised by Barrett is enough to show that Q was not a single document.

The next noteworthy book was the most important contribution to the study of the Aramaic substratum of the Gospels: M. Black, *An Aramaic Approach to the Gospels and Acts* (1946).[33] In this book, Black gathered together the best of previous work, and added many points of his own. Hence its position as the standard work on its subject. In his review of previous work, Black laid down a number of correct principles. For proposed mistranslations, he laid down that 'the mistranslation must at least be credible; and the conjectured Aramaic must be possible'.[34] This excludes a high proportion of suggestions, and in this matter Black unfailingly observed his own principles. He also followed Driver in calling for

---

[29] One or two more are given in T. W. Manson, *The Teaching of Jesus* (Cambridge, 1931, 2nd edn, 1935); 'Some Outstanding New Testament Problems. XII. The Problem of Aramaic Sources in the Gospels', *ET* 47, 1935–6, 7–11.

[30] Manson, *Sayings*, p. 93, referring to Burney, *Poetry*, p. 131.

[31] Casey, *Aramaic Sources of Mark's Gospel*, pp. 19–22; pp. 6–7 above.

[32] C. K. Barrett, 'Q: A Re-examination', *ET* 54, 1942–3, 320–3.

[33] M. Black, *An Aramaic Approach to the Gospels and Acts* (Oxford, 1946).

[34] *Ibid.*, p. 7.

the presentation of whole sentences.[35] Black also offered a sound overall summary of the range of available Aramaic sources, of Aramaic dialects, and of the languages which Jesus is likely to have known. He concluded that Jesus will have taught almost entirely in Aramaic, and that his task was to determine the extent of Aramaic influence in the Gospels.[36] He discussed whole features of the Aramaic language as well as detailed reconstructions; for example, he has a whole section on asyndeton.[37] This includes discussion of whether the extent of asyndeton in John's Gospel might be due to Jewish or Syrian Greek, rather than actual translation. Black's separation out of these possibilities was much more careful than the work of his predecessors.

It is all the more regrettable that Black was not able to make a significant positive contribution to the study of Q. He did repeat some useful suggestions from earlier work. For example, he repeated Wellhausen's suggestion that at Matt. 23.26 καθάρισον correctly represents the Aramaic *dakkau* (cleanse), whereas at Luke 11.41 τὰ ἐνόντα δότε ἐλεημοσύνην represents a misreading of the same word as *zakkau* (give alms), and he correctly defended this against Dalman's criticism.[38] Such suggestions cannot, however, take us far enough, because they deal only with single words. Black was moreover in no position to produce the much needed revolution in Q studies, not least because scholars who had written extensively on Q had not made significant use of Aramaic. Equally, of those who had written on Aramaic, only Meyer showed first-class ability, and he wrote when the study of Q was still in its infancy.[39] Black's main problem was accordingly that there was no established model of Q, nor any established methodology for studying a possible Aramaic substratum of it. Believing correctly in the historicity of much of the Q material, and knowing that Jesus spoke Aramaic, Black tried to reconstruct as many Aramaic features in the supposed source(s) of Q as he could. Unfortunately, he thereby *produced* Aramaisms rather than reconstructing them, and when they are genuinely to be found in our texts, he moved verses to put them beside each other in a supposedly original source. Too influenced by Burney, he did not always reconstruct the original Aramaic at all.

For example, Black sets out Matt. 3.12//Luke 3.17 in parallel lines in English, without reconstructing the supposed Aramaic.[40] It is, however, simply not obvious that Jesus, Q, Matthew or Luke was aware of this parallelism. Black then suggests that φυγεῖν at Matt. 3.7//Luke 3.7

---

[35] *Ibid.*, p. 12.   [36] *Ibid.*, ch. II.   [37] *Ibid.*, pp. 38–43.

[38] *Ibid.*, p. 2, referring to Wellhausen, *Einleitung*, p. 27.

[39] Meyer, *Jesu Muttersprache*: see p. 3 above.

[40] Black, *Aramaic Approach* (1946), p. 106.

represents the Aramaic '*ᵃraq*, that ῥίζα at Matt. 3.10//Luke 3.9 represents
'*iqqar*, and that 'if the word-play was to be effective, verse 10 must have
followed directly on verse 7 . . .'[41] Here Black's Aramaic is sound, but the
use he has made of it is not, for altering the text like this is quite arbitrary.
At Matt. 5.43–48//Luke 6.27–36, Black uses his ideas of parallelism to
alter the order of the text; here too this criterion is too arbitrary to be
accepted. Black also declares that 'Alliteration, assonance and word-play
are all prominent features of the Aramaic of these verses.'[42] He therefore
uses Luke 6.32–3 rather than Matt. 5.46 to 'reconstruct' these features,
including *ṭebhu* for χάρις and *ḥabbibhu* for ἁμαρτωλοί. It is, however,
most unlikely that Matthew would put μισθόν for *ṭebhu*; it is surely very
likely that Luke would alter it to χάρις (a term never used by Matthew,
but used eight times in Luke's Gospel and seventeen times in Acts), precisely because it makes the text more suitable for Gentiles. Accordingly,
we should reconstruct מה אגר איתי לכון, a probable source which has less
wordplay than that proposed by Black. Likewise, it is not probable that
Matthew wrote τελῶναι for *ḥabbibhu*, whereas Luke might well alter
מכסיא or τελῶναι to ἁμαρτωλοί, a term which he uses seventeen times
and which might make better sense for him here. Accordingly, bearing
in mind the reading οὕτως (D Z 33, with Latin and Syriac support), we
should reconstruct הלא מכסיא עבדין כן. This further reduces the extent of
the proposed wordplay.

This straining after features which do occur in Aramaic, but less frequently than in Black's reconstructions, sometimes leads to problems with
the actual Aramaic. For example, Black has an arbitrary combination
of Matt. 6.19–20 with Luke 12.33, apparently because shifting from
Matthew to end with Luke 12.33 enables him to reconstruct *qarebh*
behind the Lucan ἐγγίζει to give wordplay with *ruqba*, proposed behind the Matthean σής for 'moth', and with *marqebh*, proposed behind
the Matthean ἀφανίζει for 'corrupteth'.[43] The first problem is ἐγγίζει
at Luke 12.33, whereas Matthew has διορύσσουσιν (Matt. 6.20). That
Matthew should translate קרב or edit ἐγγίζει into διορύσσουσιν is surely
most improbable. It is, however, entirely plausible that Jesus said פלשין,
and that Luke, writing for Greeks who lived in cities, should find
פלשין/διορύσσουσιν quite strange and replace it with ἐγγίζει. More serious is *ruqba*. Black gives no attestation for this, and appears to have
repeated from an unfortunate entry in Jastrow a word which did not really
exist. סס is found at *Ahiqar* 184, and in Hebrew, later Jewish Aramaic,
Christian Palestinian Aramaic and Syriac, including the Syriac versions

[41] *Ibid.*, p. 106.   [42] *Ibid.*, p. 137.   [43] *Ibid.*, pp. 135–6.

here. סס is surely the word which should be reconstructed, and this ruins the proposed wordplay. Nor did Black give attestation for *marqebh*, which is not known to me from early sources. There is much more extensive attestation of חבל, including 4Q203 8 11. It is therefore quite impossible that Black's wordplay occurred in an Aramaic source.

It must therefore be concluded that Black did not succeed in carrying forward research into the Aramaic substratum of Q. During the next few years, both he and Bussby wrote short articles which again drew attention to the evidence that there is an important Aramaic dimension to Q.[44] These treatments were too short to achieve the massive amount of progress which was theoretically possible. The whole matter was ignored by Farrer, in a famous essay which attempted to dispense with Q altogether.[45] His argument that Luke used Matthew does not even list, among the objections which he proposed to meet, any cases in which Luke may be thought to have made or used a different translation from that of Matthew.[46] Farrer also argued very strongly against the production of an unknown source which mysteriously disappeared, suggesting that his hypothesis was better for utilising only known sources. This argument should have been forceful enough to prevent the emergence of the American view of Q, a supposedly real Gospel supposedly produced by a unique community. Such an important work would surely not have been discarded merely because it was used by Matthew and Luke. Farrer's argument did not, however, have the effect it should have had. It should not be allowed great weight against the existence of smaller sources, which no one would have such great reason to preserve after their incorporation by Matthew and Luke into their Gospels.

Taylor wrote two essays on the order of Q which are worthy of mention here.[47] They began from the fact, posed with such clarity by Barrett, that the Q material as we have it is not in common order. Taylor proposed to remove from Q some material in which the level of verbal agreement is notoriously lower than in others. While his work was not detailed enough to make his case demonstrable, it was potentially fruitful in suggesting a

---

[44] M. Black, 'Unsolved New Testament Problems. The Problem of the Aramaic Element in the Gospels', *ET* 59, 1947–8, 171–5; F. Bussby, 'Is Q an Aramaic Document?', *ET* 65, 1953–4, 272–5.

[45] A. M. Farrer, 'On Dispensing with Q', in D. E. Nineham (ed.), *Studies in the Gospels. Essays in Memory of R. H. Lightfoot* (Oxford, 1957), pp. 55–88; likewise e.g. B. C. Butler, *The Originality of St Matthew* (Cambridge, 1951), chs. 1–2.

[46] Farrer, 'Dispensing with Q', p. 63.

[47] V. Taylor, 'The Order of Q', *JThS* NS 4, 1953, 27–31; 'The Original Order of Q', in A. J. B. Higgins, ed., *New Testament Essays: Studies in Memory of T. W. Manson* (Manchester, 1959), pp. 246–69.

possible model for the Q material, with one Greek document to which a significant proportion of the Q material did not belong.

The next work to be considered important is that of Tödt.[48] Kloppenborg regards it as important because Tödt recognised that Q presented a kerygma organised along its own distinctive lines: Son of man Christology. He declares that his thesis 'marked a decisive shift in this historical, theological and hermeneutical valuation of Q'. Tuckett likewise describes it as a 'decisive contribution in the development to see Q as a self-contained entity'. He particularly notes that Tödt interpreted Q 'independently of the passion kerygma so dominant in Mark and Paul'. Hoffmann likewise regards it as 'The most incisive and significant contribution to the study of the sayings source, and also the foundation and impetus for recent discussion.'[49] Yet Tödt's work has since been shown to be deeply flawed, not least in his use of the term Son of man (Menschensohn). His chapter I is entitled 'The transcendent sovereignty of the Son of man figure (Menschensohngestalt) in late Jewish (spätjüdischen) Apocalyptic'. Both 'the Son of man figure (Menschensohngestalt)' and the description 'late Jewish (spätjüdischen)' should warn us that we are to be treated to German tradition, not to real Judaism. The discussion is carried through at the hand of German translations of Dan. 7.13–14, 4 Ezra 13 and the *Similitudes of Enoch*, without any discussion of the Aramaic בר (א)נש(א), or of the original text of any of these documents. The discussion of Dan. 7.13–14 already introduces 'the figure of a transcendent Perfecter', and bluntly casts aside the interpretative section, which is said to rob him 'completely of his individuality and puts "the people of the saints of the Most High" in his place'.[50] This arbitrarily removes the Jewish people from the original text of Dan. 7, and alters the interpretation of כבר אנש to a figure from German tradition more convenient for Tödt's work.

When he reaches the New Testament material, Tödt follows other scholars in declaring Luke 12.8–9 more original than its parallels, on the ground that it discriminates between the 'I' of Jesus and the Son of man, without any discussion of a possible Aramaic original in which this matter would

---

[48] H. E. Tödt, *Der Menschensohn in der synoptischen Überlieferung* (Gütersloh, 1959); ET *The Son of Man in the Synoptic Tradition* (London, 1965).

[49] J. S. Kloppenborg, in J. S. Kloppenborg (ed.), *The Shape of Q. Signal Essays on the Sayings Gospel* (Minneapolis, 1994), pp. 7–8; J. S. Kloppenborg, *The Formation of Q. Trajectories in Ancient Wisdom Collections* (Philadelphia, 1987), p. 23; C. M. Tuckett, *Q and the History of Early Christianity* (Edinburgh, 1996), p. 51; P. Hoffmann, 'The Redaction of Q and the Son of Man. A Preliminary Sketch', in R. A. Piper (ed.), *The Gospel Behind the Gospels. Current Studies on Q* (NT.S 75. Leiden, 1995), pp. 159–98, at 160.

[50] Tödt, *Menschensohn*, pp. 19, 21; *Son of Man*, pp. 21, 24.

look quite different.[51] At the beginning of chapter III 'The sayings concerning the Son of man's activity on earth', he sets up the question of 'how
the name Son of man came to be used in this new way', without discussing
בר (א)נש(א), which would have shown that the supposedly new usage was
in some cases the original one. His discussion of Matt. 8.20//Luke 9.58
concludes that the 'name Son of man (Menschensohnname)' is used to ex-
press Jesus' 'sovereignty, his supreme authority', without any discussion
of a possible Aramaic original in which this could hardly be the case.[52]
This inadequate methodology becomes crucial when Tödt proceeds to
argue, 'In the understanding of the Sayings Source the Identification of
Jesus with the coming Son of man is no doubt complete. Accordingly, we
find in Q a Son of man Christology (Menschensohnchristologie).'[53] This
supposed result has been produced by treating the Jewish texts only in
German and ignoring the Aramaic level of the tradition of Gospel sayings.

Tödt's specific discussion of Q in general is equally unsatisfactory. It is
largely discussed in German, with only occasional treatment of the Greek
text, and no consideration of a possible Aramaic substratum. This means
that Tödt can put together patterns which would not have occurred to any
bilingual translators. Equally, assuming Q to have been a document, he
can put forward categories contrary to the editing procedures of Matthew
and Luke. Thus freed from the major constraints under which the text
was actually produced, he can form effectively circular arguments with
his own culture. Without discussion of Aramaic source material, there
is no proper discussion of the variability in verbal overlap in different
parts of the document, nor of the extent to which this coincides with lack
of common order. Thus Tödt effectively omits consideration of the main
reasons why we should not believe that Q was a single document.

It is as a result of these unsatisfactory procedures that Tödt can imagine
a serious Gospel document which had no passion narrative. Such are his
(inherited) criteria that all he needs to come to this conclusion is for either
Matthew or Luke to follow Mark; then the evidence of other material (in
fact largely Lucan) does not count. This might have been the case even
if Q had been a single document, partly followed in the passion by Luke
but only twice by Matthew; if Q was not a document, then the document
without a passion is merely a construct of modern scholars. Tödt offers
no proper discussion of the two exceptional passages: at Mark 14.65
προφήτευσον, both Matthew (26.68) and Luke (22.64) have τίς ἐστιν

[51] Tödt, *Menschensohn*, p. 51; *Son of Man*, p. 55.
[52] Tödt, *Menschensohn*, pp. 112–14; *Son of Man*, pp. 120–3.
[53] Tödt, *Menschensohn*, p. 241; *Son of Man*, pp. 264–5.

ὁ παίσας σε, and they end the story of Peter's denial καὶ ἐξελθὼν ἔξω ἔκλαυσεν πικρῶς (Matt. 26.75//Luke 22.62). Such strong evidence of an alternative version of part of the passion narrative should surely not have been ignored.[54] Similar problems attend his assertion that the sayings about the suffering and rising *Menschensohn* 'do not occur in the Sayings Source, but first in Mark'.[55] This position is achieved without considering Aramaic originals, which would be earlier than Mark or Q; and without considering that it might simply be a consequence of Matthew and Luke feeling that they had a central group of predictions already from Mark, so they did not agree at points when they reproduced others (Luke 13.31–3) or edited in such additions as they did feel they needed (Matt. 26.2b). A document without passion predictions has been produced by assuming that some rather disparate material was a document, not by demonstrating anything of the kind. Finally, though it is not expounded as it was to be in later American scholarship, we do meet *die Gemeinde*/the community, which asserts things over against *die Juden*/the Jews.[56] Tödt did not, however, show that there was such a community, and Matthew and Luke have an unambiguous frame of reference which puts Jesus and all his earliest followers among the Jews, not over against them.

We must therefore conclude that Tödt's work was methodologically unsatisfactory from beginning to end. If this book was as important for the study of Q as subsequent Q scholars have asserted, the future of the study of Q was bound to be problematic.

From Robinson to Kloppenborg

It is generally agreed that J. M. Robinson's 1964 essay has been a fundamental influence on subsequent study of Q.[57] Kloppenborg describes it as a 'major step toward the solution of the hermeneutic of Q'.[58] What Robinson is often thought to have done is to have established the genre of Q; it is less often noticed that his apparent establishment of its genre stopped many scholars from troubling over whether Q really existed.

---

[54] See further pp. 26–9 below.

[55] Tödt, *Menschensohn*, p. 215; *Son of Man*, p. 235.

[56] Tödt, *Menschensohn*, p. 252; *Son of Man*, p. 277.

[57] J. M. Robinson, 'ΛΟΓΟΙ ΣΟΦΟΝ: Zur Gattung der Spruchquelle Q', in E. Dinkler (ed.), *Zeit und Geschichte. Dankesgabe an Rudolf Bultmann zum 80. Geburtstag* (Tübingen, 1964), pp. 77–96; revised ET '*LOGOI SOPHON*: On the Gattung of Q', in J. M. Robinson and H. Koester (eds.), *Trajectories through Early Christianity* (Philadelphia, 1971), pp. 71–113, and in J. M. Robinson (ed.), *The Future of Our Religious Past: Essays in Honour of Rudolf Bultmann* (London, 1971), pp. 84–130.

[58] Kloppenborg, *Formation of Q*, p. 27.

Evidence that it was not a unity was turned into evidence that *it* had phases of composition and the like. The title of Robinson's essay indicates the *Gattung*, or genre, which he found for Q: λόγοι σοφῶν, which he translates as 'sayings of the sages', or 'words of the wise'. Robinson sought to establish the existence of this genre by referring to a wide variety of sayings collections. While his use of late sources such as the *Apocalypse of Adam* makes one uneasy at times, he established beyond reasonable doubt from documents such as *Ahiqar* and Proverbs that collections of sayings had been made for a long time. Accordingly, the existence of such documents as *m. Abot* and the *Gospel of Thomas* showed that a collection of sayings of Jesus was a possible document: scholars who had maintained that a document in the form of the proposed Q was impossible had been shown to be wrong. That should have been an important gain, and it is regrettable that problems with this genre have prevented it from being such.

The major problem is the nature of this genre itself. If we chop a sonnet in half, we get two halves of a sonnet. A sayings collection is like a worm: if we chop it in two, we get two sayings collections, perhaps a little damaged at the ends. Similarly, if we have an epode and we add another epode, we get two epodes. A sayings collection is like a glass of *Trockenbeerenauslese*: pour it into a bigger glass with another glassful, and we still have one glass of *Trockenbeerenauslese*, and some of us like it better for being bigger; add a sayings collection to another sayings collection and we get one bigger sayings collection. In practice, this meant that all kinds of tricks could be played with Q. It could be thought to have grown in stages, or to have had different versions, merely because of differences in its supposed parts, but these might have belonged to different documents altogether.

Problems should also be found over such passages as Matt. 8.5–10// Luke 7.1–9; Matt. 26.68//Luke 22.64; Matt. 26.75//Luke 22.62, which show that, Mark apart, Matthew and Luke had access to more than 'sayings', or 'words', Robinson's translations of λόγοι in the title of his *Gattung*. The problem is not, however, the Greek word λόγοι itself. In Hebrew, the book of Jeremiah is introduced as דברי ירמיהו; in Greek, the historical account of Nehemiah is introduced as λόγοι Νεεμια (2 Esdras 11.1 LXX); a longer account of the reign of Jehoshaphat is referred to as in ספר דברי הימים למלכי יהודה, βιβλίῳ λόγων τῶν ἡμερῶν τῶν βασιλέων Ιουδα (1 Kings 22.46). It follows that a collection of λόγοι might by no means be confined to sayings: it might include chronicles and prophecy. This makes it all the more necessary to be wary of inferences to and from a supposed genre of λόγοι.

A more serious problem is to be found with the σοφῶν. Not only are λόγοι in general found abundantly without σοφῶν as well as with them; more seriously and surely quite devastatingly, Jesus is *never* described in Matthew or Luke, or in the rest of the New Testament for that matter, as a σοφός. The contents of Q are not altogether those of a wisdom collection either. Neither the narratives noted above, nor the account of John the Baptist, are generally comparable to wisdom collections. We must surely conclude that Robinson set the stage for scholarship to go down a blind alley. The breadth and manoeuvrability of the proposed form is especially to be noted; it will be recalled when we reach chreiae.

The next major development was that of redaction criticism (Redaktionsgeschichte). I propose to examine especially the work of Lührmann, which is said to have had the greatest influence on subsequent research, and that of Schulz, who wrote what is effectively the largest commentary on Q.[59] Lührmann simply assumes that Q was a single document, and never pauses to establish this. He offers no meaningful discussion of Aramaic sources. He consequently never faces the problem posed by the wide variety of agreement and disagreement between Matthew and Luke in Q passages. While he notes the variability of the ordering of the Q material, he simply infers from this that we cannot tell the original position of something in Q; he does not face the problem which this poses for his model of Q. For example, in discussing Luke 11.39–52 and its Matthean parallels, he suggests that some uncertainty about the position of this passage in Q arises from Matthew and Luke positioning it differently with respect to the Marcan context.[60] Yet this passage is not only out of sequence from any perspective of a common order, it has substantial variations between Matthew and Luke, some of which are explicable as due to two translations of Aramaic source material. These problems should have been discussed. Yet the whole book proceeds as if the existence and unity of a single documentary Q had been established, which it had not.

Lührmann's *redaktionsgeschichtliche* judgements are often unsatisfactory too. For example, he declares Luke 7.33–5//Matt. 11.18–19 secondary.[61] This saying contains the expression ὁ υἱὸς τοῦ ἀνθρώπου, the

[59] D. Lührmann, *Die Redaktion der Logienquelle* (WMANT 33. Neukirchen-Vluyn, 1969), on which I cite the verdict of Tuckett, *Q and the History*, p. 54; S. Schulz, *Q: Die Spruchquelle der Evangelisten* (Zurich, 1972). See also especially P. Hoffmann, *Studien zur Theologie der Logienquelle* (NTA 8. Münster, 1972); A. Polag, *Die Christologie der Logienquelle* (WMANT 45. Neukirchen-Vluyn, 1977).

[60] 'Da sowohl Lk als auch Mt den Komplex jeweils verschieden in den Mk-Kontext einfügen, läßt sich über seine Stellung in Q nichts Sicheres sagen' (Lührmann, *Redaktion*, p. 44).

[61] *Ibid.*, p. 29.

most notorious Semitism in the New Testament, but Lührmann offers no discussion of any possible Aramaic underlay. His supposed reasons for his judgement are quite arbitrary. He lists differences between this passage and the earlier sayings, noting for example that in this passage John and Jesus stand over against each other, without any perceptible devaluation of John.[62] This is true, but tells us nothing about the authenticity of any saying. Lührmann then focusses on the very last line (Luke 7.35), but the difficulties of this problematical saying cannot make the Son of man saying inauthentic. Lührmann then proceeds to turn 'this generation' (Matt. 11.16//Luke 7.31) into the people of Israel (das Volk Israel), so that the criticism of 'this generation' becomes the opposition between John and Jesus on the one hand and the people of Israel on the other.[63] The *Sitz im Leben* of this judgement is in German rejection of Jews, not in first-century Israel, where both John and Jesus carried through successful popular ministries in Israel. This becomes quite a theme,[64] but it is not justified by the primary source material.

Lührmann's decision to regard Luke 11.49–51//Matt. 23.34–6 as redactional is equally unsatisfactory. Lührmann begins his argument for Q redaction with the observation that this passage does not correspond to the woes (den Weherufen) in form or content.[65] This requires a source to have a degree of form-critical uniformity which is quite remote from existing texts. In Matthew, this passage forms a suitable conclusion to the woes which have gone before it, while Luke has moved one of them to form a narrative ending; the perfectly true observation that this passage is not the same as the woes cannot tell us whether it was the work of Jesus or an earlier editor or the final redaction of Q, if there was one. Lührmann adds the use of 'this generation' (Matt. 23.36//Luke 11.51), but we have seen that his interpretation of this is not satisfactory.

Lührmann begins a chapter labelled 'The Community (Die Gemeinde)' by suggesting that there are Q sayings which permit inferences about the self-understanding of the community which stood behind the redaction of Q.[66] Unfortunately, however, Lührmann has never demonstrated that there was a single Q, let alone a single community behind it. Consequently, this is not what any of his observations demonstrate. For example, he uses the word 'harvest' at Matt. 9.37–8//Luke 10.2 to show that there were Gentiles in the Q community.[67] But the metaphorical use of so normal a

---

[62] 'Hier stehen also Johannes und Jesus nebeneinander, ohne daß eine Abwertung des Johannes zu erkennen ist' (*ibid.*, p. 29).
[63] 'Der Gegensatz zwischen Johannes und Jesus einerseits . . . und dem Volk Israel' (*ibid.*, pp. 30–1).
[64] E.g. *ibid.*, pp. 43, 68, 93.   [65] *Ibid.*, p. 45.   [66] *Ibid.*, p. 49.   [67] *Ibid.*, p. 60.

phenomenon cannot be controlled by selected biblical texts. Jesus' ministry was directed at Jews, who must therefore surely be in mind, as Matt. 10.5 says and Luke evidently assumed. The sayings are therefore likely to be genuine. Moreover, even if this passage were secondary, it could only tell us about the Q community if it had already been demonstrated that there was a single Q produced by a single community.

That this book should have been so influential indicates how bureaucratised the study of Q had already become. The basic assumptions of the existence of one document, and of a community behind it, were simply taken for granted, without any attempt to demonstrate them. The document was then treated as if it had been a Gospel like Matthew, Mark and Luke, and subjected to the *redaktionsgeschichtliche* procedures then fashionable among academics.

Similar comments apply to the commentary on Q by Schulz. Schulz does not at any point argue that Q was a single document. He orders the Q material into two layers (Schichten). He labels his discussion of the older one 'The Kerygma of the Jewish-Christian Q Community (Das Kerygma der judenchristlichen Q-Gemeinden)', and of the other one 'The Kerygma of the Later Syrian Q-Community (Das Kerygma der Jüngeren Q-Gemeinde Syriens)'. He declares that these two are *traditionsgeschichtlich, formgeschichtlich* and *religionsgeschichtlich* not a unity.[68] Nonetheless, he never stops to show that the document was a unity, that either of the proposed layers was a documentary unity, nor that there was a community behind either of them. His *Forschungsberichte* is weighed down with previous German scholarship, the judgements of which are repeated in numerous footnotes throughout the book. Like that of Lührmann, this learning demonstrates only the bureaucratisation of scholarship, since many of the judgements are arbitrary and the main points, the existence of a document and the two communities behind it, were never demonstrated.

Schulz discusses the different passages of Q in an order all his own. He never justifies the validity of this order, to the point where it is not fully clear that it is meant to be an original order, or if so, of what (each layer?). He knows that the order of the material is sometimes uncertain. For example, he begins his discussion of Matt. 23.37–39//Luke 13.34 by saying that it belongs to the Q material, even if its position in the context of the Q source can no longer be determined. A massive footnote retails the judgements of previous scholars, giving reasons why Matthew and/or Luke should have moved this passage to these two places, and the

[68] Schulz, *Q*, e.g. pp. 57, 177, 481.

like.[69] At no stage, however, does he stop to demonstrate that there was a common order from which this piece was twice displaced. If Matthew and Luke be supposed to have moved it to its present places, why should we not believe that they each inserted a *separate* saying in these places?

Schulz mentions Aramaic only occasionally. He omits it for example from his discussion of Matt. 12.32//Luke 12.10. He declares Matthew's κατά secondary, on the kind of statistical comparison only with the other synoptics which is a feature of his work – Matthew likes κατά + genitive (sixteen times; Mark, eight ; Luke, six).[70] He does not even consider the possibility that it was selected as a translation variant, not even because Matthew liked it. He declares the Marcan variant secondary, with a long note on previous scholarship but without consideration of the possibility that this too is an alternative translation, perhaps indeed an edited one.[71] Yet Matt. 12.32 was reconstructed by Meyer![72] In this way Schulz refrained from discussing the possibility that some parts of the Q material derived from more than one translation of an Aramaic source.

Failure to deal properly with Aramaic evidence is generally associated with other arbitrary features. For example, he begins his discussion of verses from Matt. 23 and Luke 11 by declaring that they are prophetic threat-oracles (prophetischen Drohsprüche), originally independent woe-oracles of early Christian prophets (selbständige Wehesprüche urchristlicher Propheten).[73] While similar comments are made in a more general way in his introduction,[74] Schulz does not at any point justify the putting of sayings in this category, nor even the existence of early Jewish-Christian prophets who created sayings of Jesus and transmitted them as such. He proceeds to reject Wellhausen's suggestion that Luke 11.41 τὰ ἐνόντα δότε ἐλεημοσύνην resulted from mistranslation of an Aramaic source, but he simply declares that Haenchen and others were right about this, without discussing the Aramaic. In the very next verse, he declares the proposal that τὸ πήγανον resulted from a misreading of שׁבתא = ἄνηθον as שׁבדא (sic!) unnecessary, without discussion of whether an argument of cumulative weight might be formed from different suggestions.[75] This is especially important in this particular passage, since the degree of verbal agreement is lower, and this might be due to two different translations, which would ruin Schulz's assumption of an entirely Greek Q. In the next Matthean phrase, τὰ βαρύτερα τοῦ νόμου (Matt. 23.23), he declares τοῦ νόμου redactional on the ground that it is

[69] *Ibid.*, p. 347.   [70] *Ibid.*, p. 246, with n. 476.   [71] *Ibid.*, p. 247.
[72] Meyer, *Jesu Muttersprache*, p. 94; see above, p. 3.   [73] Schulz, *Q*, p. 94.
[74] *Ibid.*, pp. 57ff.   [75] *Ibid.*, pp. 96 (with n. 20), 100.

always redactional in Matthew. This assertion about the obvious translation of תורה is quite arbitrary, since Matthew might have increased the
number of occurrences rather than invented them all, and this is doubly
ironical because there are other reasons why it may well be right.[76]
Unable to discuss the cultural ramifications of חומריא, עבר and עבד,
Schulz could not possibly have found the *Sitz im Leben* of this saying in
the ministry of Jesus.

The combination of arbitrariness with failure to discuss the major parts
of evidence that Q was not a single document ensured that Schulz could
not achieve correct results about Q. His omission of Aramaic, a major
feature of the culture of Judaism during the ministry of Jesus in Galilee,
ensured that he could neither discuss all aspects of Q nor locate authentic
material in its original cultural context. His whole work belongs rather
to a temporary phase in scholarship, one in which there was a sociable
agreement to conduct scholarly discussion within certain parameters.

Some other features of the scholarship of this period are worth mention-
ing, before we proceed to the outstanding monograph of Kloppenborg. In
the third edition of his *Aramaic Approach to the Gospels and Acts*, Black
gathered together more evidence of Aramaic influence in Q.[77] In the long
term, the most important part was a seminal paper by Vermes, which was
to permit us to revolutionise the study of the Son of man problem, in Q
as elsewhere.[78] In the short term, the more mundane and less convincing
parts were sufficient for Kloppenborg to feel that he had to make some response to the Aramaic question. I also began to contribute the reconstruction of some son of man sayings found in Q, a fact which the major American works on Q have seen fit to ignore.[79] This work should have caused
Q scholars to rethink some of the points which they took for granted.

The other important feature of work at this time was the vigorous demolition work of Goulder, a pupil of Farrer. In several articles, Goulder

[76] See p. 75 below.
[77] Black, *Aramaic Approach* (3rd edn, 1967), including the new section 'The Source Q',
pp. 203–8.
[78] G. Vermes, 'The Use of בר נש/בר נשא in Jewish Aramaic', App. E in Black, *Aramaic
Approach* (3rd edn, 1967), pp. 310–28; reprinted in G. Vermes, *Post-Biblical Jewish Studies*
(Leiden, 1975) 147–65. See further G. Vermes, *Jesus the Jew* (London, 1973) pp. 160–6;
'The Present State of the "Son of Man" Debate', *JJS* 29, 1978, 123–34; 'The "Son of Man"
Debate', *JSNT* 1, 1978, 19–32.
[79] P. M. Casey, *Son of Man. The Interpretation and Influence of Daniel 7* (London,
1980), esp. pp. 190 (Matt. 24.44//Luke 12.40), 193–4 (Luke 12.8//Matt. 10.32), 230–1
(Matt. 12.32a//Luke 12.10a); 'The Jackals and the Son of Man (Matt. 8.20//Luke 9.58)',
JSNT 23, 1985, 3–22; 'General, Generic and Indefinite: The Use of the Term 'Son of Man'
in Aramaic Sources and in the Teaching of Jesus', *JSNT* 29, 1987, 21–56, esp. 36–7 (Matt.
12.32//Luke 12.10), 39–40 (Matt. 11.19//Luke 7.34).

pointed out many of the faults of the Q hypothesis as it was being generally pursued. In particular, he noted the two passages in the passion
narrative where Matthew and Luke have five words running in common
(Matt. 26.68//Luke 22.64; Matt. 26.75//Luke 22.62), a strong pointer to a
common source.[80] Goulder however argued that Luke used Matthew, and
this has not convinced many of us, for reasons which will be indicated
when I consider his full-scale commentary on the Lucan material from
this perspective.[81] It is all the more important that many of his arguments
against the standard form of the Q hypothesis are perfectly valid.

The main trends of the research carried out by scholars who believed
that Q was a single document reached a climax in 1987 with the major
work of John Kloppenborg, *The Formation of Q*.[82] In the foreword, J. M.
Robinson commented that his 'impressively wide-ranging survey of the
various genres of sayings collections in antiquity and his placing of Q
within that context have elevated this dimension of the study of Q to a new
niveau of sophistication. With its publication, all previous studies of the
genre of Q are rendered inadequate . . .' From a more critical perspective,
Tuckett declares that it has been 'rightly acclaimed as one of the most
outstanding of the recent attempts to unravel different strata within the
Q material, and his solution offered in his book has influenced a large
number of Q researchers who have taken up his theories very enthusias-
tically'.[83] Such verdicts are partly justified by Kloppenborg's vigorous
attempt to actually *demonstrate* that Q was a single document written
in Greek, and indeed to unravel the strata which preceded its formation.
The work is however fatally flawed, not least by Kloppenborg's handling
and/or omission of Aramaic evidence.

I begin therefore with the Aramaic evidence. There are three major
faults. Firstly, Kloppenborg ignores the fact that Jesus spoke Aramaic.
This creates a prima facie case for there having been Aramaic sources at
some stage of the tradition, and for considering whether there is evidence
of them in the Q material. Secondly, Kloppenborg ignores the Son of man
problem. Yet we all know that ὁ υἱὸς τοῦ ἀνθρώπου is not natural Greek,
and that it can hardly be explained except as a translation of בר (א)נש(א).
It follows that some sayings, including some Son of man sayings, were
translated from Aramaic. The omission of these two main points is a
major defect.

---

[80] M. D. Goulder, 'On Putting Q to the Test', *NTS* 24, 1978, 218–34. Other contributions
include the more general demolition, 'A House Built on Sand', in A. E. Harvey (ed.),
Alternative Approaches to New Testament Study (London, 1985), pp. 1–24.

[81] See pp. 45–7 below.   [82] See n. 49 above.

[83] Robinson, in Kloppenborg, *Formation of Q*, p. xi; Tuckett, *Q and the History*, p. 69.

Thirdly, there are detailed errors in the actual handling of the older arguments for Aramaic material. At Matt. 23.26//Luke 11.41, Wellhausen suggested that at Matt. 23.26 καθάρισον correctly represents the Aramaic *dakkau* (reinigt), whereas at Luke 11.41 τὰ ἐνόντα δότε ἐλεημοσύνην represents a misreading of the same word as *zakkau* (gebt Almosen). Kloppenborg contradicts this firstly by alleging that זכי means '*both* "to purify" and "to give alms"', but for the meaning 'purify' he cites only *Lev. Rab.* 34.7.[84] One occurrence in so late a source is not enough, and Kloppenborg has misinterpreted it. The final phrase, spoken by a beggar to the person whom he is asking for alms, is זכי גרמך בי, 'benefit yourself through me', 'gain yourself merit through me'. This is the only possible interpretation in a culture where giving alms was a good work which was considered meritorious, but it did not convey purity particularly. This passage cannot possibly be used to *establish* the meaning 'purify'. Kloppenborg appears to have taken an entry in Jastrow too literally, without consulting the primary sources properly. Moreover, Kloppenborg has quite misstated the force of his objection. If he had been right, we would have had to modify Wellhausen's explanation rather than drop it, since a source with זכי could simply have been read differently by Matthew and Luke, rather than a source with דכי being misread by Luke.

Kloppenborg then follows Moule in suggesting that the evidence for the currency of זכי in Palestinian Aramaic seems precarious.[85] It is not. It is attested long before our period, as for example at *Ahiqar* 46. It occurs in a derived moral sense at 11QtgJob XXXIV.4 (Job 40.8), where it renders the Hebrew צדק, with a meaning approximating to the English 'be innocent', 'be justified'. The word זכי also occurs in the fragmentary 11QtgJob IX.8 (Job 25.5). Both of these examples were available to Kloppenborg (but not to Moule!). The form זכו is now found also at 4Q542 1 ii 13. זכי then occurs in the sense 'give alms' in the Palestinian Talmud, as elsewhere, as Dalman already pointed out with abundant attestation long ago, and with a broader semantic area.[86] It does not mean 'purify' either at Qumran or in the Palestinian Talmud. The adjective דכי, on the other hand, occurs in the sense of ritually 'pure' long before the time of Jesus (Cowley

---

[84] Kloppenborg, *Formation of Q*, p. 58, criticising Wellhausen, *Einleitung*, p. 27.

[85] Kloppenborg, *Formation of Q*, p. 58 n. 67, referring to C. F. D. Moule, *An Idiom Book of New Testament Greek* (Cambridge, 1971), p. 186

[86] G. H. Dalman, *Die Worte Jesu*, vol. I: *Einleitung und wichtige Begriffe* (Leipzig, 1898; 2nd edn, 1930), p. 71. Most references are, however, omitted from the ET, *The Words of Jesus*, vol. I: *Introduction and Fundamental Ideas* (Edinburgh, 1902), where only *y. Pes.* 31b is given (p. 63), for 'act meritoriously by giving alms', 'procure [for another] that merit by asking alms'. For summary entries, see now M. Sokoloff, *A Dictionary of Jewish Palestinian Aramaic of the Byzantine Period* (Ramat-Gan, 1990).

21,6).[87] It is so used at Qumran (e.g. 4Q196 6 9, Tob. 3.14). It is also so used in the Palestianian Talmud, where the verb דכי means 'purify'. We must therefore infer that Wellhausen's hypothesis was soundly based in Aramaic.

Kloppenborg further points out that appealing to Aramaic does not explain the other differences between Matthew and Luke. This is not, however, a satisfactory criterion to use. We shall see that Luke probably misread the source because he did not understand why Jesus should tell the Pharisees to cleanse the inside.[88] This enabled him to interpret the whole verse for his Gentile readership. One misreading is surely more likely to be accompanied by editorial work than by umpteen misreadings, unless the text is virtually unreadable, and Luke's presentation of this material for his target culture is a reason for editorial work, whereas an illegible source is more likely to have been ignored.

Kloppenborg then turns to the proposal that Luke 11.42 πήγανον has resulted from Luke misreading שבתא, 'dill', correctly translated with ἄνηθον at Matt. 23.23, as שברא, 'rue'. He then suggests that 'it is doubtful whether πήγανον stands for שברא since πήγανον has an exact Aramaic equivalent, פיגם'.[89] But פיגם is Hebrew, and Kloppenborg offers no evidence that it was used in Aramaic. Kloppenborg also argues against Black that translation mistakes cannot explain the difference between כמונ(א), supposed to lie behind Matthew's τὸ κύμινον, and ירק, supposed to lie behind Luke's λάχανον. This is the same error of method as we saw in the previous example. Luke's πᾶν λάχανον might indeed be put down to Lucan editing, rather than to misreading וכמונא. This does not, however, undermine the evidence that he misread the second herb. Moreover, we shall see that Luke may not have understood כמונא, and may have put πᾶν λάχανον for what he thought should have been כל מינא.[90] Finally, having turned down both suggestions from successive sayings, Kloppenborg cannot see that he has not been able to consider an argument from cumulative weight.

By this stage, we must perceive another mistake. Kloppenborg has not conducted an *independent* investigation of a possible Aramaic substratum of part(s) of Q. He is entirely dependent on assessing previous suggestions, most of which were made before the discovery of the Dead Sea scrolls, and he could never see anything not previously noted in the secondary literature. Some comments are mistaken because Kloppenborg did not become sufficiently competent in Aramaic to assess the possibility

---

[87] See A. E. Cowley, *Aramaic Papyri of the Fifth Century B.C.* (Oxford, 1923).
[88] See p. 82 below.   [89] Kloppenborg, *Formation of Q*, pp. 58–9.
[90] See p. 74 below.

of Aramaic sources of Q. This means that he was never able to assess properly the evidence that Q consisted of at least two sources.

There are also problems with several other aspects of Kloppenborg's work. His arguments for the supposed original order of Q are not satisfactory. He notes correctly that the most secure argument is that of *already existing order*.[91] This is, however, much more problematic than he sees. Firstly, his compilation of Q in common order is highly selective; and secondly, instead of finding Q in common order he constantly has to find reasons why it is not. For example, he suggests that Luke was responsible for the placement of Luke 17.33, and that Matt. 10.39 provides the original Q setting.[92] The trouble with this is firstly that the reasons for supposing that Luke was responsible for the placement of Luke 17.33 also explain why he might put a separate saying here. This is moreover generally the case: reasons for supposing that Luke moved a saying, or a longer passage, to its present place will always explain why he should have put in that place a passage which was transmitted to him separately. Indeed, such reasons are sometimes more powerful precisely because they explain why Matthew or Luke put a saying in its present context, but do not so readily explain why it was moved away from an existing Q context. Secondly, Matt. 10.39 is now located in a group of separate sayings. Matthew might have gathered them here himself, without having found them together in Q. This is generally the case too. Reasons for finding a saying at home in Matthew's placing of it will always function as reasons why he put it there, just as well as reasons why he might have found it there in Q. Thus these explanations really *presuppose* common order, the absence of which is a fundamental point.

Kloppenborg's discussion of the original extent of Q is equally unsatisfactory. While correctly dismissing arguments that only $10^1/_2$–22 per cent of Q is preserved in the double tradition, for such calculations are indeed as precarious as he says, he does not note the equally precarious nature of his own assumption 'that the Synoptists could be expected to treat Q as they did the corresponding type of Marcan materials'.[93] They may not have done so at all. They would be particularly unlikely to do so if Q were a lot of diverse material, since they might then have preferred to follow Mark most of the time precisely because he offers a coherent collection of material in a rationally ordered composition. If they each had special material of a generally similar kind, they would not know when the other one would use Q material anyway. Kloppenborg's discussion of the passion material is especially unconvincing here. On Luke 22.48, he simply

[91] Kloppenborg, *Formation of Q*, p. 72.   [92] *Ibid.*, pp. 158–9.
[93] *Ibid.*, p. 82. See pp. 5–6 above, on the similar argument of Streeter.

quotes two scholars in whose view the verse may be pre-Lucan, and comments 'there is nothing here to suggest that the pre-Lucan source was Q'.[94] This is inadequate, for two reasons. Firstly, the kiss with which Judah betrayed Jesus is clearly attested in our oldest source (Mark 14.44–5). The saying attributed to Jesus at Luke 22.48 can be reconstructed in Aramaic:

יהודא, נשק לבר אנש ותמסרנה.

This is an example of an idiom found in Aramaic but not in Greek, the use of the term (א)שׁנא(א) בר in a general statement which refers especially to the speaker.[95] The chances of this being coincidental are surely negligible. It follows that Luke had available either an Aramaic source, or a Greek translation of an Aramaic source, for this part of the narrative. Secondly, Kloppenborg again *presupposes* that he must discuss his result, Q as a single Greek document. The demonstrable point is that Luke had a source which contained a genuine saying of Jesus. How long it was, whether it was in many respects like Mark's account, and how much of it was known to Matthew, we have no idea. This is accordingly important evidence for a more chaotic model of Q than Kloppenborg ever faces up to.

This is even more unsatisfactory with the two runs of five words which Matthew and Luke have in common. At Mark 14.65, Mark relates how the people mocking Jesus said to him 'prophesy'. Luke, whose account differs considerably from Mark and who has the incidents in a different order, adds the words τίς ἐστιν ὁ παίσας σε; (Luke 22.64). Matthew, whose account follows Mark more closely but by no means slavishly, adds ἡμῖν, χριστέ and then the same five words, τίς ἐστιν ὁ παίσας σε; (Matt. 26.68). This is surely very strong evidence that Matthew and Luke had access to a common source for this part of the narrative, that it was written in Greek, and that it related the same incident as we find in Mark. Kloppenborg declares that 'textual uncertainties abound',[96] which is quite untrue: there is no serious uncertainty in the text of either Matthew or Luke. Kloppenborg refers not to any ancient witnesses who omit these words, but rather to previous scholarly discussion which has found this

[94] *Ibid.*, p. 86.

[95] Casey, 'Jackals'; 'General, Generic and Indefinite'; 'Method in our Madness, and Madness in their Methods. Some Approaches to the Son of Man Problem in Recent Scholarship', *JSNT* 42, 1991, 17–43; 'The Use of the Term (א)שׁנא(א) בר in the Aramaic Translations of the Hebrew Bible' *JSNT* 54, 1994, 87–118; 'Idiom and Translation. Some Aspects of the Son of Man Problem', *NTS* 41, 1995, 164–82; *Aramaic Sources of Mark's Gospel*, esp. pp. 111–21.

[96] Kloppenborg, *Formation of Q*, p. 87, with n. 167. For full discussion, with full bibliography, but no new or convincing arguments, see F. Neirynck, 'ΤΙΣ ΕΣΤΙΝ Ο ΠΑΙΣΑΣ ΣΕ Mt 26,68/Lk 22,64 (diff. Mk 14,64)', *EThL* 63, 1987, 5–47.

minor agreement too difficult to explain in the light of particular scholarly theories. Equally, some manuscripts read these words in Mark 14.65, preceded by the Matthean χριστέ. Such manuscripts include W Θ f¹³ 565. This attestation is far too weak for us to accept it as original in Mark: manuscripts from which it is absent include א A B C D and many others. We must therefore conclude that this reading in a small proportion of inferior manuscripts is due to assimilation to Matthew, a very common feature of the textual tradition of the synoptic Gospels. Kloppenborg also notes the absence of καὶ περικαλύπτειν αὐτοῦ τὸ πρόσωπον from Mark 14.65 in D a f sy^sbo^mss. This evidence is not, however, strong enough to support the notion that these words were originally absent from Mark. We should rather note that this is another case of manuscripts assimilating to the text of Matthew.

Kloppenborg also takes from older scholarship the view that the absence of καὶ περικαλύπτειν αὐτοῦ τὸ πρόσωπον from Matt. 26.67–8 implies its absence from Mark, for it is regarded as a necessary presupposition of the question τίς ἐστιν ὁ παίσας σε. Thus the question must be regarded as Lucan redaction, and Matthew's question as a secondary assimilation to the text of Luke. Everything is wrong with this. In the first place, the veiling of Jesus' face is not a 'necessary presupposition' of the question τίς ἐστιν ὁ παίσας σε. Jesus was being spat on and beaten up by a whole group of violent men, at least the majority of whom he had not met previously. Whether or not he was temporarily blinded by punches and spit, he did not need to be blindfolded to be unable to recognise each of the men who hit him. Matthew thought the story was better without the blindfolding, whether or not he had independent information about this. Secondly, Matthew has τὸ πρόσωπον αὐτοῦ, only he has connected it with spitting rather than blindfolding. He might well have dropped the veiling and taken the mention of his face from Mark. Thirdly, there are no positive reasons to suppose that τίς ἐστιν ὁ παίσας σε is Lucan redaction, and that a Lucan addition would affect all manuscripts of Matthew is also very unlikely, and would be doubly so if the result were as illogical as some scholars think.

We should therefore describe the manuscripts correctly and follow the evidence which they give us. The words τίς ἐστιν ὁ παίσας σε are not textually uncertain in Matt. 26.68. They are read by all manuscripts. We should therefore read them, and come to terms with the obvious fact that at some points in the passion narrative Matthew and Luke had access to a common source other than Mark.

Similar remarks apply to Matt. 26.75//Luke 22.62. Here, where Mark 14.72 has καὶ ἐπιβαλὼν ἔκλαιεν, Matthew and Luke have five words running in common, only the first of which is Marcan: καὶ ἐξελθὼν ἔξω ἔκλαυσεν πικρῶς. Moreover the text of Mark is quite unsatisfactory from the point of view of a monoglot speaker of Greek, since ἐπιβαλών means 'throwing', which does not make sense. In Syriac, however, שׁדא is used of 'throwing' threats and curses, much as in English we may 'hurl' abuse. We must therefore infer that Mark had a written source which read וישׁרא בכא: 'And he began to weep'. He misread this as וישׁדא בכא: 'And throwing (sc. more abuse), he wept.' This made sense to him because the idiomatic use of שׁדא was already present in Aramaic, and he translated with ἐπιβαλών because he was suffering from the double level of interference inevitable in translators.[97] Matthew and Luke, however, had in front of them the text of Mark, which does not make proper sense to anyone approaching it from a purely Greek perspective. This is exactly the point at which both of them had good reason to consult another version if they knew it. Luke shows ample signs of having such evidence available to him. We should therefore infer that this included an account of Peter's denial, and that Matthew, seeing something wrong with the Marcan account which he usually follows, looked again at his alternative account, just as he had done a few verses earlier.

Kloppenborg suggests that Luke 22.62 is 'beset with textual difficulties'.[98] This is not true: it is attested by every major Greek manuscript. It has been suggested that it was omitted by a grand total of one Greek manuscript, 0171, a phenomenally fragmentary piece which certainly omitted verse 51, and seems to have omitted other material as well.[99] It certainly is omitted by some of the Old Latin. For weight of attestation, it is remarkable that this has ever been taken seriously. Kloppenborg follows Mcloughlin in arguing that 'without v. 62 Luke flows better'.[100] If this were true, it would not be an adequate criterion for imagining that it

[97] Casey, *Aramaic Sources of Mark's Gospel*, pp. 85–6.

[98] Kloppenborg, *Formation of Q*, p. 86.

[99] For the original suggestion of omission in 0171, see the editio princeps in *Papiri Greci e Latini* 2 (Pubblicazioni Della Società Italiana per la ricerca dei Papiri greci e latini in Egitto. Florence, 1913), 22–5. There is no photograph. A photograph is supplied in the now classic treatment of this manuscript, with a conjectural restoration of its text: J. N. Birdsall, 'A Fresh Examination of the Fragments of the Gospel of St Luke in ms 0171 and an Attempted Reconstruction with Special Reference to the Recto', in R. Gryson (ed.), *PHILOLOGIA SACRA. Biblische und patristische Studien für Hermann J. Frede und Walter Thiele zu ihrem siebzigsten Geburtstag*, vol. I: *ALTES UND NEUES TESTAMENT* (Freiburg, 1993), pp. 212–27.

[100] Kloppenborg, *Formation of Q*, pp. 86–7, n. 166, citing S. Mcloughlin, 'Le problème synoptique: Vers la théorie des deux sources – Les accords mineurs', in I. de la Potterie (ed.), *De Jésus aux évangiles. Tradition et rédaction dans les évangiles synoptiques* (BEThL 24. Gembloux and Paris, 1967), pp. 17–40, esp. p. 29.

was not there originally: most of us can edit ancient texts to make them flow better, and the last thing this means is that our creative editing was known 1900 years ago. But in this case the text does not flow better, because it leaves the story of Peter denying Jesus without a proper ending. Kloppenborg explains, "Ὡς in v. 61 introduces a final clause which does not require continuation in v. 62, while the αὐτόν in v. 63 refers not to the subject of v. 62 (Peter) but to that of v. 61 (Jesus). This suggests that v. 62 is an interpolation.'[101] This is not satisfactory either. Continuation is desirable so that we know what happened to Peter, not to complete a final clause. The shift represented in αὐτόν happens in Greek, and is characteristic of Aramaic narratives. Kloppenborg has proposed to improve the narrative in his own eyes; this should not be allowed to masquerade as recovering an earlier version of it.

Kloppenborg concludes by suggesting that the statement that Peter went out and wept bitterly 'is not a solid basis for a Q passion account'.[102] This illustrates again the circularity of much of his argument. The proposed standard of judgement is whether there was a complete passion narrative in a single document. That has indeed not been shown by this piece of evidence. The important point, however, is that it does demonstrate that Matthew and Luke both had access to some passion-narrative material other than Mark. A somewhat chaotic model of Q can cope with this and with all the other pieces of evidence; Kloppenborg's model cannot.

The next major feature of Kloppenborg's Q to be faulty is his proposals for layering it. He devotes the whole of chapter 5 to 'Sapiential Speeches in Q'. He argues that these formed a separate stratum, and that passages such as Q 12.8–9, 10, which rather obviously do not fit this description, are interpolations into the sapiential stratum. But the whole classification is arbitrary. Jesus and the collectors of his sayings alike had access to both prophetic and wisdom traditions all the time, as part of a whole culture. They might therefore have used and placed both wisdom and non-wisdom items together, and our ability to classify them with more formal sophistication than anyone in their culture does not imply a literary stratum. Moreover, Kloppenborg's classification of some sayings as being wisdom sayings creaks and groans at the edges. For example, he discusses Q 12.22–34 as a cluster of Q sayings in his sapiential stratum.[103] This leads him into problems with 'seeking the kingdom' at Matt. 6.33//Luke 12.31. His discussion as to whether this might be prophetic or apocalyptic, his

[101] Kloppenborg, *Formation of Q*, pp. 86–7.
[102] *Ibid.*, p. 87. [103] *Ibid.*, pp. 216–23.

criterion that ζητέω is not found with τὴν βασιλείαν in Jewish apocalyptic literature, his bringing forth evidence that seeking other things is
associated with Sophia, all this underlines the arbitrary way in which
he is determined to classify things. The kingdom of God was central to
Jesus' teaching, in which it is much commoner than in extant literature
of our period. That he should teach people to seek it did not require either him or the collectors of his sayings to be in wisdom, apocalyptic
or prophetic mode, since all these could be combined. Kloppenborg also
seeks to dismiss previous suggestions that seeking the kingdom might
be concerned with keeping the Law, but it is culturally so obvious that
a faithful Jew seeking the kingdom would keep the Law that this is not
convincing either (cf. Matt. 6.33, adding καὶ τὴν δικαιοσύνην αὐτοῦ,
probably secondary but culturally an entirely reasonable interpretation).
Moreover, the material is not really in common order.

Equally arbitrary are Kloppenborg's attempts to separate tradition and
redaction. His other stratum, The Announcement of Judgement in Q,
begins with the preaching of John the Baptist. Here, for example, he
suggests that Q 3.16b is a very early Christian gloss, predating the Q
redaction.[104] But the only reason he gives for regarding it as a gloss at
all is previous scholarship, which is supposed to have recognised that it
is intrusive. It is surely nothing of the kind: it has an excellent *Sitz im
Leben* as John the Baptist's colourful description of someone who would
succeed him. Kloppenborg regards its attestation in both Mark and Q as
a reason for regarding it as a gloss earlier than Q; this is reasonable as
far as it goes, but it should go further and be presented as attestation so
strong that it supports its genuineness.

Kloppenborg then proceeds to argue for a difference in emphasis between Mark and Q 3.7–9, 16–17. The emphasis in Mark is supposed to
fall on the two baptisms, a reasonable judgement: 'Q, on the other hand,
places the stress on judgement.'[105] This, however, assumes Kloppenborg's
overall result, that Q was a single document which did not contain even
true accounts which are also found in Mark. Both Mark and Q contained
material about John the Baptist's baptism and preaching, and the overlap is especially obvious at Mark 1.7–8, Matt. 3.11–12, Luke 3.16–17,
because at this point Mark's version of John the Baptist's prediction is
continued by both Matthew and Luke in terms which make it clear that
it stood in Q too. Accordingly, where Matthew and Luke both follow
Mark, they simply tell us that they have both followed Mark, as they so
often do. They do not tell us whether similar material also stood in Q

---

[104] *Ibid.*, pp. 104–5.   [105] *Ibid.*, p. 106.

or not. Consequently, Kloppenborg has *created* some theology for Q; he has not inferred it from the primary sources, from which we cannot tell the extent or content of Q material omitted by both Matthew and Luke as they followed Mark.

The remaining major flaw in Kloppenborg's book is his dogmatic use of the very flexible form-critical category of chreiae. On the one hand, he offers no clear definition, a possible but hardly satisfactory approach to the massive variety of sayings included under this head. On the other, when he discusses Matt. 8.19–20//Luke 9.57–8, he declares it the first of three chreiae. Subsequently, he avers that Q contains several chreiae, 'a form which is not indigenous to Jewish (or Near Eastern) collections, but very common in Greek circles'.[106] This, together with the supposed 'very fact' that Q was composed in Greek, not in Hebrew or Aramaic, is supposed to make it likely that resonances with Greek material will be found. At no point does Kloppenborg consider an Aramaic reconstruction of Matt. 8.19–20//Luke 9.57–8.[107] Yet it is precisely this which shows that it is not of Greek origin, because an Aramaic reconstruction falls properly into place in the culture of Jesus with a meaning which could not entirely be suspected by monoglot speakers of Greek. It follows that the loose definition of chreiae has let in under this head sayings which were originally Jewish and transmitted in Aramaic, and which were not originally examples of Greek chreiae. We thus end where we began: one of Kloppenborg's major weaknesses is that he is not expert in the language Jesus spoke.

It follows that the most important recent monograph on Q is seriously defective from beginning to end. It is the best attempt to show that Q was a Greek document, and it completely fails to do this. Some parts of the Q material are two translations from an Aramaic source, but Kloppenborg could not see this. Some parts are not in common order, but Kloppenborg's special explanations of why each piece was moved function to conceal this major facet of the evidence, the second major reason why the whole of Q cannot be regarded as a single Greek document. Kloppenborg consistently underplays evidence that the Q material did not consist just of sayings. I have noted the healing of the centurion's servant (Matt. 8.5–13//Luke 7.1–10), the exorcism of a dumb demoniac (Matt. 9.32–3,12.22//Luke 11.14),[108] the mockery of Jesus at the high priest's house (shown by Matt. 26.68//Luke 22.62), and Peter's presence in the courtyard, shown by his tears after he had denied knowing Jesus (Matt. 26.75//Luke 22.62). These

[106] *Ibid.*, pp. 190–2, 263.   [107] For detailed discussion, see Casey, 'Jackals'.
[108] See pp. 155–7 below.

last two are especially important because they show that the Q material contained at least part of a passion narrative; Luke's access to another account of Jesus' betrayal by Judas (Luke 22.48) amplifies this. It is accordingly regrettable that Kloppenborg has been widely believed, and his work extensively built upon. I now consider the major recent trends.

Trends from Kloppenborg to Kloppenborg Verbin

The most extraordinary recent trend has been the development of the Cynic Q community, mostly in the United Sates. Increasingly precise pictures of the Q community were partly dependent on developments in the study of other material, some of which began before the publication of Kloppenborg's monograph on Q. One was the study of the *Gospel of Thomas*, which is largely a collection of sayings; another was the study of Cynic philosophy. We must therefore turn next to the *Gospel of Thomas*.

The complete Coptic text of the *Gospel of Thomas* was discovered in 1945, identified in 1948 and properly published in 1956.[109] The first important fact about it was that it consisted almost entirely of sayings of Jesus, and was clearly labelled at the end with a title already known from patristic comments: *The Gospel according to Thomas* (ΠΕΥΑΓΓΕΛΙΟΝ ΠΚΑΤΑ ΘΩΜΑΣ). One of the standard objections to the Q hypothesis had always been that a Gospel could not consist primarily of sayings; this was now disproved. On the other hand, the *Gospel of Thomas* was generally dated in the second century and held to be Gnostic in character, like most of the documents discovered with it at Nag Hammadi, including those in the same codex. It could therefore be argued that it was not from the same environment as Q, and consequently did not really cast light on what so early a Gospel might be like. It is the original view of its setting which some scholars sought to undermine. A variety of scholars argued that its sayings were independent of the synoptics, in some cases earlier in form, and not as Gnostic as had been thought. In 1983, S. L. Davies brought all the arguments together in an attempt to show that it should be dated c. 50–70 CE.[110] If this could be

---

[109] On the discovery, see J. Doresse, *The Secret Books of the Egyptian Gnostics* (London, 1958. Rev. ET 1960), esp. ch. 3; J. M. Robinson, 'The Discovery of the Nag Hammadi Codices', *BA* 42, 1979, 206–24. The standard edition of the text is now B. Layton, *Nag Hammadi Codex II,2–7 together with XIII,2, Brit. Lib. Or. 4926(1), and P.Oxy.1, 654, 655*, vol. I (Nag Hammadi Studies 20. Leiden, 1989). For the history of scholarship, see especially F. T. Fallon and R. Cameron, 'The Gospel of Thomas: A Forschungsbericht and Analysis', *ANRW* II.25.6 (1988), pp. 4195–251; S. J. Patterson, 'The Gospel of Thomas and the Synoptic Tradition: A Forschungsbericht and Critique', *Forum* 8, 1992, 45–98.

[110] S. L. Davies, *The Gospel of Thomas and Christian Wisdom* (New York, 1983).

demonstrated, it would be important for the study of Q, since it would show that other people at the same time composed a Gospel of recognisably similar form.

Most of Davies' arguments should not, however, be accepted. He joins those who have argued for the independence of the *Gospel of Thomas* from the synoptic tradition, a rather improbable view, general discussion of which must lie beyond the scope of this book.[111] His weakest argument is from the genre. We have already seen genre being troublesome in the work of J. M. Robinson.[112] Following Robinson, Davies believes that documents such as the *Sayings of Amen-em-Opet* and the biblical book of Proverbs establish the existence of collections of sayings as a viable genre. That is a fair point. At once, however, Davies argues that the *Gospel of Thomas* should be dated at the same time as Q because of the similarity of genre.[113] This proves too much. The logic of the argument requires that Q and the *Gospel of Thomas* be also dated at the same time as both the book of Proverbs and the *Sayings of Amen-em-Opet!* The fundamental fault is the logic of the argument itself. That someone collected sayings of Jesus in Q c. 50 CE does not bear upon the question of whether someone would attribute a significantly different set of sayings of Jesus to him a little later or more than a hundred years later.

This would not, however, be the case if Q and the *Gospel of Thomas* were *very* like each other, so much so that, even if they were similar in genre to works of different date, they would be Christian documents of the only date when Christians were writing collections of the sayings of Jesus. Davies accordingly suggested that the *Gospel of Thomas* was permeated with Jewish wisdom speculation, and he pressed the absence of Gnostic ideas, influence or mythology. These contentions would make the *Gospel of Thomas* more like Q than is usually thought. There is moreover some truth in both contentions. The question of genre is genuinely relevant at this point – discussion of wisdom could be written in works which were partly collections of sayings, such as the books of Proverbs and Sirach. There are some genuine parallels with Jewish wisdom sayings. Saying 90 reads as follows:

> Jesus said: 'Come to me, for my yoke is easy (χρηστός) and my lordship is gentle, and you will find rest (ἀνάπαυσις) for yourselves.'

[111] In general, see C. M. Tuckett, 'Thomas and the Synoptics', *NT* 30, 1988, 132–57. For discussion of sayings 35, 44, 46, 78, and 89, see below pp. 80–1, 117–18, 123–4, 176, 181–2.
[112] See pp. 15–17 above.   [113] Davies, *Thomas*, pp. 13–17.

This has an obvious parallel at Sir. 51.23–7, as well as in the Jesus tradition at Matt. 11.28–30. There are, however, relatively few clear parallels of this kind, and wisdom was so much a part of Jewish culture that two documents which contain some wisdom material are not thereby very closely connected. Davies pushes some points much too hard. For example, he discusses saying 77, of which he gives the following translation:

> I am the light which is above [all things], I am [all things]; [all things] came forth from me and [all things] reached me. Split wood, I am there; lift the stone up, you will find me there.

Davies comments, 'Jesus is not a messenger or friend of Wisdom here, he is Wisdom itself, creating, illuminating, permeating all things.'[114] This is not the case. The proposed equation is quite absent from the text, and light is too common a symbol to call up wisdom particularly. Moreover there is no parallel to this kind of saying in Q, notably not to the latter part, which does not call up the wisdom tradition either.

Again, there is something to be said for Davies' view that the *Gospel of Thomas* is not really Gnostic. Most notably, specific notions of the creation of the world by the Demiurge and a mythology of syzygies are absent from this Gospel. But this merely shows that some early scholarship exaggerated the contacts between *Thomas* and Gnosticism – it does not provide a very strong connection with Q.

What is more important is that some sayings are quite remote from Jesus' position in the first century, where the evidence of the synoptic Gospels so unambiguously places him. There is for example nothing like saying 114 from such an environment:

> Simon Peter said to them, 'Let Mary leave us, for women are not worthy of life.' Jesus said, 'Look, I myself will lead her to make her male, so that she too may become a living spirit resembling you males. For every woman who makes herself male will enter the kingdom of heaven.'

Despite its use of the term 'kingdom of heaven', the same strand of tradition that we find in Matthew (the Coptic ⲘⲚⲦⲈⲢⲞ ⲚⲘⲠⲎⲨⲈ having literally the plural 'heavens' like the Matthean οὐρανῶν), this saying has its *Sitz im Leben* in second-, third- or fourth-century Christianity rather than first-century Judaism. This basic rejection of womanhood reflects the notion that femaleness is the locus of passion, earthliness and mortality, and should therefore be transcended so that a woman may return to the

---

[114] *Ibid.*, p. 87.

original state of primal perfection, which may be perceived as androgyny. Such notions are found in Gnosticism in the second and third centuries. The saying may also reflect actual ascetic practices in which women sought to appear more like men.[115]

Davies argues that this saying is a secondary addition, but this is obviously wrong if applied to the complete Coptic document which we possess, and Davies' supporting arguments are entirely spurious.[116] For example, he suggests that in 'Thomas D' we find the phrase 'Kingdom of the Father' in sayings 96, 97, 98 and 99, but 'Kingdom of Heaven' only in 114. But it is not clear that Davies' 'Thomas D' was ever a separate piece, and these different uses are characteristic of this Gospel as we have it. For example, 'kingdom of heaven' occurs in saying 20 (parallel to the secondary editing of Matt. 13.31), whereas saying 22 has 'the kingdom'. Saying 54 also has 'kingdom of heaven' (like Matt. 5.3, while other aspects are parallel to Luke 6.20), but saying 57 has 'kingdom of the Father'. When therefore we find 'kingdom of heaven' (114), 'kingdom' (107, unlike Luke 15.1–7; 109, unlike Matt. 13.44; 113, unlike Luke 17.20) 'kingdom of the Father' (96, unlike Matt. 13.33 or Luke 13.20; 97, 98; 113, unlike Luke 17.20) and 'kingdom of my Father' (99, unlike Matt. 12.50, which has 'my Father' but not 'kingdom', cf. Mark 3.35//Luke 8.21), we find the sort of variation characteristic of this complete document as we have it.

What the unusual nature of saying 114 should underline is the fact that some sayings in this complete Coptic document are likely to be later in date than the Greek fragments from Oxyrhynchus, which date from the second or early third century. Davies, however, repeatedly refers to the supposed *terminus ad quem* for these fragments as if it were a *terminus ad quem* for the whole document (minus saying 114).[117] But most of these fragments are very fragmentary versions of sayings 1–7 and 24–39, with part of saying 77 attached to a form of saying 30 significantly different from the Coptic version. What is to be dated in the second century is accordingly a collection of sayings which may have lacked a high proportion of the sayings now found in the Coptic *Gospel of Thomas*.

Some other sayings are equally remote from the environment of the historical Jesus. Saying 53 has the most straightforward rejection of an aspect of Judaism.

[115] S. J. Patterson, *The Gospel of Thomas and Jesus* (Sonoma, 1993) pp. 153–5; M. W. Meyer, 'Making Mary Male: The Categories "Male" and "Female" in the Gospel of Thomas', *NTS* 31, 1985, 554–70; E. Castelli, 'Virginity and its Meaning for Women's Sexuality in Early Christianity', *Journal of Feminist Studies in Religion* 2, 1986, 61–88.
[116] Davies, *Thomas*, pp. 152–3.   [117] *Ibid.*, pp. 18, 19, 33.

His disciples said to him, 'Is circumcision beneficial (ΡѠΦΕΛΕΙ) or not?' He said to them, 'If it were beneficial, their father would produce them already circumcised from their mother. Rather, true circumcision in spirit has become profitable in every way.'

This outright rejection of one of the basic customs of Judaism is not, however, accompanied by any significant polemic, neither the polemic against opponents characteristic of Paul, nor polemic against 'the Jews' characteristic of the Gospel attributed to John. It is therefore most unlikely to come from anywhere near the time of the split between Christianity and Judaism. The ascetic environment of Christianity in the Syriac-speaking church from the second century onwards, and of Coptic monks in the subsequent period, alike provide an excellent *Sitz im Leben* for both of these kinds of secondary sayings. The hostile use of the term 'the Jews' is found only in saying 43, which also suggests that these sayings were not collected in an environment where there was vigorous conflict with the Jewish community.

With authentic sayings of Jesus collected with sayings so absolutely remote from his ministry, it is not surprising that some scholars have suggested that *Thomas* consists of more than one layer. In a recent essay, McLean describes the final Coptic text as 'probably a cumulative product which expanded over time by the interpolation of new sayings'.[118] While this process cannot be reconstructed in detail, the basic notion that our final Coptic document reflects the gathering of sayings over rather a long time is much the most plausible model for its composition.

Attempts to find the earliest layer, and to locate this document in the Syriac-speaking church, might have been expected to make use of Aramaic and Syriac. In fact, however, rather little work of this kind has been done, and it has not been very conclusive. In the early days of *Thomas* research, Quispel was notable among scholars who did use Syriac. For example, taking up earlier work by Wellhausen and Black on the synoptic tradition, Quispel suggested that παρά in the expression παρὰ τὴν ὁδόν (Matt. 13.4//Mark 4.4//Luke 8.5) was most unlikely to be right, since one would expect the sower to have sown *on* the path rather than beside it. Quispel then noted that *Thomas* 9 has 'on' (ΕΔΝ), compared this with the reading εἰς τὴν ὁδόν at Justin, *Dialogue with Trypho* 125, and suggested that c. 150 CE there were available two translations from an Aramaic version which read אורחא על, which can mean either 'on' or 'beside' the

---

[118] B. H. McLean, 'On the Gospel of Thomas and Q', in R. A. Piper (ed.), *The Gospel Behind the Gospels. Current Studies on Q* (NT.S 75. Leiden, 1995), pp. 321–45, at p. 332, with similar quotations from Robinson and Cameron.

road.[119] The problem here is the combination of the conjectural nature of this suggestion with the possibility of an alternative conjecture. Justin's version is much shorter even than that of Thomas, and shows signs of the harmonising tendency which afflicts his quotations and appears to be related to the very difficult matter of the textual transmission of these sayings in the Fathers and in the Diatessaron.[120] It is possible that one interpreter, and the Coptic translator, independently interpreted the text to mean 'on' and rendered it accordingly, or that the Coptic translator was dependent on a harmonising reading which he found in a Greek text. This kind of problem afflicts all the examples which I have seen. Work done so long ago was, however, especially prone to looseness of method, and it may be that a fresh assault on the problems of the Semitic background of the *Gospel of Thomas* would be fruitful. It has to lie beyond the purview of the present book.[121]

More recent work, even that on very early sayings which may well have been spoken by Jesus, has tended to leave the Aramaic out. For example, in his rather influential 1990 introduction to the Gospels, Koester also dates the *Gospel of Thomas* very early. One of his reasons is the close comparison of sayings found both in *Thomas* and in the synoptics, where he regards the *Thomas* version as the more primitive. If valid in any given case, this argument is of obvious importance. For example, Koester compares *Thomas* 89 with what he calls Q/Luke 11.39–40.[122] In fact, however, he has selected for comparison only part of the Lucan version, which he has altered and given only in English. So he has Jesus tell the Pharisees 'you are full of extortion and wickedness?', following neither

[119] G. Quispel, 'The Gospel of Thomas and the New Testament', *VigChr* 11, 1957, 189–207, at 201–2.

[120] On Justin, see A. J. Bellinzoni, *The Sayings of Jesus in the Writings of Justin Martyr* (NT.S 17. Leiden, 1967), with discussion of this parable at pp. 127–30. On Justin and Tatian, W. L. Petersen, 'Textual Evidence of Tatian's Dependence upon Justin's 'ΑΠΟΜΝΗΜΟΝΕΥΜΑΤΑ', *NTS* 36, 1990, 512–34; more generally, W. L. Petersen, *Tatian's Diatessaron. Its Creation, Dissemination, Significance and History in Scholarship* (VigChr.S XXV. Leiden, 1994). For critical discussion of two of Quispel's suggestions, see T. Baarda, '"Chose" or "Collected": Concerning an Aramaism in Logion 8 of the Gospel of Thomas and the Question of Independence', *HThR* 84, 1991, 373–97; '"The Cornerstone": An Aramaism in the Diatessaron and the Gospel of Thomas?', *NT* 37, 1995, 285–300.

[121] See further A. Guillaumont, 'Les sémitismes dans l'évangile selon Thomas. Essai de classement', in R. van den Broek and M. J. Vermaseren (eds.), *Studies in Gnosticism and Hellenistic Religions presented to Gilles Quispel on the Occasion of his 65th Birthday* (Leiden, 1981), pp. 190–204.

[122] H. Koester, *Ancient Christian Gospels. Their History and Development* (London and Philadelphia, 1990), pp. 91–2. For a more reasonable comparison, see M. Fieger, *Das Thomasevangelium. Einleitung Kommentar und Systematik* (NTA NF 22. Münster, 1991), pp. 233–4.

Matthew's γέμουσιν or Luke's γέμει, but with a definite shift away from an original מלא referring to the cup and/or the dish, in favour of Luke's secondary notion that it is the Pharisees rather than the cup and/or dish which is full of these qualities, and with one eye on *Thomas* 89, 'Why do you wash the outside of the cup?' This presumably also explains why Koester has added to his Q version a question mark wholly inappropriate to the synoptic versions. His omission of Matt. 23.26//Luke 11.41 also ensures that he cannot see that Luke's extraordinary τὰ ἐνόντα δότε ἐλεημοσύνην is a literal translation of זכי נא לגוא, a misreading and misinterpretation of an Aramaic source visible in Matthew, whose logical and reasonable καθάρισον πρῶτον τὸ ἐντός is a correct reading and translation of דכי נא לגוא, naturally followed by the explicitative addition of τοῦ ποτηρίου. Nor could Koester possibly reconstruct what Jesus said. Thus Koester's *method* has removed both the linguistic and the cultural evidence that the Matthean form was earlier, and indeed part of the teaching of Jesus. Consequently, Koester has removed the linguistic and cultural evidence that the Q form was earlier than that of *Thomas*.[123] Arguments of this kind cannot possibly support Koester's main contention that the *Gospel of Thomas* should be dated back in the first century.

The use of the study of Cynicism for the study of Q must be considered next. The possibility of some connection was noted by Theissen as long ago as 1973, but it became important only with the work of Downing in the 1980s, and it has been central to the very recent work of Vaage and others on Q.[124] As the fine critical essays of Tuckett and Betz pointed out some time ago, the general background to these comparisons is unsatisfactory, and the actual comparisons are culturally inappropriate and in many cases

[123] For detailed discussion of the Q form of this saying, and demonstration that the Thomas version is a secondary abbreviation, see pp. 77–83 below. For more general criticism of Koester's other faults, see the incisive article of C. M. Tuckett, 'Q and Thomas: Evidence of a Primitive "Wisdom Gospel"?', *EThL* 67, 1991, 346–60.

[124] See especially G. Theissen, 'Wanderradikalismus: Literatursoziologische Aspekte der Überlieferung von Worten Jesu im Urchristentum', *ZThK* 70, 1973, 245–71; F. G. Downing, *Jesus and the Threat of Freedom* (London, 1987); 'The Social Contexts of Jesus the Teacher: Construction or Reconstruction', *NTS* 33, 1987, 439–51; 'Quite like Q: A Genre for "Q": The "Lives" of Cynic Philosophers', *Bib* 69, 1988, 196–225; *Christ and the Cynics: Jesus and other Radical Preachers in First-Century Tradition* (Sheffield, 1988); *Cynics and Christian Origins* (Edinburgh, 1992); L. E. Vaage, *Galilean Upstarts. Jesus' First Followers According to Q* (Valley Forge, 1994); 'Q and Cynicism: On Comparison and Social Identity', in Piper (ed.), *The Gospel behind the Gospels*, pp. 199–229. For accounts of ancient Cynicism largely independent of New Testament scholarship, see L. E. Navia, *Classical Cynicism. A Critical Study* (Westport, CT, 1996); R. B. Branham and M-O. Goulet-Cazé (eds.), *The Cynics. The Cynic Movement in Antiquity and Its Legacy* (Berkeley, 1996).

unconvincing.[125] For example, Vaage seeks to set out Cynic parallels to Q 11.42, which he gives in an English version, so shortened as to omit several of the main points which enable us to set Matt. 23.23–4//Luke 11.42 in its original cultural background:[126]

> But woe to you Pharisees, for you tithe mint and dill and cummin, and neglect justice and the love of God.

Vaage's supposed parallels include this one, from Diogenes:

> He would rebuke people in general regarding their prayers, declaring that they asked for those things that seemed good to them and not for what is truly good.

The major difference in even Vaage's drastically reduced Q is that Jesus was concerned with the tithing of mint, dill and cummin, a culturally specific concern which was absent from Cynic philosophy and which marks out Jesus as a Jewish teacher. This is even more obvious with the real Q, in which Jesus tried to lay out what were the weightier and what the lighter matters of the Law, another centrally Jewish concern, using the culture-specific term חומריא. He also used the culture-specific term חייב, and made skilful and effective use of the natural pun on עבר and עבד. Jesus ended this particular point by making fun of his opponents for straining out gnats by portraying them as swallowing a camel, a quite specifically Jewish joke. Vaage thus made a comparison by leaving most of the Q material out. When all the evidence is taken into account, supposed parallels of this kind show that Jesus was quite different from a Cynic philosopher, not that he was like one.

Other parallels are more real, but are not specific enough to show a genuine connection between Jesus and Cynicism. For example, Vaage discusses Q 7.24b–26, that is, Matt. 11.7b–9//Luke 7.24b–26, presented in English, with 'in the royal palace' for ἐν τοῖς οἴκοις τῶν βασιλέων//ἐν τοῖς βασιλείοις.[127] As a parallel to Jesus' description of what John the Baptist was not, and Herod Antipas was, 'dressed in soft clothing', Vaage

---

[125] C. M. Tuckett, 'A Cynic Q?', *Bib* 70, 1989, 349–76; H. D. Betz, 'Jesus and the Cynics: Survey and Analysis of a Hypothesis', *JR* 74, 1994, 453–75. See further B. Witherington, *Jesus the Sage* (Edinburgh, 1994), pp. 117–43; P. R. Eddy, 'Jesus as Diogenes? Reflections on the Cynic Jesus Thesis', *JBL* 115, 1996, 449–69; D. E. Aune, 'Jesus and Cynics in First-Century Palestine: Some Critical Considerations', in J. H. Charlesworth and L. L. Johns (eds.), *Hillel and Jesus. Comparisons of Two Major Religious Leaders* (Minneapolis, 1997), pp. 176–92.

[126] Vaage, *Galilean Upstarts*, pp. 75–8. For the original saying, see pp. 72–7 below.

[127] *Ibid.*, pp. 96–101.

is able to produce Cynic parallels to the rejection of soft clothing. This is not enough, because the rejection of soft clothing is found elsewhere and none of the passages, taken as a whole, is sufficiently like Jesus' comments in Q. For example, Vaage produces a passage of Pseudo-Lucian in which the representative Cynic complains that the softness of his adversary's tunics makes him like the sodomites. Jesus' comments on John the Baptist do not, however, mention sodomites. The passage of Pseudo-Lucian also says that the Cynic's appearance is to be dirty and unkempt with a worn cloak, long hair and bare feet. These points also have no parallel in the teaching of Jesus. Equally, Jesus hailed John the Baptist as more than a prophet because he was not just any prophet, but fulfilled the prophecies of the coming of Elijah before the day of the Lord.[128] Vaage's suggestion that 'not a prophet, but more' means that John defined himself as a Cynic is an extraordinary piece of eisegesis into a half-sentence in the wrong language. We must conclude that the rejection of soft clothing is one small parallel between people who were quite different from each other because they belonged to different cultures.

Vaage's omission of Aramaic is accompanied by some rather strange comments on it. For example, he complains that Jeremias '*assumes*' (sic! – my italics) 'that the historical Jesus spoke in Aramaic' without any reference to Jeremias' discussion of his reasons, with his proper references to primary sources and secondary literature.[129] When he gets to the difficult ἐπιούσιος, Vaage notes the translations 'daily' and 'sufficient', but does not discuss מחר, to which Jeremias drew well-known attention.[130]

Devastating as these faults are, however, they are not the most fundamental one. The decisive fault underlying all these suggestions is the notion that Q was *one complete* document used by Matthew and Luke. On this basic fault lies the disastrously incorrect procedure of comparing sayings without regard for their present context in Matthew and Luke; abbreviating and altering sayings to recover hypothetical Q versions which turn out to be more like, or at least less unlike, the supposed parallels elsewhere; leaving out Aramaic evidence, because the one document was apparently written in Greek; and the notion that the compilers of Q had no passion or resurrection narratives. Matthew and Luke make absolutely clear that Jesus' ministry was conducted within the framework of

---

[128] See further Casey, *Aramaic Sources of Mark's Gospel*, ch. 3.

[129] Vaage, *Galilean Upstarts* p. 58, conspicuously not referring to J. Jeremias, *New Testament Theology*, vol. I (London, 1971), pp. 3–29.

[130] Vaage, *Galilean Upstarts* p. 59, conspicuously not discussing J. Jeremias, *The Prayers of Jesus* (London, 1967), pp. 100–102; *New Testament Theology*, pp. 199–201, which is nonetheless recorded at p. 167 n. 30.

Judaism. In their significantly different accounts of his ministry, each of them retails a massive proportion of material about Jesus' words and actions which is culture-specific to this Jewish framework. Both of them, and especially the more Jewish Matthew, have specifically Jewish features in their Q sayings, which have been cut out from Q versions by scholars to compare them with their 'parallels' elsewhere. Both Matthew and Luke have passion narratives, and we have noted the two crucial pieces of evidence of at least a partial non-Marcan narrative which they provide.[131] Both of them have resurrection narratives, secondary support for the belief attested as early as the first speeches of Acts and never absent from a Christian work of sufficient length and early date. On the other hand, neither Matthew nor Luke mentions philosophy, Cynics or anything which is overtly intended to be culture-specific to Cynic philosophy. The major function of the largely American Q is to enable every single one of these main points to be left out of account. The present context of all these sayings and the few Q narratives in the Gospels of Matthew and Luke should remind us that they were all collected in an early Christian context, and that the original setting of genuine ones was that of Second Temple Judaism, not Cynic philosophers.

Two further changes in the general background setting were accordingly desirable to facilitate anything like the Galilean upstarts portrayed by Vaage. One was in the picture of Galilee. There have always been New Testament scholars prepared to exaggerate the degree of Hellenisation in Galilee, at least since the days of Diodatus in 1767, and this has been given scholarly respectability in recent years by the learned work of Hengel.[132] That there was significant Hellenisation is not in doubt. Hellenised cities included Tiberias and to some extent Sepphoris, the latter only four miles over the hill from Nazareth.[133] These Hellenised cities, however, tell us of the proximity of Gentiles and assimilating Jews – they are not mentioned in the Gospels, and tell us nothing of Jesus' mission to Aramaic-speaking Jews who were either faithful or who were prepared to respond to his call to them to return to the Lord. That there were some Cynic philosophers in

[131] See pp. 25–9 above.
[132] D. Diodati, *DE CHRISTO GRAECE LOQUENTE EXERCITATIO* (Naples, 1767; reprinted London, 1843), on which see Casey, *Aramaic Sources of Mark's Gospel*, pp. 9–10; M. Hengel, *Judaism and Hellenism. Studies in Their Encounter in Palestine during the Early Hellenistic Period* (2 vols., 1968. ET from 2nd edn, London, 1974); *Jews, Greeks and Barbarians. Aspects of the Hellenisation of Judaism in the pre-Christian Period* (1976. ET London, 1980); *The 'Hellenization' of Judaea in the First Century after Christ* (ET London, 1989).
[133] On Sepphoris, however, see now the cautionary article of M. Chancey, 'The Cultural Milieu of Ancient Sepphoris', *NTS* 47, 2001, pp. 127–45.

these near cities is possible on general grounds, but there is no evidence, either in general or in the Gospels, that such people were to be found in Capernaum and the local countryside, still less, that Jesus believed that Jews like him would learn from them.

Another significant mistake has been overdramatic interpretation of the fact that the horizon of most of the Q material is limited to Galilee. The real reason for this is that a high proportion of the Q material is genuine, and the historic ministry of Jesus really did take place in Galilee. When Q is taken to be a single document about its own community, however, this can be interpreted as evidence that the Q community was located in Galilee. In a 1995 essay, Reed discussed the evidence from this perspective at length, and inserted the piece of evidence missing from Q but needed by its American interpreters: contact with Tiberias and Sepphoris is to be regarded as certain on account of Q's 'spatial imagery'.[134] This is a classic case of interpretative method completely outdistancing the evidence of the primary sources. While some of the Q material may indeed have been written down in Galilee, perhaps even during the ministry of Jesus, most of it tells us about the ministry of Jesus, not about a community whose very existence has been inferred on such weak grounds.

What can this approach do about Aramaic? We have already noted severely defective comments in the work of Kloppenborg, Koester and Vaage. It was left to H. O. Guenther to attempt a whole essay on it in a 1991 edition of *Semeia*.[135] Guenther does not discuss a single Aramaic word, not even those embedded in our Greek Gospels. Nor does he discuss the outstanding Gospel Semitism ὁ υἱὸς τοῦ ἀνθρώπου. He repeatedly refers to the view that Jesus' sayings were originally transmitted in Aramaic as an 'assumption', but he does not discuss the reasons given for this view by Marshall, Meyer, Dalman, Jeremias, Fitzmyer or Schwarz;[136] indeed, Jeremias is the only one of these scholars whom he so much

---

[134] J. L. Reed, 'The Social Map of Q', in J. S. Kloppenborg, *Conflict and Invention: Literary, Rhetorical and Social Studies on the Sayings Gospel Q* (Valley Forge, 1995), pp. 17–36, esp. p. 30.

[135] H. O. Guenther, 'The Sayings Gospel Q and the Quest for Aramaic Sources: Rethinking Christian Origins', *Semeia* 55, 1991, 41–76.

[136] J. T. Marshall, 'The Aramaic Gospel', *Expositor*, 4th series, 3, 1891, 1–17, 109–24, 275–91; Meyer, *Jesu Muttersprache*, esp. pp. 35–72; Dalman, Worte *Jesu*, pp. 1–72; *Words of Jesus*, pp. 1–88; G. Dalman, *Jesus-Jeschua. Die drei Sprachen Jesu* (Leipzig, 1922), pp. 6–25; ET *Jesus-Jeshua. Studies in the Gospels* (London, 1929), pp. 7–27; Jeremias, *New Testament Theology*, pp. 3–29; J. A. Fitzmyer, 'The Languages of Palestine in the First Century A.D.', *CBQ* 32, 1970, 501–31, revised in *A Wandering Aramean* (SBL.MS 25. Missoula, 1979), pp. 29–56; G. Schwarz, *'Und Jesus sprach'. Untersuchungen zur aramäischen Urgestalt der Worte Jesu* (BWANT 118 = VI,18. Stuttgart, 1985, 2nd edn, 1987), esp. pp. 5–48.

as mentions. Guenther also accuses Black of an 'assumption', without noting that in the best whole monograph written for fifty years, and the best for another fifty-odd years too, Black gathered together the results of previous work on the Aramaic substratum of the Gospels and added much of his own.[137] Guenther's sweeping statement that Semitisms may be Septuagintalisms[138] does not lead him to discuss any of those Semitic features of the Gospels which are not found in LXX. He also develops further the view that Q sayings cannot have been Aramaic in language because they are Greek in genre.[139] His definitions of genre, however, including a very long definition of the chreia, are too general for this kind of inference to be legitimate. This should have been especially obvious when Guenther included *m. Abot*, which is written in Hebrew. It is a perfectly Jewish document, which illustrates as well as anything could that Guenther's definitions are so broad as to include material which is Jewish in content and Semitic in language. That Gospel material can be made to fit his definitions accordingly tells us nothing about its cultural origin or the language in which it was originally written.

Guenther also uses inappropriately emotive language, describing the search for 'the mysterious Hebrew/Aramaic core tradition' as 'nervous', and referring to 'nostalgia for Aramaic-written sources'.[140] Finally, he declares that the 'Aramaic hypothesis . . . is based on ideology', and comments on such points as 'pious emotion' suggest that he means a rather conservative Christian ideology, though this is not as clear as it might be.[141] Nonetheless, he does not discuss the monograph by the Jewish scholar Zimmermann, nor the seminal paper on (א)שׁנ(א) בר by the Jewish scholar Vermes.[142] By 1991, I had also contributed a significant amount of work from a non-religious perspective, including a monograph on the Son of man problem and the reconstruction of one Marcan pericope and

---

[137] Black, *Aramaic Approach* (1946; 2nd edn, 1954; 3rd edn, 1967). See further M. Black, 'The Recovery of the Language of Jesus', *NTS* 3, 1956–7, 305–13; 'Aramaic Studies and the Language of Jesus', in M. Black and G. Fohrer (eds.), *In Memoriam Paul Kahle*, (BZAW 103. Berlin, 1968), pp. 17–28, reprinted with corrections in S. E. Porter, (ed.), *The Language of the New Testament. Classic Essays* (JSNT.S 60. Sheffield, 1991), pp. 112–25.

[138] Guenther, 'Sayings Gospel Q', 52, 62.

[139] *Ibid.*, esp. pp. 62–65. See also an earlier and equally biassed article: H. O. Guenther, 'Greek: Home of Primitive Christianity', *Toronto Journal of Theology* 5, 1989, 247–79. For Kloppenborg's view of chreiae, see p. 31 above. For further elaboration, using ancient Greek definitions of chreiae, see B. L. Mack and V. K. Robbins, *Patterns of Persuasion in the Gospels* (Sonoma, 1989).

[140] Guenther, 'Sayings Gospel Q', 46, 49.   [141] *Ibid.*, 73, also 66, 71.

[142] F. Zimmermann, *The Aramaic Origin of the Four Gospels* (New York, 1979); Vermes, 'The Use of שׁנ בד/שׁאבר in Jewish Aramaic', pp. 310–28; reprinted in Vermes, *Post-Biblical Jewish Studies*, pp. 147–65. See further Vermes, 'Present State', 123–34; 'The "Son of Man" Debate', 19–32.

several Q sayings.[143] Guenther leaves all this out too. Guenther's conclusion is that 'The Aramaic hypothesis is thus in all its forms and at all levels based on ideology, not on textual evidence.'[144] This conclusion is based on wilful ignorance of the primary sources and secondary literature.

With Q seen so inaccurately as the first Gospel and a work of central importance, we must surely have a more elevated name. Jacobson entitled his book on it *The First Gospel*; Mack preferred *The Lost Gospel*. It was left to Broadhead to propose 'The Alpha Tradition'![145] His main arguments are based on the mistakes I have already considered – this might possibly be thought a suitable name for the important Greek document posited by the tradition which I have just reviewed. It is to be hoped that it will not catch on, and that Q will be retained as a suitable designation for source material whose exact nature remains difficult to define.

Since the influential monograph of Kloppenborg, some more sober work has been done by scholars who believe that Q is a Greek document, but who have argued for a more moderate version of it. Three scholars have been notable from this perspective – Catchpole, Tuckett and Allison.[146] For example, Catchpole notes τὰ ἔργα τοῦ χριστοῦ at Matt. 11.2 among the expressions which favour the Q hypothesis over against a model of Luke using Matthew, for it is one of those expressions which Luke is unlikely to have omitted from a text in front of him, whereas Matthew might well add it to a Q which did not contain it. In a careful discussion, Tuckett completely undermined the American view that eschatology was absent from the earliest part of Q. In another careful discussion, Allison pointed out the methodological fallacies of American arguments that there was a Q community who did not believe anything absent from scholarly reconstructions of Q.[147] It is also noteworthy that both Catchpole and Tuckett found it necessary to explicitly defend the existence of Q. In addition to these monographs, Tuckett has contributed some splendid destructive articles, and Allison played a major role in a magnificent commentary on

[143] Casey, *Son of Man*, esp. pp. 190 (Matt. 24.44//Luke 12.40), 193–4 (Luke 12.8//Matt. 10.32), 230–1 (Matt. 12.32a//Luke 12.10a); 'Jackals'; 'General, Generic and Indefinite', esp. pp. 36–7 (Matt. 12.32//Luke 12.10), 39–40 (Matt. 11.19//Luke 7.34); 'Culture and Historicity: the Plucking of the Grain (Mark 2.23–28)', *NTS* 34, 1988, 1–23.

[144] Guenther, 'Sayings Gospel Q', 73.

[145] A. D. Jacobson, *The First Gospel. An Introduction to Q* (Sonoma, 1992); B. L. Mack, *The Lost Gospel. The Book of Q and Christian Origins* (Rockport, 1993). E. K. Broadhead, 'On the (Mis)Definition of Q', *JSNT* 68, 1997, 3–12.

[146] Many articles by Catchpole were revised to form D. Catchpole, *The Quest for Q* (Edinburgh, 1993); Tuckett, *Q and the History*; D. C. Allison, *The Jesus Tradition in Q* (Harrisburgh, 1997).

[147] Catchpole, *Quest for Q*, pp. 43–5; Tuckett, *Q and the History*, pp. 139–63; Allison, *Jesus Tradition*, pp. 43–46.

Matthew.[148] None of them, however, deals adequately with the possible Aramaic level of the tradition. Tuckett's overt discussion of the language of Q repeats earlier faults and demonstrates by default that more work needs doing. Allison discusses the possibility that Q^1 was Semitic, but he shows only that a more thorough investigation is necessary.[149] These defects in the best recent scholarship on Q demonstrate the need for a new approach to the whole Aramaic question.

One of the reasons why Catchpole and Tuckett felt bound to defend the existence of Q is that an alternative paradigm has been available, and brilliantly expounded in England by Michael Goulder. This is the possibility that Luke used Matthew, expounded in many articles culminating in 1989 in Goulder's fine two-volume monograph.[150] Some of the arguments in Goulder's introduction are so powerful that they should be considered to have destroyed the typically American view of Q. He begins with a vigorous assault on Q as a paradigm, to which the majority of scholars are so attached that they put forward arguments which would otherwise be regarded as obviously wrong, and suggestions so contorted as to be unfalsifiable. Goulder hits especially hard the minor agreements in the passion narratives, the two most important of which I have already discussed.[151] He also lauches an important attack on the validity of many of the arguments conventionally used to determine which linguistic features are so characteristic of an evangelist that they can be used to determine whether he is editing a source.

The bulk of Goulder's book also has many valuable observations. In the introduction, Goulder correctly observes that many conventional arguments do not *establish* the paradigm within which they fit, they merely permit evidence to be *fitted into* that paradigm. Accordingly, we must distinguish carefully between arguments which establish any given paradigm and arguments which merely fit it. There is of course nothing wrong with fitting arguments into one's paradigm – this is the minimum requirement for any paradigm to be maintained, and inability to fit all passages into

---

[148] I have noted Tuckett, 'Thomas and the Synoptics', 132–57; 'Q and Thomas: Evidence of a Primitive "Wisdom Gospel"?', 346–60; 'A Cynic Q?', 349–76. See also W. D. Davies and D. C. Allison, *A Critical and Exegetical Commentary on the Gospel according to Saint Matthew* (3 vols, ICC. Edinburgh, 1988–97). For demolition of the Griesbach hypothesis, see also C. M. Tuckett, *The Revival of the Griesbach Hypothesis* (SNTS.MS 44. Cambridge, 1983); and for demonstration that Nag Hammadi documents other than the *Gospel of Thomas* do not contain early versions of genuine sayings of Jesus, see C. M. Tuckett, *Nag Hammadi and the Gospel Tradition. Synoptic Tradition in the Nag Hammadi Library* (Edinburgh, 1986).

[149] Tuckett, *Q and the History*, pp. 83–92; Allison, *Jesus Tradition*, pp. 47–9.

[150] M. D. Goulder, *Luke. A New Paradigm* (2 vols., JSNT.S 20. Sheffield, 1989).

[151] See pp. 26–9 above.

a paradigm shows that there is something wrong with it. This is what is so important about the two longest minor agreements in the passion narrative. We must, however, be very careful to ensure that we do in fact *establish* the paradigm at some stage of our arguments. In the bulk of the book, Goulder proceeds to demonstrate in detail that many passages, far more than had previously been thought, are perfectly comprehensible on the basis of his paradigm that Luke used Matthew. If we do not accept this paradigm, we must accordingly be much more cautious about our efforts to fit passages into a different paradigm, and we must notice how many passages will fit more than one paradigm.

There are, however, some problems with Goulder's attempt to establish an alternative paradigm, three of which must be mentioned here. One is Goulder's attempt to show that Q is so like Matthew that we must opt for his paradigm, according to which the so-called Q material is in fact simply part of the Gospel of Matthew. Goodacre has shown how doubtful this is.[152] Goulder's arguments that Matthew created Q material because of the similarities of vocabulary between Matthew and a hypothetical Q cannot be maintained. Compared with conventional scholarship, however, Goulder has shown that there are extensive similarities between Matthew and Q.[153] The detailed discussion of selected passages offered in this book shows Matthew editing Q much less than Luke did. It is entirely coherent that he used expressions found in his Q in other passages too, and entirely possible that he was right in thinking that these were approximately the words of Jesus. A second problem lies in the compositional techniques which Goulder's paradigm presupposes. They are particularly serious with Luke, whose methods of using both Matthew and Mark would be without parallel.[154]

The third problem lies in the possibility of Aramaic sources. Like other Q scholars, Goulder has only previous scholarship to go on, and this leads him to consider only traditional suggestions. His arguments in turning these down are not convincing. For example, he omits this explanation of Luke's πήγανον at Luke 11.42, and accepts πλὴν τὰ ἐνόντα δότε ἐλεημοσύνην at Luke 11.41 as possible Greek.[155] That such a bold, learned and ingenious an attempt to provide an alternative paradigm for the synoptic problem should have the same fault as conventional

[152] M. S. Goodacre, *Goulder and the Gospels. An Examination of a New Paradigm* (JSNT.S 133. Sheffield, 1996), ch. 2.

[153] See further M. D. Goulder, 'Self-Contradiction in the IQP', JBL 118, 1999, 506–17.

[154] S. L. Mattila, 'A Question Too Often Neglected', *NTS* 41, 1995, pp. 199–217; F. G. Downing, *Doing Things with Words in the First Christian Century* (JSNT.S 200. Sheffield, 2000), chs. 8–9.

[155] Goulder, *Luke*, vol. II, pp. 519–20, 526.

works underlines the need for a fresh approach to the whole Aramaic question.

In a more recent article, Goulder compared the current progress of Q scholarship to that of a Juggernaut.[156] This is a regrettably fair comparison, given the extraordinary way that Q scholarship forges ahead without taking proper regard of its critics. Among the arguments to which Goulder again draws attention is the basic fact that there is no reference to Q in any ancient source. With this argument, I recall the point forcibly made by Farrer, that it has not survived.[157] These two points should have been devastating enough to prevent the emergence of anything like the American Q, a single document, with its own theology, cherished by its own community.

A different attempt to upset the conventional paradigm was made by Horsley and Draper, who sought to uncover the oral transmission and performance of Q discourses.[158] The best feature of their book lies in its criticisms of the conventional American Q. These include Horsley's critique of the stratigraphy of Q in the work of Kloppenborg and others.[159] They are also very sound in restating the Jewish background of Q material which has been known for some time, but left on one side in some recent scholarship. Their major positive suggestions are not, however, sufficiently well grounded. The Gospels of Matthew and Luke are both texts, and the level of verbal agreement in some Q passages is so high as to make it clear that in some parts the Q source was a written text too (e.g. Matt. 3.7b–9//Luke 3.7b–9). For example, Draper attempts to recreate the oral register of Q 12.49–59 in 'Measured Verse'.[160] But Luke 12.49–59 is barely Q, the way in which Draper sets it out in verse is quite arbitrary, and there remains nothing to indicate that an edited version of a surviving *text* was orally delivered in this way. The artificiality of the supposed signs of orality runs throughout the whole book. Draper also dismisses even the possibility of reconstructing any Aramaic sources.[161] Accordingly, this book cannot be regarded as a step forward.

The fact that Q does not exist is an important aspect of studying it. It has not, however, prevented the production of *The Critical Edition of Q*.[162]

---

[156] M. D. Goulder, 'Is Q a Juggernaut?', *JBL* 115, 1996, 667–81.

[157] Farrer, 'Dispensing with Q', pp. 56–8.

[158] R. A. Horsley with J. A. Draper, *Whoever Hears You Hears Me. Prophets, Performance and Tradition in Q* (Harrisburg, 1999).

[159] Horsley, *Whoever Hears You*, pp. 61–83.

[160] Draper, *Whoever Hears You*, pp. 189–94.   [161] *Ibid.*, pp. 187–8.

[162] J. M. Robinson, P. Hoffmann and J. S. Kloppenborg (eds.), *The Critical Edition of Q. Synopsis, including the Gospels of Matthew and Luke, Mark and Thomas, with English, German and French Translations of Q and Thomas* (Leuven, 2000).

This is the edition of a single document in Greek, just what has not been shown to have existed previously. A whole series of books, *Documenta Q*, is associated with this edition.[163] These retail the comments of modern scholars on the given passage, numbered according to the convention of using Luke's numeration, and classified by their arguments for and against major positions. Each collection of comments is followed by an evaluation by the editors of each volume. All the books are structured round the frame of Q as a Greek document, and facilitate reading the comments of scholars against this background rather than against the background of attempts to recover and interpret sayings of Jesus. It is profoundly to be hoped that this will not cause a major bureaucratised distortion in future scholarship.

Throughout the last century, progress was gradually made in the understanding of ancient writing materials, including wax tablets which were common and probably involved in the origins of the codex, which became much more important than the roll in the copying of Christian documents.[164] In 1988, Sato drew this whole question into his monograph on Q.[165] Unfortunately, this did not prevent him from trying to fit the whole of the Q material into a single mould. More recently, in a notable essay in a notable book, Loveday Alexander has gathered together our knowledge of writing materials into a discussion of the transmission of the Gospels.[166] This evidence should now be prominent in the discussion of Q. It fits a chaotic model of Q perfectly. It makes excellent sense to suppose that different sets of notes on wax tablets should be made available to Matthew and Luke, and should not be kept when Matthew and Luke had edited what they needed into Gospels written with a deliberate eye on the needs of Christian communities. More recently, this work has been carried much further by Alan Millard in a fine monograph,

[163] J. M. Robinson, P. Hoffmann and J. S. Kloppenborg (eds.), *Documenta Q. Reconstructions of Q through Two Centuries of Gospel Research Excerpted, Sorted and Evaluated. The Database of the International Q Project* (Leuven, 1996–): S. D. Anderson, S. Carruth and A. Garsky, *Q 11:2b–4* (1996); S. Carruth, C. Heil and J. M. Robinson, *Q 4:1–13, 16. The Temptations of Jesus. Nazara* (1996); S. Carruth, A. Garsky et al., *Q 12:49–59. Children against Parents: Judging the Time: Settling out of Court* (1997); C. Heil, P. Hoffmann et al., *Q 12:8–12. Confessing or Denying: Speaking against the Holy Spirit: Hearings before Synagogues* (1997); C. Heil, P. Hoffmann et al., *Q 22:28, 30. You will Judge the Twelve Tribes of Israel* (1998). The dates given are those in the volumes, not the (later) dates when I was able to obtain them.

[164] See especially C. H. Roberts and T. C. Skeat, *The Birth of the Codex* (London, 1987).

[165] M. Sato, *Q und Prophetie. Studien zur Gattungs- und Traditionsgeschichte der Quelle Q* (WUNT II.29. Tübingen, 1988), esp. pp. 62–8.

[166] L. Alexander, 'Ancient Book Production and the Circulation of the Gospels', in R. Bauckham (ed.), *The Gospels for All Christians. Rethinking the Gospel Audiences* (Edinburgh, 1998), pp. 71–111.

Reading and Writing in the Time of Jesus.[167] This excellent and more comprehensive survey makes it absolutely clear that there was nothing to stop some disciples from writing down notes of Jesus' life and teaching when they encountered him, just the sort of hard data which could be sent to the diaspora and sought out by Gospel writers. If therefore we find evidence that parts of Q are best understood as brief and accurate notes from the time of the ministry, we should accept them as such.

The most important recent book on Q itself is the second monograph by Kloppenborg Verbin, *Excavating Q.*[168] This is a summary of how Q is now seen by Kloppenborg Verbin, together with some interaction with other scholars. Accordingly, I have already discussed Kloppenborg Verbin's most important points in the context of previous scholarship, especially his 1987 monograph.[169] I do not repeat most of these points here, but largely confine myself to remarks on the new material in this second monograph. Perhaps its best feature is the careful and up-to-date discussion of Galilee in chapter 5, 'Reading Q in the Galilee'. Kloppenborg Verbin proceeds to argue that Q fits perfectly well in Galilee, which is true. This leads, however, to the major fault of his earlier work – he discusses only the setting of 'the Sayings Gospel' in Galilee, he does not consider the possibility that the Q material may seem to fit in Galilee because it provides a lot of accurate information about Jesus, whose historic ministry was really located there. This stems from his earlier monograph, in which he argued so vigorously that Q was a single document that he convinced many scholars. Kloppenborg Verbin also provides very little treatment of the Aramaic dimension of Q. He attacks Wellhausen and Black on Matt. 23.25–6//Luke 11.39b–41 again, and arbitrarily declares Luke 11.42c 'obviously intrusive'.[170] It will be shown below that further work requires us to examine the Aramaic source of these verses, a step which alone permits us to fit them into the teaching of the historical Jesus.[171]

The most regrettable feature of this book is Kloppenborg Verbin's attacks on critics of his approach, especially his largely inappropriate attack on scholars who do not see Cynicism as a helpful movement for illuminating either Jesus or Q. Two points are central. The first is his failure to see the cultural inappropriateness of the comparison and its lack of empirical support. He objects strongly to scholars who draw a clear distinction between being Jewish and being a Cynic. In a longer

---

[167] A. Millard, *Reading and Writing in the Time of Jesus* (Sheffield, 2000).

[168] J. S. Kloppenborg Verbin, *Excavating Q. The History and Setting of the Sayings Gospel* (Minneapolis and Edinburgh, 2000).

[169] See pp. 22–32 above.

[170] Kloppenborg Verbin, *Excavating Q*, pp. 74–7, 153.   [171] See pp. 72–83 below.

version of this critique written in honour of James Robinson, he also notes the term 'Jewish Cynic' from Downing.[172] But his reference to Downing underlines the absence of reference to Jewish Cynics in the primary source material, whether the Gospels or other written evidence of the period. Nor does Kloppenborg Verbin offer any analysis of how being a Cynic would affect a person's Jewish identity, nor of how the identity shift which this would entail would be coped with inside the Jesus movement.

The second central point is Kloppenborg Verbin's attack on the scholars involved in criticism of the Cynic view. Kloppenborg Verbin accuses them of having a different reason from those which they give, namely that the Cynic view of Jesus could not be theologically fruitful. In this way, he seeks to explain what he calls the 'panic' induced by the work of himself, Downing, Vaage and others.[173] This is completely inappropriate. There are no signs of panic in the published work of Betz and Tuckett, nor have I seen any signs of panic in the formal and informal discussions of this which I have had with them. That any version of the Cynic hypothesis could not be made theologically fruitful may be true, since Cynic philosophy and behaviour stands basically outside Christian tradition. But that is because the Cynic subculture is not historically associated with the Judaeo-Christian tradition, not because Betz and Tuckett have panicked and missed something in the primary source material. It is regrettable that Kloppenborg Verbin has taken no notice of the main point that our primary sources place Jesus firmly within Judaism and do not mention anything to do with the Cynic subculture. It is doubly so that he has created so fictional an attack on Betz, Tuckett and others.

As I come to the end of this selective critical history of Q scholarship, I find it in a regrettably bureaucratised state. Major arguments against its elevation into one important document are conventionally ignored. From beginning to end, the Aramaic dimension of Q has never been properly examined. The discovery and publication of the Dead Sea scrolls has moreover put us in a good position to launch a fresh examination of this matter. In the next chapter, I discuss appropriate methodology for this work, before turning to a detailed treatment of three major passages.

---

[172] Kloppenborg Verbin, 'A Dog among the Pigeons: The "Cynic Hypothesis" as a Theological Problem', in J. M. Asgeirsson, K. de Troyer and M. W. Meyer (eds.), *From Quest to Q. Festschrift James M. Robinson* (BEThL 146. Leuven, 2000), pp. 73–117, at p. 92 n. 54, referring to F. G. Downing, 'Deeper Reflections on the Jewish Cynic Jesus', *JBL* 117, 1998, 97–104, at 100.

[173] Kloppenborg Verbin, *Excavating Q*, p. 421 n. 14: 'Dog among the Pigeons', 85 n. 31.

2

METHOD

In *Aramaic Sources of Mark's Gospel*, I proposed a methodology for reconstructing Aramaic sources of both sayings and narratives in the synoptic Gospels, where sources have been translated so literally that this is possible. I applied this methodology to four passages of Mark's Gospel, from which I sought to recover events and sayings from Jesus' historic ministry, and to establish their original interpretation. The purpose of this chapter is to restate, clarify and carry forward the main points of the proposed methodology, with particular reference to the Q material. I shall presuppose rather than repeat the rest of my previous work, and clarify points which have caused trouble in subsequent discussions.

Latin, Greek and Hebrew

I begin with the languages which were in use in Israel at the time of Jesus, and the question of which ones he is likely to have used. Latin was the language of the Roman imperial power. Jesus had no reason to learn or use Latin in general, and the Gospels do not imply any general use of Latin. Jesus will merely have used the occasional Latin loanword for a Roman object. So we find him asking for a δηνάριον at Mark 12.15//Matt. 22.19//Luke 20.24. This is the ubiquitous denarius, and the story does not make sense unless it was a real denarius, which could hardly be called anything else.[1]

Greek was much more widely used, throughout Israel. Some cities were completely Hellenised. Greek was the language of the Roman administration, whenever they did not use Latin. Greek was also used at the court of Herod Antipas. General evidence dictates that Greek was used somewhat more widely than this. For example, there are Dead Sea scrolls in Greek, and these include copies of some of the scriptures. At a more mundane

---

[1] See further Casey, *Aramaic Sources of Mark's Gospel*, pp. 73, 83; and for an up-to-date survey of the use of Latin in Israel at this time, Millard, *Reading and Writing*, pp. 125–31.

level, there are jar inscriptions in Greek at Masada, some and probably all of which labelled produce for Herod the Great. Such evidence reminds us that Greek was the language of international communication, and that it was used by some Jewish people, including some observant Jews, in Israel.

On the other hand, there is nothing to make us suppose that Greek was in use among normal Jews in Jewish places such as Nazareth and Capernaum. There is evidence that Aramaic was the normal language of ordinary Jews in Israel, so we would need precise evidence to persuade us that ordinary Galilean Jews spoke Greek as well. Did Jesus speak Greek? This is very difficult to determine. There is a grand total of one word, ὑποκριτής, which he seems to have used polemically (e.g. Matt. 6.2, 5). Like his father, Joseph, and the rest of his family, he might have used Greek for business purposes, especially if they worked in Sepphoris, just four miles over the hill from Nazareth. Of course the Gospels are written in Greek, but that is to communicate with Greek-speaking Christians. Moreover, they contain many features of Aramaic, which cannot be understood unless some parts of them are translations from Aramaic. This combines with the synoptic Gospels being set in largely Aramaic-speaking areas, and Jesus' normal audience being ordinary Jews, to show us that Jesus did not generally teach in Greek. It follows that, to understand his words fully, we shall have to reconstruct them in Aramaic.[2]

Hebrew was also still in use.[3] Most of the Dead Sea scrolls are written in Hebrew. They include 4QMMT, a learned and detailed halakhic letter directed to the priests who were running the Temple in Jerusalem.[4] This means that Hebrew was considered suitable by some learned and faithful Jews as a vehicle for communicating with other learned and faithful Jews. Other works include learned commentaries on scripture, and non-canonical psalms. These Hebrew texts are not marked by significant interference from Greek, and the degree of interference from Aramaic is sufficiently accounted for by a long period of diglossia. These documents therefore constitute decisive proof that some learned Jews

[2] Casey, *Aramaic Sources of Mark's Gospel*, pp. 9–12, 63–8, 73–6, 81–3. An attempt to rebut my earlier arguments has been made by S. E. Porter, *The Criteria for Authenticity in Historical-Jesus Research. Previous Discussion and New Proposals* (JSNT.S 191. Sheffield, 2000), esp. pp. 95–7, 164–80. A detailed response must be given elsewhere: most significant points are however covered either in the present chapter, or in *Aramaic Sources of Mark's Gospel* and the bibliography cited there. For an up-to-date survey of the use of Greek in Herodian Palestine, Millard, *Reading and Writing*, pp. 102–17.

[3] Casey, *Aramaic Sources of Mark's Gospel*, pp. 79–81, 86–9.

[4] A. Qimron and J. Strugnell, with Y. Sussmann and A. Yardeni, *Qumran Cave 4*, vol. V: *Miqṣat Maʿaśe Ha-Torah* (DJD X. Oxford, 1994).

wrote sound Hebrew as a living literary language. They also make it probable that some Jews spoke Hebrew. It is thus entirely possible that some people such as Pharisees and Temple scribes could not only read the scriptures in Hebrew, but could conduct learned debates in Hebrew too. Some Hebrew documents from the Dead Sea were not written by particularly learned people. These, however, contain more Aramaisms, an indication that Aramaic was almost certainly the first language of the authors. This shows that some people used Hebrew, but not that it was the first language of anyone other than scribal families. Some sayings in Hebrew are attributed to early rabbis, perhaps because they were originally spoken in Hebrew.[5]

In these circumstances, anyone with a profoundly religious upbringing might be taught to read the scriptures in Hebrew. Jesus was steeped in the scriptures, and he relied on detailed exegesis to establish major points, as I have pointed out in considering examples of this in Mark.[6] This feature of Jesus' ministry is found in Q as well, notably at Matt. 11.10//Luke 7.27[7]; see also Matt. 8.11//Luke 13.29, Matt. 10.35–6//Luke 12.53, Matt. 11.4–6//Luke 7.22–3,[8] Matt. 11.23//Luke 10.15, Matt. 12.39–40//Luke 11.29–30, Matt. 23.23–6//Luke 11.39–42,[9] Matt. 23.39//Luke 13.35. There is also the blunt statement of Matt. 5.18//Luke 16.17, both versions of which refer to small parts of individual letters in a metaphor for the enduring validity of the Torah. Thus the major evidence which implies that Jesus read the Torah in Hebrew remains that of Mark, but the Q material also supports this and is entirely consistent with it. We shall find one passage which implies that Jesus could understand spoken Hebrew – Matt. 12.24//Mark 3.22//Luke 11.15, with Matt. 12.27//Luke 11.19. The quotation of a scripture in Hebrew is also implied at Matt. 11.19//Luke 7.34.[10]

Aramaic

Aramaic was the lingua franca in Israel at the time of Jesus.[11] It was the administrative language of the Persian empire, and consequently Jewish

---

[5] For a recent survey of the use of Hebrew in Israel, Millard, *Reading and Writing*, pp. 117–25. Detailed discussion of Qumran Hebrew, including the question of the extent to which it was a spoken language, and if so who spoke it, continues: see recently, for example, T. Muraoka and J. E. Elwolde (eds.), *Diggers at the Well. Proceedings of a Third International Symposium on the Hebrew of the Dead Sea Scrolls and Ben Sira* (StTDJ XXXVI. Leiden, 2000).

[6] Casey, *Aramaic Sources of Mark's Gospel*, pp. 86–9.

[7] See pp. 118–21 below.   [8] See pp. 112–14 below.

[9] See pp. 72–7 below.   [10] See further pp. 135–6 below.

[11] Casey, *Aramaic Sources of Mark's Gospel*, pp. 76–9.

documents are extant in Aramaic from the fifth century BCE onwards. The most important are the Dead Sea scrolls, fragmentary remains of a large quantity of documents. They include popular Jewish literature which is neither sectarian nor especially learned. It follows that Aramaic was a language spoken by ordinary Jews in Israel. Other important documents include extensive remains of a Targum to Job, and 4Q156, which contains what survives of an Aramaic translation of Leviticus 16.12–21, part of the instructions for observing Yom Kippur. The people who needed these texts must have been faithful Jews who could not understand the Hebrew originals: Aramaic must therefore have been their native tongue. There are also a few non-literary works. These include ostraka from about the time of Jesus, recording details of the delivery of items such as cakes of dried figs.[12] This shows Aramaic in very mundane everyday use.

The Aramaic of documents written before 70 CE shows significant interference from Hebrew, a natural result of centuries of diglossia among learned Jews. There is, however, no significant interference from Greek, as there was to be later. We must infer that, at the time of Jesus, Aramaic was not generally spoken by people who were bilingual with Greek.

Aramaic continued to be used in Israel after the fall of Jerusalem. The Greek of the Babata archives, and the Hebrew of the letters of Simeon son of Kosiba, both contain enough Aramaisms to show that Aramaic was the first language of some Jews whose second language was Greek or Hebrew. The Palestinian Talmud contains many sayings in Aramaic attributed to rabbis long before it was written down. The Christian Palestinian Syriac lectionary shows Christians in this area continuing to use Aramaic too. The Targums show that there continued to be many Jews who wanted to understand the scriptures, and whose native tongue was Aramaic.

These points form a massive argument of cumulative weight. Jesus will have been brought up with Aramaic as his native tongue, and he will have had to use Aramaic to teach normal Jews in Galilee and in Judaea.

The Gospels provide direct and indirect evidence of Jesus' use of Aramaic. For example, Mark 14.36 records his prayer in the garden of Gethsemane. The first word is ἀββα, the Aramaic אבא, 'Father'. There are no such Aramaic words in Q. This is not, however, surprising, given the pronounced tendency of both Matthew and Luke to remove the Aramaic words found in Mark. For example, faced with ἀββα ὁ πατήρ at Mark 14.36, Matthew put πάτερ μου (Matt. 26.39), and Luke πάτερ (Luke 22.42). It follows that the absence of Aramaic words from Matthew

---

[12] A.Yardeni, 'New Jewish Aramaic Ostraca', *IEJ* 40, 1990, 130–52; K. Beyer, *Die aramäischen Texte vom Toten Meer. Ergänzungsband* (Göttingen, 1994), pp. 197–9.

and Luke's Q material does not tell us whether the authors of the original Q materials which reached these evangelists contained Aramaic words or not. The Aramaic words in Mark remain important evidence of Jesus' use of Aramaic.

As well as Aramaic words, Jesus' teaching shows features which can only be explained if he spoke Aramaic. The outstanding one is the idiomatic use of the term 'son of man'. The Greek ὁ υἱὸς τοῦ ἀνθρώπου is not known in texts previously written by monoglot Greeks. It can only be understood as a translation of the Aramaic (א)שׁנ(א) בר.[13] Some sayings, when reconstructed completely, also turn out to be examples of a particular Aramaic idiom, according to which a speaker could use a general statement with בר (א)שׁנ(א) with particular reference to himself, or himself and a group of other people. We shall see this in detailed discussions of Matt. 11.19//Luke 7.34; Matt. 12.32//Luke 12.10, cf. Mark 3.28.[14] These sayings must have originated in Aramaic.

Other signs of interference include the use of certain words. For example, in the Lord's prayer we are to ask God to forgive τὰ ὀφειλήματα ἡμῶν (Matt. 6.12), literally our 'debts', but a metaphor for our 'sins', so a literal translation of the Aramaic חובינא. We must say that we have already forgiven τοῖς ὀφειλέταις ἡμῶν, literally 'our debtors', and a metaphor for 'those who have sinned against us', so a literal translation of חיבינא. Some of Jesus' parables, in which debt functions as a metaphor for sin, show him making extensive use of this same metaphor in story mode (cf. Matt. 18.23–35; Luke 7.36–50; 16.1–9). It follows that the Matthean version of the Lord's prayer properly reflects Jesus' usage, and that this will have been the original reading of the Q version.

A more serious mistake is to be found at Luke 11.41, πλὴν τὰ ἐνόντα δότε ἐλεημοσύνην. This originated as an attempt to translate זכו נא לגוא, with זכו being a misreading for the original דכו correctly translated καθάρισον by Matthew (Matt. 23.26).[15] At this point, therefore, we find Matthew and Luke making or using two different translations of an Aramaic source, and it will be possible to cast new light on the teaching of Jesus by reconstructing it. At Matt. 12.30//Luke 11.23, on the other hand, both Matthew and Luke have a saying which is verbally identical in Greek but which ends with the quite unGreek expression σκορπίζει με.[16] We shall see that this can only be explained as a literal translation of the Aramaic בדרני. It follows that a passage of Q which reached both evangelists in an identical Greek translation was nonetheless a translation of an Aramaic

---

[13] See pp. 133–5 below.   [14] See pp. 133–6, 177–81 below.
[15] See pp. 23–4 above; pp. 82–3 below.   [16] See pp. 176–7 below.

56 *An Aramaic Approach to Q*

source. By reconstructing it, we can fit it not merely into the teaching of Jesus but into the Beelzeboul controversy, where it is normally thought to have been secondarily collected as a general statement, rather than the precisely focussed comment which we shall find it to be.

What sort of Aramaic should we use? We must suppose that Jesus spoke Galilean Aramaic. Virtually no Galilean Aramaic of the right period survives, however. Later sources are centuries later, and much of what goes under the heading of Galilean Aramaic is not specific to Galilee.[17] Moreover, there is no guarantee that Q material was transmitted in Galilean Aramaic, rather than by disciples who spoke Judaean Aramaic.

This problem is insuperable in theory, but fortunately it is no longer of great importance in practice. This is largely due to the discovery of the Dead Sea scrolls, which provide us with a large slice of Aramaic vocabulary, and standard syntax, from shortly before the time of Jesus. These words and constructions are virtually all found in other dialects too. It follows that they were known in the time of Jesus, and that they are likely to have been known in Galilee. However, the scrolls do not supply everything. What do we do when the necessary vocabulary, nuances and constructions are missing? At this point, we must use material from other dialects with caution. In the first place, Aramaic words extant in earlier documents were certainly in existence before the time of Jesus, and the Aramaic language was spread in a relatively stereotyped and official form. The probability of words extant in old sources still being extant is therefore high. For similar reasons, we should not hestitate to use later sources with care. The most important single source is the Palestinian Talmud. This is the right language and culture, only somewhat later in date. It contains many words which are also extant in the Dead Sea scrolls and earlier sources, and many sayings which are attributed to rabbis long before the final date of its composition. Finally we may turn to other later sources, including the Syriac versions of the Gospels.

The devastating effect of not using later sources may be illustrated from Matt. 23.23//Luke 11.42.[18] The first important word not found in the scrolls or in earlier Aramaic is פרישין or פרושין, 'Pharisees'. However, we know the reasons for this. This word is absent from very early sources because there were no Pharisees before the second century BCE. It is absent from a few Dead Sea scrolls for the same reason and from the others for two other reasons. Most of the scrolls do not concern such sectarian matters, and Hebrew ones which do so call them by the very

---

[17] Casey, *Aramaic Sources of Mark's Gospel*, pp. 35–6, 39, 89–93.
[18] For reconstruction and detailed discussion, see pp. 64, 72–6 below.

polemical term דורשי החלכות. The Greek term φαρισαῖοι is moreover a loanword from the Aramaic פרישין, and it occurs over sixty times in the Gospels. This is accordingly a particularly clear example of a word from later Aramaic and Hebrew sources which it is entirely legitimate to use in reconstructing sayings of Jesus.

The next important words absent from the Dead Sea scrolls are those for mint, dill, rue and cummin. נונא, 'mint', is not found in the Dead Sea scrolls or in earlier sources. They do not, however, have a different word: they simply do not contain discussions of herbs. נונא is found in the Palestinian Talmud, in Christian Palestinian Aramaic and in Syriac; hence it is used at Matt. 23.23 by cur pesh hark palsyrlec, and at Luke 11.42 by sin cur pesh hark. There is no alternative. We should therefore be confident that נונא was the word used by Jesus. Similar remarks apply to שבתא, 'dill'. This is not found in earlier Aramaic sources for the same reason as נונא. It is however a loanword from the Akkadian *šibittu*. Loanwords from Akkadian are important because of their age. The use of Akkadian began to decline already when Aramaic became important during the time of the Babylonian empire. It continued to decline under the Persians, who also used Aramaic as the lingua franca of their empire, and under the Seleucids, who governed their empire in Greek. The last Akkadian inscriptions, c. 50 BCE, are merely survivals of a bygone era being preserved by temple priests, some half a millennium after Akkadian was a significant spoken language. It follows that words borrowed into Aramaic from Akkadian must have been borrowed before the time of Jesus, regardless of the date at which they are first attested. שבתא is found in Syriac, and as שובתא in Christian Palestinian Syriac. Hence its use at Matt. 23.23 by sin cur pesh hark palsyrlec. It is also found, as שבת, in Hebrew in the Mishnah and the Talmuds. It is unfortunate that the Gemara to passages such as *y. Peah* 3.2/3 (17c) is in Hebrew rather than Aramaic, as discussion in Aramaic would surely have given us attestation of שבתא in Jewish Aramaic from Israel. Finally, there is no alternative to שבתא. We should therefore conclude that שבתא was the Aramaic word for 'dill' at the time of Jesus, and that he used it in this saying.

Similar remarks apply to שברא, 'rue', כמונא, 'cummin', and חומריא, literally 'heavy', so 'weighty' or 'stringent' (things), the other important Aramaic words which are required for a reconstruction of the sources of Matthew and Luke for this verse, and which are not attested in the Aramaic of Dead Sea scrolls and earlier (שברא, כמונא), or not in the figurative sense required here (חומריא). In each case an argument of cumulative weight can be put forward for supposing that they were in use earlier, and that possible alternatives can be eliminated.

These examples illustrate how essential it is to use Aramaic later than the time of Jesus to reconstruct his sayings, as well as sources of Gospel narratives. Even taking all the Dead Sea scrolls and the whole of earlier Aramaic together, our sources provide us with part of a language, not a whole one. To imagine Jesus speaking *only* such Aramaic is to confine him to Aramaic which is too early in date, as well as too small in compass. There is nothing authentic in imagining Jesus and the disciples talking to each other in the imperial Aramaic of previous centuries. The importance of the Dead Sea scrolls is accordingly twofold. Firstly, they provide us with a lot of the words and constructions which Jesus will have used. Secondly, one of the reasons why we can be confident that such Aramaic was still in use is that such a high proportion of words and constructions in the scrolls recur in later Aramaic. Accordingly, the scrolls show us what a generally stable language Aramaic was. They therefore enable us to use later Aramaic with care to fill out the *whole* of the language which Jesus used, and thereby complete our approximations to what he actually said.

This does not of course justify the *indiscriminate* use of later sources characteristic of earlier scholarship, let alone the naughty tricks which were played using Aramaic of earlier and later date alike. It is important to recall briefly the errors of method from which we must refrain.[19] For the simplest kind of mistake, I cite Schwarz's reconstruction of סוטרא behind μισθόν at Matt. 6.2.[20] Schwarz cites only what he calls 'Tg Jer', and should call *Tg. Pseudo-Jonathan*, at Leviticus 19.13 for סוטרא. סוטרא is, however, unlikely because it is not attested in earlier Aramaic at all. אגר is attested in earlier and later Aramaic, and we now have it with the right meaning at 4Q196 16 1 (Tob. 12.1). We should surely infer that אגר was the word which Jesus used, where Matthew has μισθόν.

At least, however, this does not involve changing the meaning of the text. This has often been done. For example, Burney altered the meaning of John 6.50 using the particle ד, which in one form or another was common in the Aramaic of all periods.[21] In John's text, the Greek word ἵνα introduces a purpose clause: 'This is the bread which comes down from heaven, *in order that* one may eat of it and not die.' Burney used the wide semantic area of ד to argue that this was originally a relative clause: '*which* a man shall eat thereof and shall not die'. This is quite

---

[19] For a selective *Forschungsberichte*, highlighting problems of method, see Casey, *Aramaic Sources of Mark's Gospel*, ch. 1.

[20] Schwarz, '*Und Jesus sprach*', p. 202.

[21] C. F. Burney, *The Aramaic Origin of the Fourth Gospel* (Oxford, 1922), p. 76; for more detailed discussion, Casey, *Aramaic Sources of Mark's Gospel*, pp. 21–2.

misplaced creativity, and is here used to misinterpret a text which was not originally written in Aramaic. This process is greatly facilitated by using Aramaic of any period, or even of no period at all. For example, C. C. Torrey suggested that at Mark 7.3 πυγμῇ was a translation of לִגְמֹד, 'with the fist', whereas the translator should have read לִגְמָר, and should have translated this 'at all'.[22] Here it is relevant that neither expression occurs in Aramaic of anything like the right period, and important that as far as I know there is no Aramaic word גמד = 'fist'. Torrey appears to have used the Syriac לגמר, and to have invented לגמד from the meaning 'fore-arm' taken from the Syriac גורמידא and assumed to lie behind the biblical Hebrew גומד, 'cubit'. Using Aramaic of all periods in this creative manner produces novelty of no value.

This kind of methodology is so uncontrolled that it can be used for ideological distortion. For example, the Christian scholar Burney proposed that an accidental doubling of the letter ו from the beginning of John 1.14 caused איתיליד, 'was born', at the end of John 1.13 to be read as איתילידו, 'were born'; by this means he got the virgin birth *into* his original version of the Johannine prologue. The Jewish scholar Zimmermann, on the other hand, used equally arbitrary methodology to get the deified λόγος *out of* his original version of the Johannine prologue. He proposed that ὁ λόγος was a translation of אמרא, which was intended to mean 'lamb'.[23] Such wild methodology should never be employed, least of all on a document which does not seem to be a translation from Aramaic at all.[24]

The problems involved in finding the most suitable Aramaic for reconstructing sayings of Jesus cannot be solved by heading for Targums in particular.[25] In the first place, it will be noted that they are *not* oral sources. In the form in which we encounter them, they are written texts. Secondly, they are translations *into* Aramaic, and they therefore contain features which are not typical of natural Aramaic. For example, in discussing Matt. 6.3, Schwarz proposed the Aramaic שוי as the underlay for ποιεῖ, citing *Tg. Neof.* Exod. 10.2, with *Tg. Onq.* Gen. 44.1, for שוי.[26] But

[22] C. C. Torrey, *Our Translated Gospels* (London, 1937), pp. 93–4, discussed at Casey, *Aramaic Sources of Mark's Gospel*, p. 25.

[23] Burney, *Aramaic Origin*, pp. 34–5, 41–2, followed by Torrey, *Translated Gospels*, pp. 151–3; Zimmermann, *Aramaic Origin*, pp. 169–70; discussed in more detail by Casey, *Aramaic Sources of Mark's Gospel*, pp. 22, 44.

[24] See further P. M. Casey, *Is John's Gospel True?* (London, 1996), pp. 87–97.

[25] For a survey of significant attempts to do this, L. T. Stuckenbruck, 'An Approach to the New Testament through Aramaic Sources: The Recent Methodological Debate', *JSP* 8, 1994 (sic!), 3–29, esp. 17–28.

[26] Schwarz, '*Und Jesus sprach*', p. 202, discussed in more detail by Casey, *Aramaic Sources of Mark's Gospel*, pp. 45–6.

שׂוּי is the wrong word. It is used in these two passages as a translation of the Hebrew שׂים because the translator was suffering from interference from Hebrew as he worked. We must not proceed like this, but we must prefer the common Aramaic עבד, well attested in Aramaic both before and after the time of Jesus with the correct meaning. This does not mean that Targums are to be avoided altogether, only that, like other Aramaic documents, they must be used with care. Perhaps the most interesting piece of work of this kind has been Chilton's use of the Targum of Isaiah. I shall seek to carry a small part of his work further forward in discussing the very difficult saying Matt. 11.12 (cf. Luke 16.16).[27]

Finally, it should be obvious that the criticisms which we must make of our predecessors' methods are criticisms of their methods, not of their integrity. Knowledge cannot advance if the methodological weaknesses of earlier work are not exposed. Such criticisms however presuppose that our predecessors *did* believe what they wrote, not that they were guilty of any kind of wrongdoing.

Method

In *Aramaic Sources of Mark's Gospel*, I sought to lay down methodological principles for uncovering some written Aramaic sources of Mark's Gospel.[28] I now offer a modified version of these principles with a view to approaching the Aramaic dimension of Q.

1. The first step is to select passages which show some signs of having been translated literally from an Aramaic source. This is the logic of the passages selected for discussion in this monograph. Matt. 23.23–36//Luke 11.39–51 contains features which have led previous scholars to suggest that at least parts of it are two translations of a single Aramaic source, somewhat misread and misunderstood by Luke. We shall see good reason to carry this hypothesis much further forward. Matt. 11.2–19//Luke 7.18–35 consists largely of material which has an excellent *Sitz im Leben* in the life and teaching of Jesus and of John the Baptist. Its peculiarities include a son of man saying which appears to be a literal translation of a saying which makes proper sense only in Aramaic. The passages selected for study in chapter 5, Mark 3.20–30, Matt. 12.22–32, Luke 11.14–23, 12.10 also have an excellent *Sitz im Leben* in the life and teaching of Jesus. They

[27] B. D. Chilton, *GOD in STRENGTH. Jesus' Announcement of the Kingdom* (StNTU B1. Freistadt, 1978. Reprinted Sheffield, 1987); *The Glory of Israel. The Theology and Provenience of the Isaiah Targum* (JSOT.S 23. Sheffield, 1983); *A Galilean Rabbi and His Bible. Jesus' Own Interpretation of Isaiah* (London, 1984); see further pp. 125–8 below.

[28] Casey, *Aramaic Sources of Mark's Gospel*, pp. 107–10.

include one mistake (σκορπίζει με at Matt. 12.30//Luke 11.23), and a son of man saying which appears to have been translated no fewer than three times, and which makes proper sense only when the original Aramaic has been reconstructed.

All these passages, therefore, make an excellent start for considering the Aramaic dimension of Q. If it be adjudged successful, the next task will be to consider the rest of the Q material from the same perspective, to see how fruitful the methods proposed here can be for the rest of this predominantly early source material.

2. The second task is to begin the detailed work of making up a possible Aramaic substratum. For this purpose, we must use in the first instance the Aramaic of the Dead Sea scrolls. We have seen that it is close to the right date and cultural environment, which is of central importance. It is the wrong dialect for Jesus' speech, but this is much less important than has generally been thought.

Where words are not found in the scrolls, we must use other Aramaic with care. We have already seen how to proceed with words such as פרישׁין, נגעא and שׁבתא.[29] The judicious use of Aramaic of earlier and later date enables us to recover a good approximation to the language of the historical Jesus, despite the fragmentary nature of early remains. It is only at this stage that we should use the Syriac versions. We should never begin with them, because they are translations *into* the wrong dialect. At a late stage, however, they may alert us to possibilities which we had not thought of, because they are in the right language and derive from a significantly similar culture.

3. The third task is to check that the draft reconstruction is sufficiently idiomatic. Some specifically Aramaic locutions are bound to have been removed during the process of translation into Greek, and they have to be recreated. For example, confronted with the quite Greek οὐκ ἔχει ποῦ at Matt. 8.20//Luke 9.58, I suggested לא איתי לה אן ד... בה.[30] We cannot normally infer that such suggestions are accurate verbatim. What we should claim is that Jesus must have spoken, and our sources must have written, idiomatic Aramaic. If therefore this is what we reconstruct, we will obtain an accurate impression of the source even where details are uncertain. My fifth procedure is a particularly important check and balance against too much creativity.

4. The resulting reconstruction must be interpreted from a first-century Jewish perspective. Particular attention must be paid to any respect in which it differs from the Greek translation. This is most striking with

---

[29] See pp. 56–9 above.   [30] Casey, 'Jackals,' 3–22, at 7.

(א)נשׁ(א) בר, a normal term for 'man' with a general level of meaning, quite different from ὁ υἱὸς τοῦ ἀνθρώπου, a Christological title of Jesus alone. Sometimes it is later exegetical tradition which has to be removed. For example, at Matt. 8.20//Lk 9.58, I suggested מַשְׁכְּנִין for Q's κατασκηνώσεις, and discussed the alternative possibilities מְמַלְלִין and מְדָרִין.[31] This enabled me to consider the natural provision of roosts for birds, instead of being hidebound by the traditional translation 'nests'; in Aramaic this would be קִנִין, which would have given rise to the precise Greek equivalent νοσσιάς.[32] The erroneous nature of traditional exegesis should however already have been clear from Q's κατασκηνώσεις. Moreover, the mere fact of an Aramaic source takes us one stage back in the tradition, but not necessarily back to Jesus himself. All the necessary criteria must then be used to determine whether Jesus said and did what our sources attributed to him. The Aramaic sentences will be found especially helpful in reconstructing the cultural context of Jesus' ministry. They cannot, however, function properly without a full cultural context.

5. We must go through the passage again from the perspective of an ancient translator. If s/he was faced with the proposed reconstruction, might s/he reasonably have put what we have? Careful attention must be paid both to the overall sweep of the translation, and to all the small details. In doing this, we must make use both of research into the known habits of ancient translators, and from modern insights into the nature of the translation process itself. We shall feel happiest when the translator could *only* have done what we posit, but we must not impose this as a general standard of judgement, because there are many situations in which translators have a genuine choice. We must be on the look-out both for consistent habits and for strategies, but we must be careful not to invent either of them.

6. We must isolate as far as possible deliberate editing by the Gospel writers themselves. This is especially important with 'Q' passages, where we have to determine in the first place whether we are dealing with one translation or two. In Matt. 23.23–36//Luke 11.39–51, we shall find two translations. Luke 11.39–51 has been vigorously edited throughout, with some Aramaic words being misread in a way that fits in with the editorial aims throughout the passage. Matthew's version also shows some signs of editing, especially towards the end. Other editorial features include omissions, notably of Mark 3.20–1 by both Matthew and Luke, and the interpolation of small narrative pieces (e.g. Matt. 12.23, but more characteristically by Luke, e.g. 7.20–1).

---

[31] *Ibid.*, 8, 20–1.
[32] See further Casey, *Aramaic Sources of Mark's Gospel*, pp. 21, 50, 61, 69–71.

7. Having completed a whole hypothesis, with a reconstruction interpreted in the light of Jesus' Jewish culture and a translation plotted out in accordance with the needs of a translator who belonged to the target culture, an overall assessment must be made of the probability of what I have suggested. I shall suggest that in the case of the passages studied in chapters 3–5 of this book, the probability that we can reconstruct abbreviated but accurate accounts written by Jews from Israel who were present at the time is quite unassailable. Accordingly, I propose that the methods expounded here are an essential element in any reasonable attempt to recover the Jesus of history, and an essential complement to the proposals which I previously made in *Aramaic Sources of Mark's Gospel*.

8. Finally, the results must be written up in a way that is as reader-friendly as possible. It should be obvious that this does not involve following the order of events in which the investigation was conducted. As in my previous monograph, I have presented reconstructed source material at or near the beginning of each of chapters 3–5. After any necessary introduction, I have proceeded through the source material in the order in which the sayings are presented, with discussion of that order when necessary. I have also discussed any Aramaic words which might be considered difficult or controversial, the proposed behaviour of the translators in difficult or controversial circumstances, and editorial behaviour by Matthew and Luke. I have not, however, given the attestation of every Aramaic word, nor every detail of the behaviour of the translators, as this would make this book very lengthy and tedious. I hope the result is sufficiently learned, and yet intelligible.

3

SCRIBES AND PHARISEES: MATTHEW
23.23–36//LUKE 11.39–51

The purpose of this chapter is to reconstruct the Aramaic source of Matt. 23.23–36//Luke 11.39–51, and to discuss the interpretation and historicity of this source. I do not offer a Greek reconstruction of Q, because we do not have sufficient reason to believe in one. I argue that there were two translations, one used by Matthew and the other used by Luke. We cannot disentangle the processes of translation and editing, which may or may not have been done as a single piece of work. I also reflect on the importance of a passage like this for our model of Q.

In presenting the Aramaic source, I follow Matthew's order, because Luke shows heavy Gentile editing. We shall also see that a first-century Jew might assume a connection between verses 1 and 4, still perceptible in Matthew and removed by Luke. I have numbered our source in verses for convenient reference. The editing of both evangelists has been too great for us to use the conventional verse numbering of either of them.

1 אוי לכון, ספרין ופרישין, די עשׂרין נגעא ושבתא וכמונא ועברתון על חומריא, די דינא ורחמיא והימנותא.

2 אלין נא חייב הוה למעבד, ואנון לא למעבר.

3 נגדין עוירין, דמצללין יתוש ובלעין גמלא.

4 אוי לכון, ספרין ופרישין, די דכין בריתא דכסא ודמזרקא, וגוא מלא מן חטוף ושרחות.

5 ריקין. הוא דעבד בריתא, הלא עבד אף גוא.

6 דכו נא לגוא והא בריתא דכא.

7 אוי לכון, ספרין ופרישין, דמפתין תפיליכון ומרבין ציציא ורחמין כורסותא רברביא בכנישתא ושלמיא בשוקיא.

8 אוי לכון, ספרין ופרישין, דדמיתון לקברין מתטשׁין, דלבר שפירין ובגוא מליין גרמי מיתין וכל טמאה.

9 אוי לכון, ספרין ופרישין, דבנין קבריא דנביאיא ומצבתין נפשתא דצדיקיא.

10 ואמרתון, אן איתינא ביומי אבהתנא לא איתינא חבריהון בדמא דנביאיא.

11 ושהדתון לכון דבנין אנתון די קטליהון.

12 כל־קבל דנה אמר אף חכמתה די אלהא, אשלח נביאין וחכימין וספרין ומנהון
יקטלון וירדפון,

13 די יאתא עליהדן כל דם קשיט מתאשד על ארעא מדם דהבל קשיטא לדם זכריה
דאבד בין ביתא למדבחא.

14 אמן אמר אנה לכון, יתבעא מן דרא דנה.

Woe to you, scribes and Pharisees, who tithe mint and dill and cummin,
and transgress/pass over the 'heavy' (things), which (are) justice and
mercy and trust. [2]These, surely, (one) was liable to do, and (one was
liable) not to pass over them (i.e. the others). [3]Blind guides, who strain out
the gnat and swallow the camel! [4]Woe to you, scribes and Pharisees, who
cleanse the outside of the cup and dish, and the inside is full from robbery
and excess. [5]Fools! (lit., Empties!) He who made the outside/creation,
did he not make the inside too? [6]So cleanse the inside, and look! the out-
side/person/everything is clean. [7]Woe to you, scribes and Pharisees, who
broaden your tefillin and lengthen (the) tassels, and love the important
seats in the synagogues and greetings in the streets. [8]Woe to you, scribes
and Pharisees, who are like whitewashed tombs, which (are) beautiful
on the outside and inside are full of dead people's bones and of all uncleanness. [9]Woe to you, scribes and Pharisees, who build the tombs of
the prophets and decorate the monuments of the righteous, [10]and you say
'if we were in the days of our fathers, we would not be their associates in
the blood of the prophets.' [11]And you bear yourselves witness that you
are the sons of their murderers.[12]Because of this the Wisdom of God said,
'I will send prophets and sages and scribes, and some of them they will
kill and put to flight, [13]so that all the righteous blood shed on the earth
will come upon them, from the blood of Abel the righteous to the blood of
Zechariah, who perished between the House and the altar.'[14]Amen I say
to you, it will be sought from this generation.

Orthodox Jews

It is evident from the first part of this passage that some of Jesus' opponents were what I call 'orthodox' Jews. I use this term advisedly, for
three reasons. Firstly, we need a term for analytical purposes. Secondly,
there is no term in the primary source material, so we must produce one.
Thirdly, their central life-stance was very similar to that of some people
in the modern world, where they are universally known as orthodox Jews.
If we do this, however, we must be careful to produce a definition which
is applicable to orthodox Jews in the ancient world, and we must not read

back aspects of modern Judaism which do not apply to them. I offered such a definition in *From Jewish Prophet to Gentile God*:

> Orthodox Jews accepted as divinely inspired the accounts of the history and halakhah of the Jewish people recorded in the written and oral Laws, and codified in sacred books such as the Pentateuch. In the face of threats of assimilation, they stood firm as guardians of the Law, seeking to ensure that it was observed and applied to the whole of life. This led them to discuss and codify additional enactments, both orally and in written collections such as the Zadokite document and the book of Jubilees. This was a central concern of their lives, and in this way they embodied and defended Jewish identity. Orthodox Jews thus included both Pharisees and Essenes. A significant proportion of Jews did not observe the additional enactments of the orthodox, and some Jews did not obey the halakhah at all. The difficulties which this caused for the orthodox world-view are evident in works such as Daniel 9 and 4 Ezra.[1]

My discussion was criticised by some reviewers, who maintained the older view that there was no orthodoxy in Second Temple Judaism. In so doing, however, they used Christian assumptions about what orthodox people should be, a group of people who agreed with each other and who were in some sense normative. The above definition is not of this kind. It is based on the embodiment and defence of Jewish identity by applying the Law to the whole of life, a process which has always involved the expansion of detailed enactments. I did not suggest that orthodox Jews thought and/or acted in the same way as each other, since that would be patently false, in the ancient and modern worlds alike. On the contrary, I explicitly included Pharisees and Essenes in my definition, and I did not confine my discussion of orthodox opposition to Jesus to Pharisees.[2]

To see how fruitful this definition can be, we may consider sabbath observance. Sabbath observance is so important that I isolated it as one of eight identity factors of Second Temple Judaism.[3] It is commanded in scripture. Its observance is one of the ten commandments, which declares

---

[1] P. M. Casey, *From Jewish Prophet to Gentile God. The Origins and Development of New Testament Christology* (The Edward Cadbury Lectures at the University of Birmingham, 1985–86. Cambridge and Louisville, 1991), pp. 17–18, with discussion at pp. 18–20.

[2] *Ibid.*, p. 17 and e.g. 61–5.   [3] *Ibid.*, pp. 12–13.

that it is to be observed by the people, children, slaves, animals and guests (Exod. 20.8–11//Deut. 5.12–15), so that the whole Jewish community should observe it. The penalty for not observing it is said to be death (Exod. 31.14; 35.2), and its importance is further indicated by its legitimation from the creation (Exod. 20.11) and the Exodus (Deut. 5.15). The book of *Jubilees* declares that sabbath observance is a mark of being Jewish (*Jub.* 2.31). The same perception was found among Gentiles. Josephus records a number of Gentile measures permitting Jews to keep the sabbath (e.g. Jos., *A.J.* XIV.263–4).

Such a clear marker of Jewish identity naturally functions also as an index of assimilation. When Trito-Isaiah gives a brief description of foreigners who join themselves to the Lord, that is, of Gentiles assimilating into Judaism, he specifies 'everyone who keeps the sabbath' (Isa. 56.6). When 1 Maccabees relates how some Jews gladly left Judaism, that is, assimilated into the Gentile world, it records that they 'profaned the sabbath' (1 Macc. 1.43). This is the importance of the untrue statement that Jesus 'abrogated the sabbath' (John 5.18). This means that Jesus has been wrongly portrayed as taking a Gentile view of the sabbath.

It is precisely because the sabbath was so important in the Judaism of our period that orthodox Jews vigorously developed additional enactments to observe on it. We can see this orthodox perspective in the additional sabbath halakhoth found in the collections of *Jub.* 50.6–13 and CD X.14–XII.6. These contain numerous additional judgements, including for example the prohibition of sex and of warfare on the sabbath. The judgement that warfare is not permitted on the sabbath (*Jub.* 50.12) is drastically illustrated by 1 Macc. 2.29–41. This relates how a thousand Jews were killed on the sabbath, when they refused to defend themselves. This is an orthodox expansion of sabbath Law, unknown from the earlier period, when it would have caused equal havoc and could therefore not have gone unrecorded. In response to it, a deliberate decision to fight on the sabbath is recorded, the response of the Jewish community as a whole when orthodox expansion of halakhah grew quite out of hand. The prohibition of sex with one's wife on the sabbath has never been normal in the Jewish community either. Both prohibitions resulted from applying the biblical prohibition of work on the sabbath to the whole of ordinary daily life.

This distinction between orthodox and other Jews is essential for understanding sabbath observance in the historical ministry of Jesus.[4] When Jesus first healed on the sabbath, there were no objections. One

---

[4] *Ibid.*, pp. 70–1.

incident was an exorcism in public at a Jewish meeting in Capernaum (Mark 1.21–7): the second was the healing of Peter's mother-in-law at home (Mark 1.29–31). We know that Capernaum Jews were observant, because they brought other sick people to him, but only when the sabbath was over. Mark's note of time is very careful: 'When evening came, when the sun had set' (Mark 1.32), that is, when the sabbath was clearly over. This makes sense only if Mark's source made the standard Jewish assumption that we do not carry sick people on the sabbath under the rubric of not carrying burdens (Jer. 17.21–2). It follows that observant Jews did not generally object to healing on the sabbath.

It was different when some of Jesus' disciples took Peah on the sabbath.[5] This is not forbidden in the written Law. However, there were some Pharisees present, and they objected that the behaviour of the disciples was not lawful (Mark 2.24). This illustrates the orthodox Jewish life-stance, which was expanding the regulations governing sabbath observance. Whether or not anyone had previously suggested or ruled that Peah should not be taken on the sabbath, these Pharisees felt that it was work and they objected accordingly. Coming in from a prophetic perspective, Jesus defended his disciples with two classic arguments. The first went in from the example of the patriarch David, the second from the purpose of God at creation. A further conflict followed at a Jewish meeting.[6] Mark records that people, probably Pharisees (cf. Mark 2.24; 3.6) and certainly orthodox, watched to see if he would heal on the sabbath. From their perspective, as from that of later orthodox sources, healing on the sabbath was wrong (cf. *m. Shab.* 14.3–4; *t. Shab.* 12.8–14). Equally, they will have held something like the later orthodox view that people could not be prosecuted for sabbath violation unless they had been warned (*Sifre Num.* 113.5 on Num. 15.33; *t. Sanh.* 11.1–3; cf. e.g. *m. Sanh.* 5.1), and they were watching for a further violation. Jesus healed the man, because he believed that healing released a person from the bond of Satan (Luke 13.16), and it is not against the written Law. He therefore defended his actions with a classically Jewish argument by analogy, based on the halakhic judgement that saving life overrides the sabbath (Mark 3.4). This follows from the decision of 1 Macc. 2.41, so we should infer that it was already accepted and perhaps codified (cf. *m. Yoma* 8.6; *Mek.* I (Exod. 31.12–17), 7–30). The term used was נפש, which means both 'life' and 'person', so the argument involves a typical shift of meaning, extending the accepted

---

[5] For detailed discussion, see Casey, *Aramaic Sources of Mark's Gospel*, pp. 138–68.

[6] For detailed discussion of Mark 3.1–6, see Casey, *Aramaic Sources of Mark's Gospel*, pp. 138–9, 173–92.

view, that saving life overrides the sabbath, to saving a person overrides the sabbath. The Pharisees then gave counsel to destroy him (Mark 3.6). This is extremely logical, because from their perspective he had violated the sabbath twice, the second time quite deliberately. Equally, no court case follows, because from a more normal Jewish perspective he had not broken the Law.

This distinction between orthodox and other Jews also enables us to see how seriously sabbath healing has been rewritten in the fourth Gospel. In the sabbath healing of John 5, Jesus orders the healed man to carry his pallet (John 5.8). This is obviously contrary to the biblical prohibition of carrying burdens on the sabbath (Jer. 17.21–2). Jesus has thus acted like a Gentile. The subsequent discussion is entirely coherent. The objection to this behaviour comes from 'the Jews', who point out that it is unlawful for the man to carry his pallet on the sabbath (John 5.10). It is, for all Jews, so the opposition has been correctly delineated. When therefore 'the Jews' seek to kill Jesus, that is, to carry out the biblical penalty for sabbath-breaking (Exod. 31.14; 35.2), the fourth Gospel correctly says that one reason was that Jesus abrogated the sabbath (5.18). The discussion is thus in a quite different realm from the synoptic disputes. Whereas Jesus disputed with orthodox Jews as to *how* the sabbath should be observed, the fourth Gospel has him break it like a Gentile and thereby dispute with 'the Jews'. A concept of orthodoxy is essential in clarifying this difference.

The most extensive criticism of my analysis of Jewish identity in the Second Temple period is that of Dunn, so I must consider here in more detail his criticism of my use of the concept of orthodoxy.[7] Dunn's first objection concentrates on the differences between Qumran Essenes and other Jewish groups. He notes that they regarded themselves as 'the only truly "orthodox", the only truly loyal to the covenant and to the law' (sic), and he sees similar factionalism in other writings such as *1 Enoch* and *Jubilees*. Dunn's facts are right, but as an objection they presuppose that orthodox Jews should have a degree of uniformity characteristic not of orthodox Jews, but of the imaginations of Gentile Christians. Moreover, he replaces my definition of orthodoxy with his, which is not a satisfactory way of discussing anything. The differences between different groups of Jews should not prevent us from isolating what they have in common. Dunn also confuses the issue by imagining our terms

[7] J. D. G. Dunn, 'The Making of Christology – Evolution or Unfolding?', in J. B. Green and M. Turner (eds.), *Jesus of Nazareth: Lord and Christ: In Honour of Prof. I. H. Marshall* (Carlisle, 1994), pp. 437–52, at p. 441.

'orthodox' and 'unorthodox' being used by ancient groups who do not use these terms. For example, he asserts that 'different groups within late Second Temple Judaism regarded themselves as in effect the only truly "orthodox"'. There are no such statements in the primary sources. We should not confuse our analytical categories with ancient evidence like this. Dunn's second objection is that by using the term 'orthodox' of the Pharisees, 'Casey is viewing the time of Jesus from a post-70 rabbinic perspective, with inevitably distorting effect.' I did not, however, claim that the Pharisees were the only orthodox group, nor that they were more orthodox than other Jews who expanded detailed enactments as they applied the Law to the whole of life. This was a significant feature of Second Temple Judaism, and therefore cannot be regarded as a 'post-70 rabbinic perspective'.

Dunn's criticisms presuppose that analytical categories should be used in a Christian sense when we analyse Second Temple Judaism. He ignores my definition of orthodoxy altogether. His notion that factionalism makes orthodoxy an unsuitable category depends on replacing my definition with one in terms of uniformity. Hence his use of 'unorthodox' as the opposite of 'orthodox'. I did not use 'unorthodox' because it is not the opposite of 'orthodox' in a Jewish sense – in discussing Jesus' conflict with some of his orthodox opponents I used 'prophetic' as the opposite of 'orthodox', to locate the nature of Jesus' opposition to Jews who used their expansion of enactments to damage the Jewish lives of others.[8] The notion that by using the term 'orthodox' of the Pharisees I am looking from 'a post-rabbinic perspective' further equates orthodoxy with what has been thought to be normative. This assumption that concepts should be used in a Christian sense should not be accepted, indeed it should not be regarded as a properly academic view at all. All scholars should be free to use analytical categories in senses that seem fruitful to them, and they should be judged by whether such uses are genuinely fruitful. The use of Jewish categories for the analysis of Second Temple Judaism is an especially obvious ploy, and one which should be judged on its own terms, not by imposing Christian assumptions on it.

I shall therefore proceed to use the term 'orthodox' in explicating the nature of Jesus' opponents in this passage. My discussion of the orthodox view of the sabbath has shown how orthodox Jews observed a much stricter halakhah than later became normative. This is a more general feature of orthodox Judaism at this time, and part of the explanation of the conflict between Jesus and orthodox Jews.

[8] Casey, *From Jewish Prophet to Gentile God*, pp. 61–5, 70–3.

Edited introductory comments

The Lucan version of this passage has an introduction, setting it in the house of a Pharisee who was surprised that Jesus did not immerse before breakfast. This setting is evidently secondary. It has probably been formed on the basis of Mark 7.1ff., which Luke omitted as part of his great omission of Mark 6.45–8.27a. Luke has inferred from Mark 7.2 the setting of a meal suitable for the Q teaching, since the Pharisees and some of the scribes could see the disciples eating with unwashed hands only if they were at a meal with them. Mark 6.48 gives the time as the fourth watch of the night, and the next incident takes place εὐθύς (Mark 6.54), so Luke has inferred that the meal was ἄριστον, the first meal of the day. Immersion is from Mark 7.4, and Luke's editing of Q has given him a version of the Marcan teaching on inside and outside (Mark 7.15–23) intelligible and meaningful to civilised Gentiles, yet remaining within the parameters of what they regarded as Judaism.

This opening is also associated with Luke 11.45, which is also purely Lucan. Thus ספרין must be right for Matthew's γραμματεῖς. Luke removed it from verses 1 and 4 to fire a second section at τοῖς νομικοῖς (Luke 11.45–52), his rendering of ספרין for Greek-speaking Gentiles. Matthew, or his source, may be schematised, but the underlying tradition should be accepted. Jesus' opponents throughout the ministry were not *only* Pharisees. The accusation that he cast out demons by Beelzeboul was made by 'scribes who came down from Jerusalem' (Mark 3.22), and such people came again with Pharisees and asked him about purity Law (Mark 7.1). His opponents were orthodox, in the sense in which I use that term. It is therefore entirely appropriate that he should have fired some of his criticisms of them at ספרין ופרישין.

I have not kept the purely Matthean ὑποκριταί. When sayings of Jesus were first translated into Greek, the Greek word ὑποκριτής meant 'actor' rather than 'hypocrite'. We should suppose that Jesus used this actual Greek word in some Aramaic sentences. This makes excellent sense in passages such as Matt. 6.2, 5, where its use with reference to overtly observant Jews will have formed extremely sharp polemic, for the theatre symbolises especially well the Hellenism against which they sought to protect Jewish observances. The Aramaic חנף, sometimes thought to be the underlying word,[9] does not occur in Aramaic texts until later. It does

---

[9] See e.g. J. Barr, 'The Hebrew/Aramaic Background of "Hypocrisy" in the Gospels', in P. R. Davies and R. T. White (eds.), *A Tribute to Geza Vermes. Essays on Jewish and Christian Literature and History* (JSOT.S 100. Sheffield, 1990), pp. 307–26; Casey, *Aramaic Sources of Mark's Gospel*, pp. 82–3.

not mean 'actor', and the Hebrew חָנֵף is properly rendered with ἀσεβής in LXX (Job 8.13; 15.34; 20.5; 27.8; Prov. 11.9; Isa. 33.14), rather than with ὑποκριτής (Job 34.30; 36.13, neither really original to LXX, but from Theodotion), because of the much bigger overlap in semantic area. The sharper force of ὑποκριτής also fits the dramatic imagery of Matt. 6.2, 5, which clearly refers to the sort of behaviour found in cities. We should therefore conclude that Jesus used the Greek word ὑποκριτής polemically in passages such as Matt. 6.2, 5: Matthew has added it and used it schematically in Matt. 23.

Tithing

עשׂר, 'tithe', עבר, 'overlook', or 'transgress', and עבד, 'do', form a series of puns. They are quite unavoidable, and have not been produced by selecting one word rather than another possible one. Moreover, that on עבר and עבד is so basic that it cannot have been unintentional. The tithing of herbs is not explicitly commanded in the biblical text. For example, Deut. 14.23 specifies corn, wine and oil, that is to say, basic food and drink. Tithing provided for priests and Levites, for Jerusalem and for the poor.[10] Tithing basic food and drink would ensure the survival of priests, Levites and the poor, all of whom received tithes directly in kind. At the same time, the tithing of herbs is a natural interpretation of biblical Law from an orthodox perspective. Some of the biblical regulations are quite general in kind. For example, Lev. 27.30 specifies זרע הארץ and פרי העץ. Such general expressions would encourage people who applied the Law to all the details of life to provide herbs with everything else. They might reason that the priests and Levites obviously deserved some dill with their fish, and/or their cucumbers needed pickling, so dill should be included in general expressions such as those of Lev. 27.30. Hence later orthodox sources provide for dill and cummin to be tithed (*m. Dem.* 2.1, cummin; *m. Maas.* 4.5, dill). The tithing of mint, not registered in rabbinical sources, reflects the same approach to life. Scribes and Pharisees will have seen it commanded in the general statements of scripture, to provide priests and Levites with mint, which perhaps they might eat with their lamb or goat in the Temple. A general principle, which could have had the same effect, was written down later:

אמרו במעשׂרות כל שׁהוא אוכל ונשׁמר וגידוליו מן הארץ חייב במעשׂרות. כלל

---

[10] See especially E. P. Sanders, *Judaism: Practice and Belief 63 BCE – 66CE* (London and Philadelphia, 1992), ch. 9.

They stated a general principle concerning tithes: everything
which is eaten and kept and which they grow from the earth is
liable for tithes.   (*m. Maas.* 1.1)

It is accordingly probable that mint is not mentioned as subject to tithe
in the Mishnah because it grew wild. Scribes and Pharisees will have
tithed it all the same, whether because they did cultivate it, or because
the priests in the Temple needed it, and were not helped by the fact that
it grew wild miles away. In either case, or both, the view of these scribes
and Pharisees is perfectly logical, but stricter than that of later sources
legislating for all Israel. This was often the case.

Jesus evidently believed that orthodox Jews were failing to observe the
main points of the Law, and that this was combined with commitment
to observing these details. His concern has an excellent *Sitz im Leben* in
his ministry, and does not have one in the early church, which was not
concerned about the details of tithing. The general situation is confirmed
by *t. Men.* 13.22. This looks back on the Second Temple period in trying
to explain the fall of the Temple, and says that people laboured over the
Torah and were careful about tithes.

Luke generalised with πᾶν λάχανον in place of the third herb, to make
the main point clear to people coming in from a Gentile Christian perspective. The second herb has been misread, and to very good effect. The
original was שבתא, 'dill', correctly translated with ἄνηθον by Matthew.
This is a common herb, which scribes and Pharisees will have tithed,
as Jesus said. It has been misread as שברא, 'rue', and so translated as
πήγανον in Luke. Whether Luke imagined exactly what sort of rue was
tithed is unclear, and hardly mattered. The word שברא does not survive
in the Aramaic of our period, but this is merely because the few extant
texts do not include any discussions of herbs. It was already in existence
in Akkadian as *šib-bur-ra-tú*,[11] so there should be no doubt that it is early
enough in date. It is found in later Aramaic, and abundantly attested in
Syriac. The late dictionary of Bar Bahlul[12] comments ארמלא או בשושא.
The first of these means that it has been identified as *peganum harmala*,
an edible herb used by some people in the East as a spice for food. If Luke
knew this, he is likely to have thought that it stank dreadfully, which portrays the scribes as very silly. Bar Bahlul's second definition means that
שברא has been identified as wild rue. This is also indicated at *b. Shebu.*
20b, where it is used as a one-word definition of the wick of the desert. It is
because it is wild that, as פיגם, it is forbidden to be tithed at *m. Shebu.* 9.1.

---

[11] R. C. Thompson, *A Dictionary of Assyrian Botany* (London, 1949), p. 76.
[12] *Lexicon Syriacum auctore Hassano bar Bahlule*, ed. R. Duval (Paris, 1901).

If Luke thought that scribes and Pharisees were tithing a wild plant with woolly leaves used for making wicks, he thought they were very silly indeed. Luke rejected their habits: the more bizarre they seemed, the better. We should not however follow him. They were sensibly tithing dill!

This is part of the evidence that this part of the Q material was transmitted in Aramaic and translated twice, so that Matthew and Luke each inherited a different translation. Older versions of this explanation of why Luke read πήγανον have accordingly been challenged by Kloppenborg, who believes that Q was a Greek document.[13] He argues that שברא is not 'rue', since πήγανον has an exact Aramaic equivalent פיגם. He does not, however, provide evidence that the Hebrew פיגם was used in Aramaic as well as Hebrew, and we have seen that the evidence of שברא is perfectly sound. Kloppenborg also argues against Black that translation mistakes cannot explain the difference between (א)כמון, supposed to lie behind Matthew's τὸ κύμινον, and ירק, supposed to lie behind Luke's λάχανον. This is true as far as it goes, but it does not go far enough. Luke's πᾶν λάχανον might indeed be put down to Lucan editing, rather than to misreading וכמונא. This does not, however, undermine the evidence that Luke misread the second herb. Equally, moreover, כמונא is the sort of word which may not have been known to a man who did not do the cooking. He may therefore have read the ו as a י, since these two letters might be indistinguishable, and thought his source ought to have read כל מינא, 'every species'. Luke's πᾶν λάχανον, 'every herb', would then be a good interpretative translation of what he thought his source really meant.

The term חומריא, literally 'heavy', did require definition. It was an Aramaic word, though many surviving discussions are in Hebrew. From our perspective, it has two meanings, which we generally represent by two different words, in English perhaps 'weighty' and 'stringent'. So the heavy of heavies (חמורה מן החמורות) may be 'Honour thy father and mother' (Abba bar Kahana at *y. Qid.* 1.7/22(61b)), or the commandment isolated as חמירא may be 'Thou shalt not take the name of the Lord thy God in vain' (*b. Shebu.* 39a). These are obviously very important commandments, and the Jewish community would suffer very badly if they were not kept. The opposite of 'heavy' was 'light'. Thus the 'light of lights' (קלה שבקלות) may be the prohibition of taking a mother bird at the same time as her young or eggs (Deut. 22.6–7: Abba bar Kahana as above). Most people are not tempted to do this, and the Jewish community would not suffer serious damage if some people did. The other aspect of 'heavy' is illustrated by the judgement that Rabban Gamaliel's house were מחמירין, 'stringent' with

---

[13] Kloppenborg, *Formation of Q*, pp. 58–9. For detailed discussion of Kloppenborg, see pp. 22–32, 49–50 above.

themselves, and מקילין, 'light', or rather 'lenient', towards Israel. This was because they let Jews in general bake large loaves on festivals, the ruling of Bet Hillel, while they themselves baked only thin cakes, the ruling of Bet Shammai (*m. Besah.* 2.6//*m. Eduy.* 3.10). It follows that orthodox Jews will have thought they were 'doing the stringent things, עבדין חומריא' when they tithed mint, dill and cummin. From their perspective, people who overlooked (עבר) mint, dill and cummin, transgressed (עבר again) the stringent things of the Law.

We can now see the point of Jesus' definition. It defines the centre of the Law in accordance with the main thrust of the prophetic tradition, over against people who were expanding its enactments. His definition of חומריא has its proper *Sitz im Leben* in the ministry of Jesus, for whom this was a central concern. It does not have a proper *Sitz im Leben* in the early church, which dropped such things as tithing altogether, and consequently was not concerned about this kind of contrast. This applies also to למעבר at the end of verse 2. Jesus had no reason to prevent the tithing of herbs. He will have known people who were devoted to justice, mercy and trust, and who automatically tithed their herbs with everything else, people like his brother Jacob rather than those scribes and Pharisees to whom he objected.

The translation of חומריא into Greek is very difficult, because the Greek language does not have equivalent terminology with the same cultural associations. This is why I have attributed τοῦ νόμου to the translator. Jesus might have said חומריא די אוריתא, but די אוריתא is unnecessary in Aramaic, whereas Matthew might well feel that it was an explicitative translation which would help to focus the minds of Greek-speaking Christians in the right place. He inserted νόμος at Matt. 12.5; 22.36, 40, and he is likely to be responsible for it also at Matt. 5.17 and perhaps elsewhere, so this addition is in accordance with his probable habits. Matthew also did his best with the translation τὰ βαρύτερα: he will have suffered from interference, and will have known very well what חומריא were. He was also familiar with the LXX, where βαρύς represents some form of כבד, the Hebrew equivalent of חמר, in the overwhelming majority of cases. Monoglot Greeks, however, may not have thought of two senses for βαρύτερα, since βαρύς was not in general use meaning 'weighty', 'important', though it was used figuratively. Matthew could not, however, do better without writing a long explanation, and he will have hoped that this would be supplied by someone when his Gospel was read.

Luke dropped this piece of Jewish culture, and made sure his Gentile audience realised that they should put first their duties to God and their neighbour, accusing Pharisees, and subsequently scribes, of not doing so. His alteration of רחמיא והימנותא to τὴν ἀγάπην τοῦ θεοῦ involved another misreading of the Aramaic source, since τὴν ἀγάπην could render רחמתא rather than רחמיא, and this is not likely to be coincidental. This also puts these misreadings in their cultural context: Luke so misread his source because he saw what fitted the needs of his congregations, not merely because the ancient source was squiggly and a bit difficult to read. This verse is strong evidence that, in this passage, translating and editing were part of the same process. This is not consistent with the view that Luke used Matthew. Nor are the variant translations of עברין in verse 1, and למעבר in verse 2. Here Luke has the more literal παρέρχεσθε and παρεῖναι, while Matthew has the freer ἀφήκατε and ἀφιέναι. It is most improbable that Luke would edit Matthew into being a more literal translation of their Aramaic source, so this is further evidence that there were two independent translations, one for each Gospel writer.

Verse 3 has an extraordinary hyperbole, and it presumably made people laugh. Guides were necessary for the blind, and for camels. Blind people cannot strain gnats out of liquids. Camels are unclean, as food (Lev. 11.4). Gnats are not mentioned explicitly in biblical dietary laws. Some people will have thought they were forbidden as שֶׁרֶץ הָעוֹף (Lev. 11.20: Deut. 14.19). We should infer that scribes and Pharisees strained liquids such as water and wine to ensure that they did not eat insects. Hatching larvae may have been considered a significant danger. I have reconstructed יתוש for Matthew's τὸν κώνωπα: some uncertainty as to the exact term should not allow us to miss the main point. Some earlier scholars suggested קלמא;[14] the major objection to this is not its late attestation, which is almost inevitable with some of the words for such things, but doubt as to whether it has the right meaning. Jastrow, for example, spelling it כלמא, reasonably translated it 'vermin'. As to the customs involved, *m. Shab.* 20.2 records the practice of straining wine. At *b. Hul.* 67a, יבחושין may or may not be removed by this process. Aristotle evidently believed that gnats came from larvae found in second-rate wine: οἱ δὲ κώνωπες ἐκ σκωλήκων οἳ γίγνονται ἐκ τῆς περὶ τὸ ὄχος ἰλύος (*Historia Animalium* 5.19.552b). This is natural, because the larvae always lie in water and other such liquids.

The Damascus Document interprets Levitical texts to prohibit the eating of creeping things, from the larvae of bees to every living thing which creeps in water:

אל ישקקץ איש את נפשו בכל החיה והרמש לאכל מהם מעגלי הדבורים עד
כל נפש החיה אשר תרמוש במים.

---

[14] E.g. Black, *Aramaic Approach* (3rd edn, 1967), pp. 175–6.

A man shall not defile himself with any living creature or creeping thing by eating them, from the larvae of bees to any living
creature which creeps in water.

(CD XII.11–13, cf. Lev. 11.10, 44, 46)

This is the right culture at an earlier date than Jesus, and shows the mindset
of his opponents already established. Whereas Lev. 11.10 has שׁ החיה נפשׁ
אשׁר במים, Lev. 11.44 has בכל השׁרץ הרמשׂ על הארץ, and Lev. 11.46 has
כל נפשׁ החיה הרמשׂת במים, the Damascus Document carefully applies these
texts not only by amalgamating them, but by specifying the larvae of bees,
which would require people to strain honey. This is an exceptionally strict
judgement, like the following requirement to drain the blood from fish.
Orthodox Jews will have strained water and wine also to remove the
larvae themselves, even before they became שׁרץ העוף. Jesus' picture of
blind guides, trying to strain gnats out of wine or the like, and swallowing
an unclean animal larger than themselves is as ludicrous as possible,
and presented with extraordinary economy. It has an excellent *Sitz im
Leben* in the teaching of Jesus, where it indicates the profundity of his
rejection of his most legalistic opponents, who sought to guide others in
the interpretation of the Law. The saying does not have a proper *Sitz im
Leben* in the early church, which was not concerned about which form of
Judaism to have, and whose Gospels do not notice jokes when they pass
them on. This one was too Jewish for Luke.

Cleansing outside and inside

The next saying takes off from circumstances in which scribes and Pharisees might cleanse the outside of vessels. Later orthodox sources do have
a distinction between the inside and outside of vessels. *M. Kel.* 25.6 con-
templates liquids falling on certain parts of vessels such as the handles,
in which case you wipe them and they are clean:

כני כלים ואוגניהן ואזניהן וידות הכלים המקבלים שנפלו עליהן משקין מגנבן והן
טהורין...כלים שנטמאו אחוריו במשקין אחוריו טמאים תוכו ואוגנו ואזניו וידיו
טהורין.

The bases of vessels and their rims and their hangers, and the
handles of vessels which have a receptacle, if unclean liquids
fall on them, they dry them and they are clean . . . Vessels whose
outsides are unclean from unclean liquids, their outsides are
unclean, their insides and rims and hangers and handles are
clean.

We should infer that Jesus knew orthodox Jews who in certain circumstances wiped only the outside of cups and bowls, and thereby removed
limited impurity. The insides were not ritually unclean. The accusation
involves extortion, for the accusation that the vessels are full from robbery
and excess shifts straight from ritual impurity to moral wickedness. It fits
most easily into a temple context, as does *As. Mos.* 7.3–10. Here men who
will rule over Israel are described as impious, but are said to proclaim
themselves righteous. Their faults include devouring the possessions of
others and extravagant banquets, at which they eat and drink. They are
said to have their hands and minds on impurities, while they tell other
people not to touch them, in case other people make them unclean. Like
Jesus' opponents, they thought they lived in a state of ritual purity, which
they were determined to maintain. The author(s) of the *Assumption of
Moses* thought they were wicked, in much the same way as Jesus viewed
the people whom he criticised.

The priestly context of the Q passage follows from careful study of
some of its details. Of course, some of the scribes may have been priests,
and there was nothing to stop priests from being Pharisees. But priests are
not isolated for particular mention by the text in front of us, so corruption
in the priesthood alone cannot be the main point. We must therefore
ask ourselves a more difficult question, bearing in mind that Matthew's
introduction is stylised, so we might really be dealing with priestly scribes
rather than Pharisees. What would orthodox Jews support, as righteous
observance of the Law, that Jesus of Nazareth might describe as filling
cups and dishes from robbery and violence? And the answer to that, surely,
is the halakhah to tithing, which had the effect of enabling rich priests
to extract produce from the poor. Josephus writes as if the extraction
of tithes was a morally debatable business. He presents himself as not
taking tithes to which he was due (*Life* 80), while his fellow priests
took lots (*Life* 63). Shortly before the Roman war, he also records the
forcible extraction of tithes (*A.J.* XX.181, 206–7). *T. Men.* 13.21 records
woes against important families, attributed to Abba Saul ben Bitnith, a
shopkeeper in Jerusalem before its fall, and Abba Yose ben Yohanan, who
lived in the city at the same time. Among the families condemned are that
of Annas, on account of their whispering. These woes conclude, 'For
they are chief priests, and their sons treasurers, and their sons-in-laws
supervisors, and their servants come and beat us with staves.' This can
only refer to extortion by rich priests, and its *Sitz im Leben* is certainly
before the destruction of the temple (cf. *t. Zeb.* 11.16; *b. Pes.* 57a). The
passage goes on to suggest that the Second Temple could not have been
destroyed like the first, because they laboured over the Torah and were

careful about tithes. We must also remember that the second tithe was to be spent in Jerusalem. High prices would make some people richer without their being priests, and orthodox Jews would necessarily support the spending of the second tithe in Jerusalem because of the biblical regulation at Deut. 14.22–6.

We now have the full cultural context for verses 4–6. Jesus objected to orthodox Jews who supported an oppressive tithing system, and who participated in consuming the results. This did indeed involve robbery and excess. This also tells us what is wrong with tithing mint, dill and cummin. At one level, nothing; there is no need to pass over them. But failure to exercise justice, mercy and trust could mean guiding the poor into the belief that they should tithe ever more strictly to rich priests, and supporting violent collection of the tithes deemed to be due, in accordance with a stringent interpretation of the Law.

We now have a connection between verses 1–3 and 4–6 which is absent from the surface meaning of the text, and obvious when the Jewish assumptions of the second saying have been uncovered. This shows that the sayings were collected together in a Jewish setting, which points to an early date.

While there are no translation errors in verse 4, the lack of precise verbal agreement in a verse so close in meaning is consistent with the hypothesis that Matthew and Luke inherited different translations of this passage. For מזרקא Matthew has παροψίδος, which is a perfectly adequate translation, whereas Luke has the better Greek πίνακος. Matthew's ἐξ, which is not necessary after γέμουσιν for the Greek equivalent of 'full of', must be a translation of the Aramaic מן, which is not necessary after מלא for the Aramaic equivalent of 'full of.' It means 'full from', so that חטוף ושרחות refers to the robbery and excess of which Jesus' opponents were guilty. Luke's addition of ὑμῶν after ἔσωθεν, and his removal of ἐξ, are obviously alterations by Luke. The addition of ὑμῶν removes the end of the verse from the sphere of Jewish purity Law altogether. It is therefore clearly the Matthean version which has a *Sitz im Leben* in the cultural environment of Jesus, while the Lucan version is a deliberate modification in the interests of the target culture. Luke's alterations of both the language and the culture of his source are thus consistent testimony to the vigour and clear purpose of his editorial activity. There is no common word for us to supply where Matthew has ἀκρασίας. The Harklean, striving hard to be as literal as possible, went for שריחותא. The form שרחותה is found already at *Ahiqar* 85 (cf. 170), so this must surely be the right word, correctly translated by Matthew. Luke has changed to the more general πονηρίας, so that he opens with severe criticism of the Pharisees, rather than the complexities of Jewish purity Law. If the rarely attested שרהות was a genuinely unusual word, Luke may also not have known it.

This also provides us with an argument for supposing that Matthew is following his Aramaic source in putting verses 4–6 after 1–3, while Luke has changed the order. With a saying about tithing written down, a Jewish collector of Aramaic sayings of Jesus had a reason for adding verses 4–6, for he would know that it was partly about the proceeds of tithing. Luke's editing of the saying has dropped some of the original level of meaning, and thereby produced a general attack on the Pharisees which is more suitable for opening this collection of sayings for the benefit of Gentile churches, rather than a saying about the Jewish custom of tithing. We must infer that Matthew has followed the original order of the Aramaic source. Care must of course be taken in fitting the discussion of this verse into a general hypothesis: taken on its own, the vigorously edited Lucan version is consistent with Goulder's hypothesis that Luke used Matthew. It is the evidence of original Luke, and of variants which can *only* be due to two translations, not the evidence of verses like this one, that compel us to prefer a hypothesis of two translations instead.

The next verse is probably an example of this. The epithet ריקן is very sharp, like נגדין עוירין. It is therefore much the most likely word to underlie Luke's ἄφρονες. Luke will have continued to translate for the benefit of his Greek-speaking Gentile audiences. The argument also has a good *Sitz im Leben* in the teaching of Jesus. It is a blunt declaration of the unity of vessels, over against people who were separating them into different parts and cleansing the outside. Matthew dropped it. He surely considered it an unsuccessful argument, perhaps because he agreed with Jesus' opponents that the inside and outside of cups and dishes are separate areas from the perspective of purity Law. At least he will have known that such an argument had no effect on orthodox Jews. It is difficult to imagine Luke adding this verse from a Gentile perspective.

Verse 5 alone has a parallel in saying 89 of the *Gospel of Thomas*.[15]

> Jesus said: 'Why do you wash the outside of the cup (ΠΟΤΗΡΙΟΝ)? Do you not understand that he who made the inside is also he who made the outside?'

Here the Jewish context of Jesus' original comments has been completely removed. The question is quite new, and comes from an environment altogether remote from Jewish Law. There is no mention of Jesus' opponents,

---

[15] See further pp. 32–8 above.

nor of the corruption to which he objected. Nor does the passage end with any instructions as to what to do. The compilers of the tradition found in the *Gospel of Thomas* will have been interested in the saying because of the importance of the inside and outside to their tradition. For example, saying 22 has making the two into one, making the inside like the outside, and the outside like the inside, as among the things that the disciples will do in order to enter the kingdom.

We should also note that the form of this text has 'inside' and 'outside' in the opposite order to that of Luke. The mention of the inside first is, however, also found in a minority of Lucan manuscripts, including P[45] C D and some of the Old Latin. Since saying 89 cannot have been transmitted independently in the original Jewish context of Jesus' comments, we must infer that it is secondary to Luke, either directly as transmitted in this minority of manscripts, or indirectly.

Verse 6 of the Q passage carries further the moral criticism begun with the accusation of extortion. Here I have supposed that there were already two words בריתא in the definite state, one of which means 'outside', while the other, literally 'creation', may be used of people. This is undisputed in later source material. ברי occurs before the time of Jesus at 5Q15 1 ii 2, where it appears to mean 'outside'. בריתה also occurs before the time of Jesus at 4Q529 line 11, where it appears to mean 'his creation', in the sense of people created by God. I have therefore reconstructed, as verse 6, a somewhat shorter saying than we find in either evangelist. This enables us to make polyvalent sense of Jesus' comment, and to see both evangelists translating and editing in accordance with their different understandings of what the original might have meant.

I turn next, therefore, to the original saying. At one level, Jesus affirms the normal Jewish view that vessels are uniform in matters of purity. At another level, God made people's inner beings, or whatever we call them, not just their visible bodies. The view which Jesus was rejecting evidently regarded different parts of these vessels as independent from the perspective of purity Law. Verse 6 was obviously true as a matter of purity Law. To cleanse the inside, you must immerse the vessel in a *miqveh*, and that cleanses the outside. Secondly, if they stopped supporting robbery and excess, their vessels would no longer be associated with the moral uncleanness that Jesus was attacking. At a different level, if they repented and became pure in heart, cleansing the insides of themselves, scribes and Pharisees would be wholly pure as people, fulfilling the intentions of their creator. The whole saying has an excellent *Sitz im Leben* in the ministry of Jesus, whose attacks on orthodox opponents are a significant feature of the traditions in our earliest sources. It does not have a satisfactory *Sitz im Leben* in the early church, which was not concerned about the details of purity Law.

The different levels of meaning make the latter part of the saying very difficult to translate. Both Matthew and Luke decided to clarify the meaning on one of the possible trajectories at the expense of dropping some of the associations. We have seen that Matthew dropped verse 5 altogether, probably because he considered it an unsuccessful argument. He clarified verse 6 by relating it closely to the cup of verse 4, adding τοῦ ποτηρίου and αὐτοῦ, good examples of 'explicitation' in translation. The particle בא is difficult to translate. Matthew replaced it with πρῶτον, which he uses a further seven times (in addition to fifteen examples of some form of πρῶτος). Πρῶτον means 'in the first place', 'above all'. The saying now has only two levels. As a matter of purity Law, it remains obviously true. If the inside of a cup was unclean, the whole cup was unclean. The way to make the outside clean was to immerse the cup in a *miqveh*, and by making the cup clean you remove the impurity from the inside and make the outside clean. At a moral level, the cup is unclean because it has been filled from the proceeds of extortion. Scribes and Pharisees are urged to cease from robbery and excess. That will leave the inside of the cup clean, and hence the outside will be clean too. Matthew also replaced the abuse of ריקין by adapting the abuse of verse 3, to produce a blind Pharisee. This does not have the sharpness of עורין נגדין. The result, however, remains perfectly well adapted to a Jewish Christian context, in which the nature of the original dispute was still understood.

Luke produced a Gentile interpretation, heading vigorously for the target culture, not just the target language. For the difficult בא, he put πλήν, which he uses some thirteen more times. Reading זכו rather than דכו, he instructs the Pharisees to give their ill-gotten gains as alms. Wellhausen's explanation of δότε ἐλεημοσύνην, as a translation of זכו misread for the original דכו that was correctly translated καθάρισον by Matthew, should be accepted.[16] Building on his work, we can give a coherent account of Luke's editorial behaviour. As with πήγανον, ἀγάπην and πᾶν λάχανον at Luke 11.42, Luke's misreading is not merely due to defective understanding of a written source, but also to his perspective. He misread דכו partly because he could not imagine why Jesus would tell the Pharisees to cleanse the inside of a cup or dish.

Luke also took בריתא to mean the creation in general, and rendered with the very explicitative πάντα καθαρά, all things are clean. He also

---

[16] Wellhausen, *Einleitung* (2nd edn, 1911), p. 27.

added ὑμιν to show that everything should be clean for the Pharisees. As a statement of purity Law about cups and dishes, this would be nonsense, so that Jewish level of meaning has been removed altogether. The selection of moral rather than ritual content is further ensured by the insertion of ὑμῶν into verse 4 at Luke 11.39. Your inside is full of, not from, robbery and quite general πονηρία. The saying now declares that Pharisees are morally wicked, and a Jewish and Christian activity which Luke approved of, giving alms, would cleanse *them*, which matters, not cups and dishes, which do not. Verse 5 is retained, and in this context it must be God who makes the inside and outside; the level of reference to the manufacturer has gone too. The Pharisees cleansing the outside of the cup and dish is now little more than a setting which illustrates how stupid they are. Luke changed the order of our source to preface this with Jesus going to eat with a Pharisee, who was amazed that Jesus did not immerse before eating. This intensifies Gentile rejection of living in a state of Jewish purity. He nonetheless retained καὶ ἰδού as a translation of והא, for it is a Septuagintal expression which he uses a full twenty-six times, whereas Matthew has gone for the more fluent Greek ἵνα γένηται. This is further evidence of two independent translations.

Tefillin, tassels, seats and greetings

The next verse in Luke (11.43) has no parallel at this point in Matthew. It does have one at Matt. 23.6–7, but that appears to be partly dependent on Mark 12.38–9, since it follows the order of Mark's text, with Matt. 22.41–5 being an edited version of Mark 12.35–37a, and Matt. 24.1–3 an edited version of Mark 13.1–4. Luke follows Mark closely with his version of the saying at that point, Luke 20.41–21.4 being an edited version of Mark 12.35–44. The relationships between the different text-forms are very complex. Luke is not likely to have gone to Mark 12.38–9, quite out of order, to re-edit that saying into Luke 11.43, as well as keeping it at Luke 20.46. Matthew, however, might well have conflated Mark and Q at the beginning of Matthew 23. He will have put Matt. 23.5–6 where it is because he was conflating Mark and Q before arriving at the point where he followed Q along in the order in which he knew it. This was probably before Matt. 23.23, the first saying in Matt. 23 which is also found in Luke and not in Mark, because the immediately preceding verses are culturally so Jewish that Luke is likely to have omitted them. We should therefore infer that the Aramaic source of Matthew and Luke read something where Luke has 11.43. I have accordingly reconstructed verse 7.

For this purpose, I have used the same introductory formula as I have suggested for the rest of this source. We have seen good reason to suppose that Luke was altering it all the way through. Matthew is likely to have altered it as he moved the saying. I have also used the second half of Matt. 23.5 as the first part of verse 7 of the reconstructed source. It is the kind of thing that Luke often omits, but Matthew keeps, and Matthew is likely to have had something to conflate when he decided to move verse 7 to its more or less Marcan position at 23.5–6.

It will be obvious that the degree of certainty in some of these judgements is lower than we would like. This is due to the vigorous editing of both Matthew and Luke, a constant problem in reconstructing Q. At the same time, there should be no doubt that I have reconstructed with certainty some main points from the polemic between Jesus and his orthodox opponents, and with reasonable probability the approximate form of this saying. I therefore proceed to interpret it.

Both *tefillin* (טוטפה) and tassels are commanded in the Hebrew bible. *Tefillin* are commanded at Exod. 13.16; Deut. 6.8; 11.18, and could be seen at Exod. 13.9. The four tassels (ציצית), each with a cord of blue, were put on the four corners of a garment, in obedience to Num. 15.37–9 and Deut. 22.12, which can easily be run together. None of these passages specifies the size of these items, nor any times when they should be worn. The translation φυλακτήρια, a word which otherwise means 'amulet', implies that God would protect people who wore them. This is reasonable, since they contained scriptural passages which promised God's protection, and amulets were in analogous use among Gentiles. Matthew is likely to have accepted this, since he wrote φυλακτήρια; Jesus is not. Some of the earlier secondary literature has made the interpretation of this passage unnecessarily difficult. Some scholars declared that *tefillin* could not be made broader because they were cubic in shape: others that φυλακτήρια are quite unJewish.[17] Fortunately, a number of *tefillin* have been found at Qumran.[18] They confirm that the ten commandments were originally

[17] E.g. J. Bowman, 'Phylacteries', in K. Aland et al. (eds.), *Studia Evangelica*, vol. I (TU 73. Berlin, 1959), 523–38.

[18] G. L. Harding, 'Minor Finds' with D. Barthélemy, 'I.13.Phylactère', in D. Barthélemy et al., *Qumrân Cave I* (DJD I. Oxford, 1955) pp. 7, 72–6; K. G. Kuhn, *Phylakterien aus Höhle 4 von Qumran* (AHAW.PH.Heidelberg, 1957); G. Vermes, 'Pre-Mishnaic Jewish Worship and the Phylacteries from the Dead Sea', *VT* 9, 1959, 65–72; M. Baillet, 'V. Grotte 8. I. Textes Bibliques. 3. Phylactère' with J. T. Milik, 'III. Textes de la Grotte 5Q. I. Textes Bibliques. 8. Phylactère', in M. Baillet et al., *Les 'Petites Grottes' de Qumrân* (DJD III. Oxford, 1962), pp. 149–57, 178; Y. Yadin, *Tefillin from Qumran (X Q Phyl 1–4)* (Jerusalem, 1969); J. T. Milik, 'Introduction', and 'Phylactères A-U (**128–48**)', in R. de Vaux and J. T. Milik, *Qumrân Grotte 4*. vol. II (DJD VI. Oxford, 1977), pp. 34–79.

among the passages written in the *tefillin*, and in the light of them, we should be able to clear up all the outstanding problems of interpreting this passage of Matthew, though it is unfortunate that we do not have discussions of *tefillin* in the scrolls, as well as the objects.

One major point is that the *tefillin* are of different sizes, and some of them are rectangular rather than cubic. There should therefore no longer be any doubt that the people whom Jesus was attacking did broaden their *tefillin*, as an overt display of piety. We should also note the methodological flaw in the scholarly objection to this straightforward explanation, that the boxes were cubic and could not be broadened. It came originally from a Jewish perspective,[19] and consists in imposing standardised later Jewish practice on documents from an earlier period. We should not do this.

The next major point is that I have put in Jesus' mouth the normal word in later Jewish Aramaic, תפילין. Neither this nor any other word for these objects has been recorded from the fragmentary Jewish texts of the Second Temple period. The word תפלה does occur in an earlier papyrus, where there is an object, תפלה זי כסף.[20] This might be a phylactery case made of silver, but the text is too brief and uninformative for certainty. תפ(י)לין is the normal Aramaic rendering of the Hebrew טוטפות in the Jewish Targums to the three scriptural passages held to command them: Exod. 13.16 *Tg. Onq. Ps.-J. (Neof. mg.* תפלם): Deut. 6.8 *Tg. Neof. Onq. Ps.-J.*; 11.18 *Tg. Neof. Onq. Ps.-J.* In the same way, τὰ φυλακτήρια αὐτῶν at Matt. 23.5 is rendered תפילין by sin cur pesh. תפילין is the normal word for them in the minor tractate *Tefillin*, and it has no serious competitor. Later documents use it of Gamaliel's slave Tabi, who put on *tefillin* (*Tefillin* 62b(4)//*Mekhilta Pisḥa* XVII (Exod. 13.5–10), 154), and transmit a saying of Shammai using it: שמאי הזקן אומר אלו תפילין של אבי אימר (*Mek.* XVII (Exod. 13.5–10), 157). We should infer that Jesus called them תפילין.

The next objection is that Matthew's φυλακτήρια cannot be תפילין. Bowman put it strongly: 'One is all the more amazed when one knows the difference between phylacteries and *Tefillin*, that any Jew could ever think of calling *Tefillin* phylacteries.'[21] Bowman, duly went on to suggest that Matthew was not referring to *tefillin*, but to amulets. Tigay concluded that the use of φυλακτήριον at Matt. 23.5 reflects the use of קמיע for

---

[19] E.g. I. Abrahams, *Studies in Pharisaism and the Gospels* (2nd series. Cambridge, 1924), pp. 203–5.

[20] A. Cowley, *Aramaic Papyri*, p. 192 number 81 line 30.

[21] Bowman, 'Phylacteries', 523–4.

תפילין, and Newport took this seriously, though he did not accept it.[22] We should reject Bowman's view completely. It arises from a common error, that of translating φυλακτήρια *back into* Aramaic; we should not do this, but rather reconstruct something appropriate for which a translator might put φυλακτήρια. This leads us to Bowman's central mistake: his proposed word, קמיע meaning 'amulet', based on analogy with later Samaritan practice, has no *Sitz im Leben* in our passage. Jesus' most orthodox opponents must have worn *tefillin*, obeying the commandments in the same way as orthodox Jews at Qumran: we should not accuse them of wearing amulets. Had they done so, Jesus would surely have objected to the very practice of wearing amulets, not to their size.

The small quantity of early evidence equating תפילין with φυλακτήρια is simply due to the small quantity of literature extant. We have noted the equation of the two in the Syriac translations of Matt. 23.5 (פולאקטריא in the Harklean is merely too literal, as so often with this version). There is further evidence in Justin and Jerome. In criticising his Jewish interlocutor, Justin comments: καὶ φυλακτήριον ἐν ὑμέσι λεπτοτάτοις γεγραμμένων χαρακτήρων τινῶν, ἃ πάντως ἅγια νοοῦμεν εἶναι, περικεῖσθαι ὑμᾶς ἐκέλευσε (*Dialogue with Trypho* 46.5). This is a perfectly clear reference to *tefillin*, called φυλακτήριον. Jerome comments on 'phylacteria' equally clearly, noting that they were seen as having a protective function (*In Mattheum* IIII.92–4).[23] The earlier sources which mention them do not seem to have a word for them. The *Letter of Aristeas* refers to them as σημεῖον (158–9), while Josephus simply has φέρειν ἐγγεγραμμένα ἐπὶ τῆς κεφαλῆς καὶ τοῦ βραχίονος (*A.J.* IV.213). In the crucial passages, LXX has ἀσάλευτον (Exod. 13.16) or ἀσάλευτα (Deut. 6.8; 11.18). We should probably infer that before the fall of Jerusalem they were not generally worn in the Greek-speaking diaspora, and that the translator whose work was used by Matthew probably regarded the rendering of תפילין as a difficult problem, with which he had done as well as possible, bearing in mind the analogies between תפילין and amulets.

It follows that we should not read Bowman's interpretation of later passages back into the texts of our period. The word קמיע does not occur in the Aramaic of the period, or earlier, though this may be accidental, as

[22] J. H. Tigay, 'On The Term Phylacteries (Matt 23:5)', *HThR* 72, 1979, 45–52; K. G. C. Newport, *The Sources and Sitz im Leben of Matthew 23* (JSNT.S 117, 1995), pp. 86–8.

[23] *S. Hieronymi Presbyteri Commentariorum in Matheum Libri IV*, cura et studio D. Hurst and M. Adriaen (CCSL LXXVII. Turnholt, 1969): Pictaciola illa decalogi phylacteria vocabant quod quicumque habuisset ea quasi ob custodiam et munimentum sui haberet...

always. It first occurs in Hebrew in the Mishnah, where it generally means 'amulet', and subsequently it is found in Aramaic. For example, a fifth- or sixth-century Jewish amulet found near the synagogue at Kanaf begins קמיע טב.[24] קמיע is also found in Syriac, in which it means both 'phylactery' and 'amulet'. This was not normally the case in Jewish Aramaic nor in Hebrew, so it is natural that תפילין and קמיע are normally used for distinctly different things: the two words really did have different meanings. So, for example, the second section of tractate *Tefillin*, dealing with תפילין which are unfit (פסולים), has an unfit category of those which are made like a sort of amulet (כמין קמיע). From this normative distinction, it does not, however, follow that Matthew's φυλακτήρια were not תפילין, for the reasons given. There are two exceptional occurrences of קמיע in tractate *Tefillin*. Whereas תפילין is the word for the objects as a whole, קמיע is used twice of the actual box into which the passages of scripture were put (*Tefillin*, 9 and 12). The tractate also forbids the use of phylacteries to calm children (*Tefillin*, 5), just the kind of usage which clarifies our translator's use of φυλακτήρια.

We must therefore turn down these scholarly objections to the culturally natural interpretation of Matt. 23.5. Orthodox scribes and Pharisees wore broader *tefillin* than normal, and Jesus objected to their overt displays of religiosity because their lives as a whole were not properly devoted to God and their neighbours. There are some profoundly parallel passages in later rabbinical literature, though they are not literally the same. For example, the third commandment is interpreted to mean that a person should not put on *tefillin* and wrap themselves in a garment which has tassels on, and then go and commit transgressions (*Pesiq. R.* XXII.5). This is the same kind of religious hypocrisy which Jesus was hitting at. This is culturally central, whereas the fact that the particular complaint about broad phylacteries is not repeated is more incidental.

It is also quite normal for such passages to link *tefillin* and tassels. Jesus' complaint about them has caused less difficulty to scholars. There is no doubt as to what the tassels were, and Jesus appears to have worn them himself (Mark 6.56//Matt. 14.36, cf. Matt. 9.20//Luke 8.44). Different-sized tassels on garments are known the world over.[25] We must infer that Jesus did indeed know and criticised people who wore exceptionally large tassels as well as broad *tefillin*.

---

[24] J. Naveh, 'A Recently Discovered Palestinian Jewish Aramaic Amulet', in M. Sokoloff (ed.), *Arameans, Aramaic and the Aramaic Literary Tradition* (Ramat Gan, 1983), pp. 81–8; K. Beyer, *Die aramäischen Texte vom Toten Meer* (Göttingen, 1984), pp. 397–8.
[25] For some of the ancient background, S. Bertman, 'Tasseled Garments in the Ancient East Mediterranean', *BA* 24, 1961, 119–28.

The accusation about seats in the synagogues is a little problematical, for we do not know very much about the layout of synagogues at the time of Jesus.[26] For the word συναγωγαῖς, I have reconstructed כנישתא. There is no doubt that this is the right word for 'synagogue' in later Jewish Aramaic, in which it also means 'gathering', 'assembly'. The root כנש is extant long before the time of Jesus, as well as in Daniel (3.3, 27) and the Dead Sea scrolls (e.g. 1QapGen XII.16). The form כנשת, meaning 'assembly', is found in 4QGiants (4Q530 ii 5; 6 i 8). There is therefore no serious doubt about the word used by the Aramaic source of Q. We should imagine distinctive buildings used for Jewish meetings of all kinds (cf. Mark 1.21–9; Luke 7.5). Those excavated at Gamla, Masada and Herodium seem to have been equipped with benches. Of the three evangelists, Matthew certainly knew for himself what synagogues were like, and he has the plural πρωτοκαθεδρίας (Matt. 23.6), like our oldest source (Mark 12.39). We should infer that this is right, and that some sort of seats for the elders were already in use. They would be very visible to the congregation, and the scribes and Pharisees will have enjoyed being distinguished. Exactly what the word was is uncertain, for there are no early Aramaic discussions of such things extant. I have suggested כורסותא רברביא, because רב was in widespread use in figurative senses, as well as literally meaning 'big', which connects nicely to the previous criticisms. In this context, no sensible translator would go for μέγας, and πρωτοκαθεδρία may have been the Greek word for them, as well as a sound translation.

A public display of distinction is also the point of the public greetings. The Aramaic שוק has a somewhat broader range of meaning than

26 See especially M. Hengel, 'Proseuche und Synagoge. Jüdische Gemeinde, Gotteshaus und Gottesdienst in der Diaspora und in Palästina', in G. Jeremias, H-W. Kuhn and H. Stegemann, eds., *Tradition und Glaube. Festgabe für K. G. Kuhn* (Göttingen, 1971), pp. 157–84, reprinted in J. Gutman (ed.), *The Synagogue: Studies in Origins, Archaeology and Architecture* (New York, 1975); A. T. Kraabel, 'The Diaspora Synagogue: Archaeological and Epigraphic Evidence since Sukenik', *ANRW* II.19.1 (1979), 477–510; L. I. Levine, 'The Second Temple Synagogue: The Formative Years', in L. I. Levine (ed.), *The Synagogue in Late Antiquity* (Philadelphia, 1987), pp. 7–31; S. J. D. Cohen, 'Pagan and Christian Evidence on the Ancient Synagogue', in Levine (ed.), *Synagogue*, pp. 159–81; H. C. Kee, 'The Transformation of the Synagogue after 70 C.E.: Its Import for Early Christianity', *NTS* 36, 1990, 1–24; E. P. Sanders, *Judaism: Practice and Belief*, 198ff.; D. A. Noy, 'A Jewish Place of Prayer in Roman Egypt', *JThS* NS 43, 1992, 118–22; R. E. Oster, 'Supposed Anachronism in Luke–Acts' Use of συναγωγή: A Rejoinder to H. C. Kee', *NTS* 39, 1993, 178–208; H. C. Kee, 'The Changing Meaning of Synagogue: A Response to Richard Oster', *NTS* 40, 1994, 281–3; H. C. Kee, 'Defining the First-Century CE Synagogue: Problems and Progress', *NTS* 41, 1995, 481–500; L. I. Levine, 'The Nature and Origin of the Palestinian Synagogue Reconsidered', *JBL* 115, 1996, 425–48; K. Atkinson, 'On Further Defining the First-Century CE Synagogue: Fact or Fiction?', *NTS* 43, 1997, 491–502.

the Greek ἀγορά, being used for large streets as well as actual squares. It does however include market-places, so ἀγορά is a sound translation. By the middle of the first century CE, על שקיא was also used idiomatically to mean 'publicly'.[27] Despite some uncertainty over details, therefore, there should be no doubt about the main points. Jesus criticised scribes and Pharisees for their overt and public behaviour, which was pious in form, and not consistent with their lack of full commitment to God and their neighbours. This is a profound link with the following saying.

Whitewashed tombs

The next saying is difficult, not least because the Matthean and Lucan forms are very different from each other. Since the Matthean and Lucan versions are in the same position relative to the other sayings, and since we can produce a convincing hypothesis that the differences are due to variant translations of the Aramaic source for the opening words but not for the rest, I conclude that most of the variations are once again primarily due to heavy editing. It will be clear that I have reconstructed the source on the basis of Matthew's version: I argue that Luke's version is once again due to his failure to understand Jewish customs – he has edited towards the understanding of his Gentile congregations.

After the stylised opening, דמיתון has given rise to two different translations, the very unusual παρομοιάζετε in Matthew, and the simpler ἐστὲ ὡς in Luke. The next point is τάφοις. This must go back to קברין, which means 'graves', 'tombs', so often that we should not imagine that it really refers to ossuaries.[28] The reconstruction of a word behind κεκονιαμένοις is more difficult. The semantic area of κονιάω does include to whitewash, to plaster with lime. Hence the traditional interpretation with reference to the whitewashing of tombs, especially near the time of Passover. This interpretation should be accepted. There is ample evidence of this being done. The custom of marking the graves is dated on 15th Adar, in time for Passover. At *m. Sheq.* 1.1, מציינין על הקברות is associated with other things which were done at that time, beginning with the warning that the Temple tax was due, issued on 1st Adar. This is surely an old and accurate tradition. Some other passages also refer to graves being marked, without explaining how (e.g. *m. Moed Q.* 1.2). It is therefore particularly important that one mishnaic passage (m. *Maas. Sh.* 5.1) provides a description

---

[27] Beyer, *Ergänzungsband*, nV 7, 13.50. On שוק, see further p. 130 below.
[28] Pace S. T. Lachs, 'On Matthew 23:27–28', *HThR* 68, 1975, 385–8.

of doing this. This deals with how things are marked (מצײנין), and says of graves:

ושל קברות בסיד וממחה ושופך

and of graves, with lime and one dissolves and pours.

We must infer from this that at least some of the people who marked the graves mixed lime with water and poured the resulting whitewash onto the graves, since only such a custom could cause our source to say exactly this. This is the proper background to the custom referred to and used by Jesus in his criticism of scribes and Pharisees. It is commented on at *b. B. Qam.* 69a:

ושל קברות בסיד סימנא דחיור כעצמות וממחה ושופך כי היכי דניחוור טפי

'And of graves, with lime', the mark (being) of white, like bones. 'And one dissolves and pours', to make it more white.

This implies that they marked the graves, rather than whitewashing them all over. This is right, since the point was to enable people to avoid them, and a clear whitewashed mark would do this, without the extraordinary labour involved in whitewashing the lot. This massive labour would not make most tombs beautiful, either. The discussions of later rabbis at *b. Moed Q.* 5a–6a reinforce the main point that the purpose of the custom was to warn people away from uncleanness, and their details should not be read back into our period. Unfortunately, we do not have appropriate discussions from our period. Later Jewish Aramaic has טוש, 'smear', 'plaster', and this is used also in Christian Palestinian Aramaic and in Syriac, with the same kind of semantic area. I have used it in the proposed reconstruction, as it helps to explain the variant saying in Luke.

The next problem is φαίνονται ὡραῖοι. The word φαίνω is characteristically Matthean, and it is difficult to see what Aramaic word could be reconstructed for it. I have therefore supposed that Matthew has added it, perhaps as a piece of explicitative translation. It is however possible that the Ithpa'el of חזה, used here by pesh hark, was used with an adjective like this, as it is not in early extant sources. The semantic area of ὡραῖος includes 'seasonable', its original meaning, as well as 'fair, beautiful, lovely'. The underlying Aramaic can hardly be anything but שפיר, as at Dan. 4.12 Theod. (MT 4.9), and pesh hark here at Matt. 23.27, as it is the only word with a sufficient overlap in semantic area. Many tombs were splendid marble monuments, highly ornamented and much venerated. They were accordingly considered beautiful all the time, not particularly when they were marked with whitewash. They remained beautiful when they were marked with whitewash, a process deliberately intended to draw attention to the uncleanness inside them, to enable people to avoid incurring corpse uncleanness.

We should probably also infer that some scribes and Pharisees wore mostly white garments. This is a symbol of purity all the world over. Josephus notes that one group of orthodox Jews, the Essenes, made a point of wearing white clothing (*B.J.* II.123). It is difficult to see why they should do this except as a symbol of purity. They are not likely to have been unique in this, because other orthodox Jews shared their concern for purity (cf. also Rev. 3.4), and obtaining white garments was not difficult. Some cultic references to linen seem likely to have assumed it was white, as with the garment of the High Priest on the Day of Atonement (cf. Lev. 16.4; *b. Yoma* 35a), and probably the linen robes which the Levitical singers were later to wear on equal terms with priests (Jos. *A.J.* XX.216). It may therefore be that, in wearing white robes, Jesus' opponents thought they were symbolising their attempt to live in a state of purity like priests. It is difficult to know quite how far to carry this argument, which could intensify the sharpness of 'whitewashed tombs'. In any case, we know with certainty that scribes and Pharisees were drawing attention to their distinguished status as exceptionally observant Jews, but in Jesus' view they symbolised their unsatisfactory way of life, their insides being equivalent to the dead people's bones in the tombs.

Scholars have had great difficulty with the logic of Jesus' polemic. In an influential comment, Manson argued that 'the comparison breaks down at the vital point. For in this verse the outward appearance of righteousness is assumed in order to *conceal* the evil condition within; whereas the whitewashing of the tombs *advertises* the fact that they are full of corruption.'[29] This underestimates the severity of Jesus' polemic. Scribes and Pharisees did indeed think that they had the outward appearance of righteousness. Jesus thought otherwise. He effectively declared that their white garments advertised the uncleanness within them. He completely rejected their concern with purity, which made them appear decent but in fact, to anyone who knew their whole way of life, drew attention to their sins.

To understand the point of the Matthean saying, we have to delve sympathetically right into the conflict between Jesus and his opponents. This is not the sort of thing that the early church was concerned about.

---

[29] Manson, *Sayings*, p. 237. Similarly already A. H. McNeile, *The Gospel of Matthew* (1915), ad loc.; cf. D. E. Garland, *The Intention of Matthew 23* (NT.S 52, 1979), pp. 153–7. Garland makes a number of good points, but his discussion suffers from treating Jewish sources in English, so I have not interacted with his comments in detail.

It follows that the Matthean version must be basically correct, and hence I have used it in the proposed reconstruction. I have not, however, reconstructed Matt. 23.28. This is a correct explanation as far as it goes, but it is likely to have been felt to be necessary when Matthew edited Matt. 23, whereas Jesus will not have needed it because everyone in his environment knew enough to understand his polemic without explanation. The Lucan version is very different, and this makes it all the more improbable that Luke was informed by a source of Matt. 23.28, and omitted it. Faced with the Aramaic source, Luke or his translator did not understand it, because they did not know about whitewashed tombs. Moreover, the word for 'whitewash' is just the sort of term which a bilingual might not know. Consequently, he read מחטשין as if it were from טמא, meaning 'hide', 'conceal'. It is extant in this sense already at 11QtgJob XIV.2 (Job 29.8). He rendered דדמיתון with ὅτι ἐστὲ ὡς, as opposed to Matthew's ὅτι παρομοιάζετε, and קברין with τὰ μνημεῖα, differently from Matthew's τάφοις. He thought he could understand מחטשין, and rendered it with τὰ ἄδηλα. This is because he did know that graves might be concealed, so that one was unaware of walking on them. He could also read the bible, and he knew from Num. 19.16 that touching a grave made one unclean. He could have checked with Jewish sources that this mattered. He then explained it. He omitted the tombs being beautiful, because hidden tombs are not beautiful. The resulting polemic is much less sharp, and intelligible to Gentiles. Once again, we find that Luke's misreading of his Aramaic source was intelligent, and in accordance with the needs of his target audience. This further strengthens the reasons for believing that there was a very close relationship between Luke's translator and the final editor of his Gospel, to the point where they may have been one and the same person.

Murderous decorators

The next saying evidently follows because it too is about tombs. Here too, the logic of Jesus' polemic has caused problems to scholars. Moreover, the Matthean and Lucan versions are again very different from each other. I have reconstructed an Aramaic source from Matt. 23.29–31, because this gives us a piece with an excellent *Sitz im Leben* in the teaching of Jesus. It makes a piece which Matthew will have been basically satisfied with in Greek, but to which he reasonably added Matt. 23.32–3 to make a link with the following saying. The reconstruction includes one word which Luke might not know, one which is too Jewish for him to want, and two more which he might misunderstand. I conjecture that he then edited vigorously.

The account I shall give of Luke is accordingly rather conjectural, and made in accordance with what we know with greater certainty from his handling of verses earlier in this passage. The reconstruction of Matthew's source should be regarded as a close approximation to what Jesus said.

The content of verse 9 is mostly straightforward. A lot of tomb building was in fact being done at the time, so the cultural background to Jesus' opening comment is unproblematical.[30] Major tombs from the late Second Temple period include that of Zechariah, a very large structure over twelve metres high. In the north of Jerusalem are a number of tombs known as the tombs of the Sanhedrin: the main entrance is 'crowned by a gable with acroteria... Stylized acanthus leaves fill the entire triangle, with pomegranates and other fruit scattered among them.'[31] There is ample evidence that people did indeed build the tombs of the prophets and decorate the monuments of the righteous, and it is entirely natural that scribes and Pharisees should have been involved in this. From the perspective of Jesus' ministry, this is a quite irrelevant thing to do to the prophets, whose message the Jewish leaders should have been following and taking to all Israel, as Jesus did. For κοσμεῖτε, I have reconstructed מצבתין. It is not found in the Dead Sea scrolls, which do not contain any discussions of decorating buildings, nor in later Jewish Aramaic. It is, however, the precise term for decorating buildings in Palmyrene Aramaic, as well as in Syriac (hence its use here by sin pesh hark). I suggest therefore that Jesus used the correct technical term, and that it was probably not known to Luke. This helped him to go for a shorter expression, using the appropriate μνημεῖα, which is a correct translation of קבריא as well as of נפשתא, for which it was used by Matthew.

Jesus' criticism of scribes and Pharisees is clarifed in verse 10, which is essential to the argument. There is comparatively little evidence in the Hebrew bible of prophets being killed, but what there is is fairly blunt (1 Kings 19.10, 14; Jer. 2.30; 26.20–4; Neh. 9.26), and constitutes an established tradition. This was more developed by the time of Jesus: in particular, Isaiah was supposed to have been sawn in half (*Mart. Isa.* 5.1–14), and the following tradition about Zechariah should be seen in the same light. That those who built and decorated the tombs dissociated themselves from those who slew the prophets is only to be expected.

---

[30] J. Jeremias, *Heiligengräber in Jesu Umwelt (Mt.23,39; Lk.11,47): Eine Untersuchung zur Volksreligion der Zeit Jesu* (Göttingen, 1958); L. Y. Rahmani, 'Jewish Rock-Cut Tombs in Jerusalem', *'Atiqot* 3, 1961, 93–120; Y. Yadin (ed.), *Jerusalem Revealed: Archaeology in the Holy City 1968–74* (Jerusalem, 1975); and for a brief recent summary, Newport, *Matthew 23*, pp. 107–11.

[31] Yadin, *Jerusalem Revealed*, p. 20.

For αὐτῶν κοινωνοί I have reconstructed חבריהון. The Hebrew חבר is rendered with κοινωνός by the LXX at Isa. 1.23; Prov. 28.24, as is חברת at Mal. 2.14, which properly indicates the overlap in semantic areas between these words. Moreover, it is probable that חבר had a particularly sharp point when Jesus used it here. It had been in use for a long time in a favourable sense to refer to a person's 'companions', or 'associates'. At Dan. 2.17, for example, Daniel is the subject of the sentence, and Hananiah, Mishael and Azariah are described as חברהי. By the rabbinical period, it was in general use to describe groups of orthodox Jews who joined together to keep an expanded version of the Law carefully. For example, the following passage lays down certain rules which must be followed by a חבר, which assumes that he must keep certain tithing and purity laws with great care:

> He who undertakes to be an associate (חבר) may not sell to a *'am ha-aretz* wet (produce) or dry, or buy from him wet, and he may not be the guest of an *'am ha-aretz* nor may he receive him as a guest in his own clothing. (*m. Dem.* 2.3).

However far this usage had developed at the time of Jesus, and regardless of whether his opponents really used the term like this to repudiate very strongly the murder of ancient prophets, Jesus' use of this term is likely to have been very sharp. These people will have thought of each other as חברין in a very righteous sense. Jesus' repudiation of their claim not to have been associates in murder is therefore both sharp and strong. Luke is not likely to have found such cultural ramifications helpful in communicating with Gentile Christians. Hence he dropped this verse as a whole, and put τῶν πατέρων, from אבהתנא, in his edited version of the next verse.

It is the logic of verse 11 which has caused most trouble. We should first note that neither Matthew's ὥστε nor Luke's ἄρα has any close Aramaic or Hebrew equivalent. There are only three examples of ὥστε + indicative in the LXX. At Esther 7.8, it is an extraordinary elliptical rendering of הגם; 2 Kings 21.12 and Job 21.27 are more relevant, because in both cases the translators have rendered freely in accordance with the sense (one might say they were rendering אשר and הן respectively). Luke's ἄρα is easier to insert, but it is still not common, and Hatch and Redpath properly give no word which it may be said to translate. It follows that both Matthew and Luke were interpreting their source. I have reconstructed the ubiquitous ו. This makes good sense: translators must interpret it at least some of the time if they are to write reasonable Greek, and both Matthew and Luke are known to decrease the occurences of καί when they found it in their Marcan source.

To make full sense of the reconstructed saying, a cultural assumption must be restored, something which was obvious at the time, and too obvious for our source to insert it. This is surely the plot to kill Jesus, seen in the light of the death of John the Baptist. For this, we have to go back to Mark 2.23–3.6.[32] Here, Pharisees took counsel with Herodians, followers of Herod Antipas, to destroy Jesus. Herod Antipas had already put to death John the Baptist, the next most outstanding prophet of the time after Jesus, hailed by him as Elijah (Mark 9.11–13; Matt. 11.7–15//Luke 7.24–8).[33] For Jesus, that was already enough to implicate Pharisees in the death of one major prophet. The opposition of scribes and elders, together with chief priests, was obvious enough for Jesus to use the ministry of John the Baptist as a standard of judgement when they questioned him about his authority to cleanse the Temple (Mark 11.27–33). Jesus must have had the same audience in view when he declared that tax-collectors and prostitutes would precede them into the kingdom of God: 'for John came to you in the way of righteousness, and you did not believe him, but tax-collectors and prostitutes believed him, but you, when you saw this, did not repent afterwards to believe him' (Matt. 21.32). This vigorous opposition to a major prophet who came in the way of righteousness, stretching to collaboration with those responsible for his death, is what made building the tombs of the prophets and decorating the monuments of the righteous a major offence rather than a serious irrelevance.

It was also no more than a foretaste of the plot to kill Jesus. I have noted that at Mark 3.6, Pharisees took counsel with Herodians to destroy Jesus. Jesus was already aware of the depths of their opposition, so much so that as he defended his right to heal on the sabbath as saving a person, he contrasted it with the evil of killing someone (Mark 3.4). Some Pharisees were so disturbed at this plot that they went to warn Jesus that Herod Antipas wanted to kill him (Luke 13.31). This split among the Pharisees again illustrates the depth of the opposition to Jesus by those Pharisees who plotted with the Herodians, a normally unlikely alliance brought together by shared and ferocious opposition to the two major prophets of the time. Jesus' response to this warning is equally instructive. He made reference to his intention to continue his healing ministry without being caught by Herod, for 'it would not be fitting for a prophet to perish outside Jerusalem' (Luke 13.33).[34] Further evidence of vigorous opposition is provided by the behaviour of scribes who came down from Jerusalem and

[32] For detailed discussion, see Casey, *Aramaic Sources of Mark's Gospel*, pp. 138–92.
[33] For detailed discussion of Mark 9.11–13, see Casey, *Aramaic Sources of Mark's Gospel*, pp. 111–37; on Matt. 11.7–15//Luke 7.24–28, see pp. 115–29 below.
[34] On Luke 13.31–33, see Casey, *Aramaic Sources of Mark's Gospel*, pp. 188–9.

accused him of being in league with the devil in his ministry of exorcism (Mark 3.22). Jesus accused them of having committed an unforgivable sin (Mark 3.28).[35]

All this was before he cleansed the Temple, the vigorous prophetic act which precipitated the measures to kill him.[36] Mark immediately records chief priests and scribes plotting to destroy him (Mark 11.18), and Jesus was fully aware of their opposition. We have noticed his use of John the Baptist in response to the question about his authority from chief priests, scribes and elders. Pharisees were not especially prominent at this stage, but they can hardly have been completely absent from scribes and elders. Jesus told a parable which makes oblique reference to his death, and the subsequent replacement of the current leadership of Israel (Mark 12.1–12). He had predicted his death some time previously, and assured Jacob and John that they would share it (Mark 10.35–45; Luke 12.50).[37]

It is in the light of this vigorous opposition to John the Baptist and Jesus that we must see verse 11. The word בְּנֵי has a double significance. Scribes and Pharisees have just been reported as referring to their fathers being responsible for the deaths of the prophets, and the word 'sons' just confirms that they are indeed descended from those who killed the prophets. Its second significance is that it means that they were like them, 'sons' in a metaphorical sense. This Jesus believed that they were, because of their murderous opposition to John the Baptist and himself.

Finally, we can now see what is wrong with building the tombs of the prophets and decorating the monuments of the righteous. It is not merely irrelevant; in the light of their opposition to the prophets of their time it is absolutely hypocritical, a display of external veneration of prophets by men bent on murdering prophets. It is thus profoundly connected with the other sayings of this passage, which will have been put together when their assumptions were obvious, as they would be to Jewish Christians at an early date.

Some details of the Aramaic reconstruction require comment. I have again supposed that Matthew has a fairly literal but slightly explicitative translation. I have suggested as the final word קטליהון, 'their murderers', as at 4Q530 6 i 4. The resulting sentence has what we feel to be a slight vagueness of reference, which characterises Aramaic documents as opposed to Greek and English ones. Thus the original author will have been content with what he wrote, and Matthew understood it perfectly well.

[35] For detailed discussion, see chapter 5 below.

[36] For detailed discussion, see P. M. Casey, 'Culture and Historicity: the Cleansing of the Temple', *CBQ* 59, 1997, 306–32.

[37] On Mark 10.35–45, see Casey, *Aramaic Sources of Mark's Gospel*, ch. 5.

He used τῶν φονευσάντων as the most precise equivalent of קטליהון, and reasonably felt that a Greek audience would understand the passage more easily if he added the explicitative τοὺς προφήτας.

The Lucan version is considerably shorter, and has been considered a complete *non sequitur*.[38] Luke omitted verse 10, only putting τῶν πατέρων for אבהתנא into Luke 11.48, his version of verse 11. We have noted that he might well have had difficulties with חבריהון. He may well not have seen the point of the verse as a whole either, since the death of John the Baptist was literally carried out by Herod Antipas, and Luke believed that Jesus was much more than a prophet. He may therefore have considered the disclaimer too obviously true to be stated, and very unhelpful in the middle of Jesus' criticism of these people. In verse 11, he read בנין, the same letters as בנין in verse 9. In verse 9, he interpreted it correctly as from בנה, the verb for 'to build'. He took it the same way in verse 11. He has therefore no reference to sons, and has edited vigorously to bring out the killing and building as equivalent activities.

We can now see that there is a much closer relationship between Luke and his source than between Luke and the surface text of Matthew. Where Matthew has μαρτυρεῖτε, Luke's μάρτυρές ἐστε is a perfectly reasonable alternative rendering of שהדתון. With בנין assumed to be from בנה as in verse 9, where Luke correctly used οἰκοδομεῖτε, his ὑμεῖς . . . οἰκοδομεῖτε is a perfectly reasonable rendering of בנין אנתון. At the end of the verse, he read קטליהון as קטלוהון. Reading י as ו can hardly be called a misreading in those days, because these two letters could be written so alike. Knowing הון as the third-person masculine plural suffix on nouns, he inferred that it could be used on verbs as well, and interpreted קטלוהון as 'they killed them'. This is correctly rendered αὐτοί . . . ἀπέκτειναν αὐτούς. Luke has then proceeded to edit vigorously. The words καὶ συνευδοκεῖτε τοῖς ἔργοις have been inserted, with τῶν πατέρων from the previous verse, to make a point of comparison clear, and the order of the references to building and killing have been changed to obtain a clear result. Once again, vigorous editing is part and parcel of the same process as translating the Aramaic source. Either Luke did his own translating from Aramaic, or he used a bilingual assistant who worked very closely with him.

The result of this vigorous editing has a perfectly consistent logic of its own. Luke also believed that the lawyers had failed to take the message of the prophets to all Israel. From his perspective, therefore, the building of the tombs of the prophets was a monumental piece of irrelevance. It drew attention to the deaths of the prophets, which had been accomplished

---

[38] Garland, *Matthew 23*, p. 164; Goulder, *Luke*, p. 522.

by the fathers of the lawyers, who no more obeyed the message of the prophets than their fathers had done.

Where Luke abbreviated as he edited, Matthew expanded for clarity. I have suggested that Matt. 23.32–3 is part of his expansions, further commenting on Jesus' message and looking forward to the next saying.

Once again, some details are probably beyond certain reconstruction. At the same time, I have again been able to probe behind the editing of Matthew and Luke to find the main points of Jesus' polemic. I have found once again an extremely fierce attack on scribes and Pharisees, and to understand it fully I have had to take their opposition to Jesus into account. When this has been done, we can see that they are accused of murderous disregard of the message of contemporary prophets, John the Baptist and Jesus, combined with a massive degree of irrelevant veneration of conveniently dead prophets. This fits perfectly into Jesus' general condemnation of them for their purely external mode of religiosity, and takes for granted his expectation of his death. It therefore leads up naturally to the last of this group of woes.

Forthcoming judgement

In the conclusion to the series of woes, Matthew's editing has been so extensive as to make reconstruction more difficult than ever, since Luke continued to edit as before. This illustrates how completely the whole process of reconstruction depends on at least one of the evangelists translating literally and not editing too much. Matthew has Jesus deliver the saying in his own name, whereas Luke has Jesus attribute it to the Wisdom of God. This is not likely to be a Lucan alteration, so I have reconstructed חכמתה די אלהא in their common source. At Wis. 7.27, Wisdom enters into holy souls and makes them friends of God and prophets, and at 8.8 she works out the future. In the book as a whole, she takes over several functions of God, which is more generally a characteristic of the development of the figure of Wisdom, and even more broadly of messianic and intermediary figures in Second Temple Judaism.[39] It is therefore entirely reasonable that Jesus should have attributed to her the divine function of sending messengers to Israel. It is also not at all likely that he would claim to have sent the prophets himself. Matthew, however, wrote after a significant period of Christological development, and the immediately following words suggest that he has interpreted the sending of 'prophets and wise men and scribes' to include the period of the early church. He

---

[39] Casey, *From Jewish Prophet to Gentile God*, ch. 6, esp. pp. 88–90.

therefore did hold Jesus responsible for sending these people, just as he has him authorise the Gentile mission (Matt. 28.18–20). I have therefore also followed Luke in using the third person, rather than have Jesus address his generation in the second person.

According to Luke, the people sent will be 'prophets and apostles'. Here the prophets, common to both Matthew and Luke, must be original, for they clearly are the messengers whom God repeatedly sent to Israel, and this fits with 'the blood of the prophets' in the next verse. 'Apostles' are likely to be secondary, for they have an excellent *Sitz im Leben* in the early church, and Matthew is most unlikely to have omitted them. An original שליחין would not moreover have been very meaningful as a category used by Jesus. I have accordingly followed Matthew at this point. His καὶ σοφοὺς καὶ γραμματεῖς can only be original. The wise men link up remarkably with the use of Wisdom in Luke, and it is not probable that Matthew would insert καὶ γραμματεῖς in a passage which is so vitriolic in its criticisms of scribes. In the mouth of Jesus, however, this makes excellent sense, because נביאין וחכימין וספרין is a good summary of all the sorts of people, other than the institutionalised priesthood, who had been sent, from a law-orientated spectrum as well as from Jesus' own prophetic viewpoint. God had sent them scribes, so they could have learnt the scriptures, including the main points of the Torah and the message of the prophets.

We must, however, follow Luke in the description of the fate of these messengers. Matthew has ἐξ αὐτῶν ἀποκτενεῖτε καὶ σταυρώσετε, καὶ ἐξ αὐτῶν μαστιγώσετε ἐν ταῖς συναγωγαῖς ὑμῶν καὶ διώξετε ἀπὸ πόλεως εἰς πόλιν. This has evidently been expanded midrashically in the light of the crucifixion of Jesus and the persecution of Jewish Christians. Luke has simply ἐξ αὐτῶν ἀποκτενοῦσιν καὶ διώξουσιν. This makes excellent sense, so I have reconstructed יקטלון וירדפון. We have seen that the killing of messengers to Israel was part of the teaching of Jesus, and the same theme occurs in the parable of Mark 12.1–12. The addition of וירדפון may seem anticlimactic, but in fact simply represents what people did when messengers whom they sought to kill fled.

Verse 13 then portrays the judgement which will come upon the present leadership of Israel. I have followed Matthew in the way in which this is expressed, except that I have continued with the third person rather than the second, since there was good reason in the previous verse to regard the second-person mode of address as due to Matthean editing. I have consequently also reconstructed דאבד for Luke's τοῦ ἀπολομένου, taking Matthew's ὃν ἐφονεύσατε as part of his editorial changes. It will be evident that much doubt surrounds these detailed judgements, but that they do not affect the main points.

The reference to the blood of Abel is not problematical: he was the first person killed in the bible, he was righteous, and his blood cried from the ground (Gen. 4.10). This is vividly portrayed at *1 En.* 22.5–7. Enoch is in the underworld, and sees the spirit of a dead man (רוח אנש מת) making accusation and his lamentation ascending up to heaven and crying out unceasingly. In response to Enoch's question, Raphael identifies this as the spirit which went forth from Abel. The reference to Zechariah has, however, caused serious problems, not least because Matthew has 'Zechariah son of Berachiah' (Matt. 23.35). Three of the many Zechariahs must be discussed in detail.

Firstly, Zechariah the priest, the son of Jehoida. The account of the murder of this Zechariah is found at 2 Chron. 24.20–2. The spirit of God clothed him (ורוח אלהים לבשה את־זכריה) when he rebuked the people for transgressing the commandments of the LORD, beginning כה אמר האלהים. This is behaviour so much in the prophetic tradition that he was obviously liable to be thought of as a prophet, the more so since the previous verse says that prophets (נבאים) were sent to testify against the people to bring them back to the LORD. So we find that Josephus says that on this occasion God had appointed him to prophesy (προφητεύειν, *A.J.* IX.168–9). He is the last person in *The Lives of the Prophets*, a brief biography which shows no clear trace of specifically Christian influence. At *Tg. 2 Chron.* 24.20, we are told more specifically that it was a spirit of prophecy which dwelt on Zechariah (רוח נבואה מן קדם ייי). He is also mentioned as a prophet in the Talmud (*b. Git.* 57b//*Sanh.* 96b). While some of this evidence is late, it is securely based in what the biblical text says, and records how central Jewish tradition was bound to treat this incident. Therefore we must not treat this evidence as *merely* late: in our period already, Zechariah the priest, the son of Jehoida, passes muster as a prophet.

At the king's command, this Zechariah was stoned בחצר בית יהוה (2 Chron. 24.21). This must surely mean in the court of the priests. This is transmitted much later as the opinion of R. Acha (*y. Taan.* 4, 8/43, (69a)), but this should not be dismissed as a late tradition, because it is the obvious interpretation of the scriptural expression בחצר בית יהוה. This gets the death of this Zechariah in the right place. As he died, he said: ירא יהוה וידרש (2 Chron. 24.22). This prediction of vengeance makes Zechariah an especially suitable prophet for mention in the present context, and ידרש accounts for the particular terminology preserved by Luke. Finally, this is the last death of a prophet recorded in the Hebrew bible in its present canonical order. This explains Jesus' choice of this Zechariah to combine with Abel, the first person wrongfully killed in the bible. It is true that we do not have independent confirmation that 2 Chronicles was already regarded as the last book in the bible,[40] but we have no evidence to the contrary either. We must remember that it cannot possibly belong to the Torah or the Prophets, and that with Daniel regarded as a sixth-century-BCE prophet, it was one of the last of the writings to be completed, and could hardly have been included in the canon unless it was already of great authority.[41] We must therefore infer that the position known to us first from a baraitha at *b. B. Bat.* 14b was already known to Jesus.

All this forms a massive argument of cumulative weight. Jesus intended a reference to Zechariah, son of Jehoida, a priest who was considered to have performed also the role of prophet. His death is recorded in the last book of the Hebrew bible, and his dying words predicted that God would demand vengeance. He thus made an excellent inclusio with Abel.

This evidence does not at first sight fit the evidence of Matthew, who has Ζαχαρίου υἱοῦ Βαραχίου. This must refer to Zechariah, the son of Berachiah, son of Iddo, the eleventh of the twelve minor prophets. There is no early evidence that he died a violent death, still less that this happened between the sanctuary and the altar, so he does not fit the definition. The point is that he was the famous prophet Zechariah, and we must therefore infer that the two Zechariahs have been identified. This is very clear in the late source *Tg. Lam.* 2.20:

אם חזי למקטל בבית מקדשא דיי כהנא ונבייא כמא דקטלתון לזכריה בר עדוא כהנא רבא ונביא מהימן בבית מקדשי דיי ביומא דכפוריא על דאוכח יתכון דלא תעבדון דביש קדם יי.

Is it proper to kill in the Temple of the Lord a priest and a prophet as you killed Zechariah son of Iddo the high priest and the faithful prophet in the Temple of the Lord on the Day of Atonement, because he admonished you not to do what was evil before the Lord?

This is a reference to the incident of the death of Zechariah who was really son of Jehoida, wrongly referred to as son of Iddo because that was a normal way of referring to Zechariah the well-known prophet (e.g. Ezra 5.1; Neh. 12.16; *b. Yoma* 39b). We must infer that Jesus, the translator or Matthew was responsible for the identification of the two different characters. It is not, however, likely to have been Jesus, since he

[40] Cf. J. S. Kennard, 'The Lament over Jerusalem: A Restudy of the Zacharias Passage', *AThR* 29, 1947, 173–9; J. M. Ross, 'Which Zechariah?', *IBS* 9, 1987, 70–3.

[41] R. Beckwith, *The Old Testament Canon of the New Testament and Its Background in Early Judaism* (Grand Rapids, 1985), pp. 211–22.

produced the inclusio with Abel in the first place. We must infer that it was Matthew, or the translator before him.

We must note a third Zechariah, because so many scholars have argued that Matthew was referring to Zechariah son of Bareis.[42] This Zechariah was a distinguished citizen of Jerusalem accused by Zealots of treasonable communications with the Romans (Jos. *B.J.* IV.334–44). After being acquitted by seventy judges, he was slain by Zealots in the middle of the Temple (ἐν μέσῳ τῷ ἱερῷ). This was in 68 CE. This Zechariah has the wrong patronymic, which is a decisive point in considering a deliberately interpretative reference to a recent figure. He surely would not be identified with the eleventh of the twelve prophets. He was not a prophet, and he was not slain between the altar and the sanctuary. This interpretation must be dismissed.

We must therefore conclude that Jesus was referring to Zechariah the priest, the son of Jehoida, the last prophetic figure to be slain in the Hebrew bible. Matthew or his translator identified him with the eleventh of the twelve prophets, Zechariah son of Berachiah.

We can now see the meaning of the saying more clearly. The blood of traditional prophets and other righteous figures has not been avenged. Israel has now rejected so many messengers, including John the Baptist and Jesus, that the righteous blood of all these figures will be sought from 'this generation'. This means that judgement is at hand, but not that no one will be exempted from it. Jesus' mission to the people of Israel necessarily entails the salvation of the members of the Jewish movement and its poor Jewish followers. This fits in with later evidence using the term דור.[43] So, for example, רשע Prov. 10.25 is interpreted of דור המבול, while צדיק is interpreted of Noah (*Gen.Rab.*XXX.1). In quite a real sense, therefore, Noah is separate from the generation of the flood. Accordingly, this passage emphasises the message of judgement on the conventional leaders of Israel elsewhere in the teaching of Jesus, and on cities such as Capernaum where he did not feel his message had been sufficiently successful (Matt. 11.21–4//Luke 10.12–15). It is at this time that God would finally establish his kingdom.

The details of the final verse are also different in Matthew and Luke. I have suggested יתבעא under Luke's ἐκζητηθήσεται. This picks up on ידרש, used by Zechariah at 2 Chron. 24.22, when he predicted vengeance. Luke is not likely to have originated this kind of reference (though I

[42] E.g. Wellhausen, *Einleitung*, pp. 118–23; Kennard, 'Lament', 176–8.
[43] E. Lövestam, *Jesus and 'This Generation'. A New Testament Study* (CB.NT 25. Stockholm, 1995).

have supposed that he repeated it in the previous verse). This makes ταῦτα πάντα Matthean editing, which is coherent because he uses this expression several times.

I therefore suggest that Matthew and Luke provide evidence of an Aramaic source, part of which can be approximately recovered. The contents of the source are genuine, and illustrate the depth of the controversy between Jesus and his orthodox opponents. Like parts of Mark's Gospel, this source was written down by one or more well-informed Jews from Israel, the only sort of people who could be responsible not only for what it does say, but also for omitting its assumptions. While some details are uncertain, or capable of an alternative explanation, there is an argument of cumulative weight which is so strong that it should be accepted. That argument can be seen and reasonably discussed only if a complete reconstruction of the source is offered.

When this source has been reconstructed, some unexpected light can be cast on the editorial work of Luke. In some passages, Luke edited vigorously in the direction of the target culture, and misread some Aramaic words as part of this process. It follows that either Luke himself was bilingual and did his own translating, or that the processes of editing and translation were done by people who worked closely together. It also follows that Luke was not editing Matthew, and this is a new argument for this conventional but important result.

Another important result is that part of the Q material was transmitted in Aramaic, and translated twice as part of the process of becoming what we now read in Matthew and Luke. This has been suggested before, but never properly investigated, and should now be regarded as proven. It has, however, often been noted that parts of Q are verbally identical in Matthew and Luke, so that some parts of the Q material were translated once and transmitted in Greek. It follows that we must opt for a relatively chaotic model of Q. These facts alone require at least two layers of Q, one Aramaic layer translated into Greek twice, and one Greek layer which had been translated from Aramaic once. They are consistent with a much more chaotic model than this. I shall pursue this further in chapters 4 and 5, before considering exactly what model of Q is appropriate.

Finally, we have again and again seen good reason to believe that, when we have been able to reconstruct the original Aramaic source from behind the vigorous editing of Matthew and Luke, we have a source whose contents are genuine. We may contrast with this, for example, the verdict of Beare on Matt. 23: 'It should be clear that there is very little in this chapter that can be regarded as language ever used by Jesus, or at all in accordance with his spirit. It is manifestly impossible to imagine him as delivering such a scathing denunciation in the temple.'[44] This verdict is in accordance with a cultural circle, concealing the Jesus of history who did not speak in accordance with current notions of what is politically correct. Quite to the contrary, I have in this chapter, by means of historical research devoted to recovering part of an alien culture, uncovered the fierce polemic of a man who was under permanent threat of death from opponents who were dangerous as well as vitriolic. When historical research uncovers such results, we should accept them, not find devious means of producing someone whose image we might prefer. One fundamental factor is precisely that this is Q material, and having seen that Luke was not using Matthew, we cannot imagine that the polemic was due to the problems in Matthew's church. Jesus was not gentle, meek and mild; he was physically peaceful, but verbally ferocious. We shall see more evidence of his interactions with other people in chapters 4 and 5.

[44] F. W. Beare, *The Gospel according to Matthew* (Oxford, 1981), p. 461.

4

JOHN THE BAPTIST:
MATTHEW 11.2–19//LUKE 7.18–35

The purpose of this chapter is to reconstruct the Aramaic source of Matt. 11.2–19//Luke 7.18–35, and to discuss the interpretation and historicity of this source. I also reflect on its importance for our model of Q. I keep Matthew's verse divisions: this is convenient, since I argue that he made relatively few alterations to the source, whereas Luke edited more heavily, both adding and omitting whole verses. I also argue that there was a single Greek translation of this source, which both evangelists inherited, whether directly or already in an edited form. I offer a reconstruction of this too.

Reconstructed sources

2 ושלח יוחנן ביד תלמידוהי

3 ואמר לה, אנתא הוא אתה או נסכא אחרן?

4 וענה ואמר להון, אזלו אודעו ליוחנן מה די שמעין וחזין:

5 עוירין חזין וחגירין מהלכין, מצרעין מתדכין וחרשין שמעין, ומיתין מתקימין ועניין מתבשרין.

6 ובריך הוא מן דלא יתתקל בי.

7 ושרי למאמר, מה נפקתון למדבר? למחזה קנה זיע ברוח?

8 אלא מה נפקתון למחזה? אנש לביש רכיכין? הא לבישין רכיכיא בביתהון דמלכיא.

9 אלא מה נפקתון למחזא? נביא? אין אמר אנה לכון, ויתיר על נביא.

10 הוא דכתיב עלוהי, ארו אנא שלח מלאכי קדם אנפיך דיתכן אורחך קדמיך.

11 אמן אמר אנה לכון, לא קום בילידין דנשין רב מן יוחנן, וזעירא במלכותה דאלהא רב מנה.

12 ומן יומי יוחנן תקף מלכותה דאלהא ותקיפין אחדין יתה.

13 כל נביאיא ואוריתא אתנביו עד יוחנן,

14 ואן תצבון למקבלה, אליה הוא דעתיד למאתא.

15 הוא דאיתי לה אדנין, ישמע.

16 למא אדמא דרא דן? דמא הוא לינוקין דיתבין בשוקיא וקריין לאחריא,

17 אמרין זמרנא לכון ולא רקדתון, הולילנא ולא ספדתון.

18 אתה יוחנן לא אכל ולא שתא ואמרין: שיד איתי לה.

19 אתה בר אנש אכל ושתה ואמרין: הא אנש זולל וסבא, חבר למכסין ולחטיין.
וזכת חכמה מן עובדה.

[2]And John sent by the hand of his disciples [3]and said to him, 'Are you him coming, or shall we wait for another?' [4]And he answered and said to them, 'Go inform John of what (people) see and hear: [5]blind (people) see and lame (people) walk, people-with-skin-diseases are cleansed and deaf (people) hear, and dead (people) are raised and poor (people) have good news preached to them. [6]And blessed is whoever does not stumble over me.'

[7]And he began to say, 'Why did/have you gone/come out into the wilderness? To see a reed shaken in a/the wind? [8]But what have/did you come/go out to see? A man dressed in soft clothing? Ha! (People) dressed in soft clothing (are to be found) in kings' palaces! [9]But what have/did you come/go out to see? a prophet? Yes, I tell you, and more than a prophet. [10]This (is/was) he of whom it is written, 'Look! I am sending my messenger before your face, who will prepare your way before you' [Mal. 3.1]. [11]Amen I tell you, there has not risen from those born of women one greater than John, and a junior (person) in the kingdom of God (is) greater than he. [12]And from the days of John the kingship of God grows strong and strong people take hold of it. [13]All the prophets and the Torah prophesied up to John, [14]and if you are willing to receive him/it, he is Elijah who is going to come. [15]He who has ears, let him hear! [16]To what shall I liken this generation? It is like children who sit in squares and call to others, [17]saying, 'We have piped for you and you do not dance, we wailed and you have not lamented'. [18]John has come not eating and not drinking and they say, "He has a demon." [19]A/the (son of) man comes eating and drinking and they say, "Look, a man 'glutton and drunkard', an associate of tax-collectors and sinners. And Wisdom is not responsible for his work."'

2. καὶ ὁ Ἰωάννης ἔπεμψεν διὰ τῶν μαθητῶν αὐτοῦ

3. καὶ εἶπεν αὐτῷ, Σὺ εἶ ὁ ἐρχόμενος ἢ ἕτερον προσδοκῶμεν;

4. καὶ ἀποκριθεὶς εἶπεν αὐτοῖς, Πορευθέντες ἀπαγγείλατε Ἰωάννῃ ἃ ἀκούετε καὶ βλέπετε·

5. τυφλοὶ ἀναβλέπουσιν καὶ χωλοὶ περιπατοῦσιν, λεπροὶ καθαρίζονται καὶ κωφοὶ ἀκούουσιν, καὶ νεκροὶ ἐγείρονται καὶ πτωχοὶ εὐαγγελίζονται·

6. καὶ μακάριός ἐστιν ὃς ἐὰν μὴ σκανδαλισθῇ ἐν ἐμοί.

7. καὶ ἤρξατο λέγειν τοῖς ὄχλοις περὶ Ἰωάννου, Τί ἐξεληλύθατε εἰς τὴν ἔρημον θεάσασθαι; κάλαμον ὑπὸ ἀνέμου σαλευόμενον;

8. ἀλλὰ τί ἐξεληλύθατε ἰδεῖν; ἄνθρωπον ἐν μαλακοῖς ἠμφιεσμένον; ἰδοὺ οἱ τὰ μαλακὰ φοροῦντες ἐν τοῖς οἴκοις τῶν βασιλέων.
9. ἀλλὰ τί ἐξεληλύθατε ἰδεῖν; προφήτην; ναί, λέγω ὑμῖν, καὶ περισσότερον προφήτου.
10. οὗτός ἐστιν περὶ οὗ γέγραπται, Ἰδοὺ ἐγὼ ἀποστέλλω τὸν ἄγγελόν μου πρὸ προσώπου σου, ὃς κατασκευάσει τὴν ὁδόν σου ἔμπροσθέν σου.
11. ἀμὴν λέγω ὑμῖν, οὐκ ἐγήγερται ἐν γεννητοῖς γυναικῶν μείζων Ἰωάννου· ὁ δὲ μικρότερος ἐν τῇ βασιλείᾳ τοῦ θεοῦ μείζων αὐτοῦ ἐστιν.
12. ἀπὸ δὲ τῶν ἡμερῶν Ἰωάννου ἕως ἄρτι ἡ βασιλεία τοῦ θεοῦ βιάζεται, καὶ βιασταὶ ἁρπάζουσιν αὐτήν.
13. πάντες γὰρ οἱ προφῆται καὶ ὁ νόμος ἕως Ἰωάννου ἐπροφήτευσαν·
14. καὶ εἰ θέλετε δέξασθαι, αὐτός ἐστιν Ἠλίας ὁ μέλλων ἔρχεσθαι.
15. ὁ ἔχων ὦτα ἀκουέτω.
16. Τίνι δὲ ὁμοιώσω τὴν γενεὰν ταύτην; ὁμοία ἐστὶν παιδίοις καθημένοις ἐν ταῖς ἀγοραῖς ἃ προσφωνοῦντα τοῖς ἑτέροις.
17. λέγουσιν, Ηὐλήσαμεν ὑμῖν καὶ οὐκ ὠρχήσασθε· ἐθρηνήσαμεν καὶ οὐκ ἐκόψασθε.
18. ἐλήλυθεν γὰρ Ἰωάννης μήτε ἐσθίων μήτε πίνων, καὶ λέγουσιν, Δαιμόνιον ἔχει·
19. ἐλήλυθεν ὁ υἱὸς τοῦ ἀνθρώπου ἐσθίων καὶ πίνων, καὶ λέγουσιν, Ἰδοὺ ἄνθρωπος φάγος καὶ οἰνοπότης, φίλος τελωνῶν καὶ ἁμαρτωλῶν. καὶ ἐδικαιώθη ἡ σοφία ἀπὸ τῶν ἔργων αὐτῆς.

John's question and Jesus' reply

The opening of the underlying Q passage is difficult to reconstruct because of the obvious editorial activity of both Matthew and Luke. Matthew's introduction includes a reference to the deeds τοῦ Χριστοῦ, and Luke has John send πρὸς τὸν κύριον. These Christological titles illustrate well what the evangelists missed in their source material. We can safely exclude them from Q. Matthew's shorter introduction is likely to be right because Luke is patently creating a setting for the following piece. Both agree on some form of πέμπω, and that the message went through τῶν μαθητῶν. I have therefore supposed that we can reconstruct idiomatic Aramaic mostly with the help of Matthew: ושלח יוחנן ביד תלמידוהי. This makes Matthew's διά a smooth translation of the idiomatic ביד. I have used תלמיד for μαθητής, despite the fact that it has not survived in the Aramaic of the preceding period. It is used abundantly in later Jewish Aramaic, Christian Palestinian Aramaic and Syriac. What is more, it is derived from the Akkadian *talmīdu*,[1] and it occurs in biblical Hebrew at 1 Chron. 25.8. We should infer that it was already available for our narrator to use. The reference to John being in prison is in Matthew alone. It should be regarded as secondary, for three reasons. Firstly, it is not probable that John would be imprisoned under conditions which made it possible to communicate like this. We know from Josephus that Herod Antipas imprisoned him in Machaerus, a fortress miles away on the other side of the Jordan (*A.J.* XVIII.116–19). The chances that John could send disciples from there are surely not good. Secondly, the information has an excellent *Sitz im Leben* in the work of Matthew, who took literally Mark's report that Jesus came into Galilee preaching after John's arrest (Mark 1.14–15), and amplified it greatly (Matt. 4.12–17). The actual expression ἐν τῷ δεσμωτηρίῳ is also closely associated with the obviously editorial τὰ ἔργα τοῦ Χριστοῦ. Thirdly, Luke had no reason to remove a reference to John's imprisonment, since his narrative also inherited Mark's information and consequently assumed that this is where John was. Finally, we shall see that some parts of this passage presuppose that John was still alive. We should infer that the ministries of Jesus and John the Baptist overlapped. The contrary impression is derived only from literal interpretation of Mark 1.14 in its present position. It will originally have contained perfectly true information about what Jesus did after John's arrest – he preached in Galilee, despite the obvious dangers from Herod Antipas (cf. Mark 3.6; Luke 13.31–3).[2] Only Mark's arrangement implies that Jesus had never done so before, and this is no more reliable than Mark's placing of Jesus' baptism after his abbreviated version of John's prediction of someone else coming.

There is a problem over the term ὁ ἐρχόμενος. This is not a known title, either in Judaism at the time of Jesus or in the early church. It must therefore be a reference to John the Baptist's own prediction, the earliest recorded version of which is in the Greek text of Mark 1.7, which is continued in the Greek text of Matt. 3.11–12//Luke 3.16–17:

> Ἔρχεται ὁ ἰσχυρότερός μου ὀπίσω μου, οὗ οὐκ εἰμὶ ἱκανὸς κύψας
> λῦσαι τὸν ἱμάντα τῶν ὑποδημάτων αὐτοῦ· ἐγὼ ἐβάπτισα ὑμᾶς
> ὕδατι, αὐτὸς δὲ βαπτίσει ὑμᾶς ἐν πνεύματι ἁγίῳ καὶ πυρί·
> οὗ τὸ πτύον ἐν τῇ χειρὶ αὐτοῦ, καὶ διακαθαριεῖ τὴν ἅλωνα
> αὐτοῦ, καὶ συνάξει τὸν σῖτον αὐτοῦ εἰς τὴν ἀποθήκην, τὸ δὲ
> ἄχυρον κατακαύσει πυρὶ ἀσβέστῳ.

---

[1] S. A. Kaufman, *The Akkadian Influences on Aramaic* (Assyriological Studies 19. Chicago, 1974), p. 107.

[2] Casey, *Aramaic Sources of Mark's Gospel*, pp. 185–91.

I suggest the following reconstruction of the opening words:

אתה תקיפא ברא מני בתרי די לא אנה שוא למגהן למשרא ערקא דמסאנה ...

This means literally 'A/the one stronger than I is coming after me, whom I am not worthy/sufficient to bend down to undo his sandalstrap . . . ' The Aramaic תקיף is well attested from before the time of Jesus, and it is a very suitable word. For example, at 1QapGen XXII.31 God promises to be a shield over Abraham, as at Gen. 15.1, and to protect him from תקיף ברא מנך, 'he who is stronger than you'. At *1 En.* 89.30 it is said of God, חזיה תקיף ורב, 'his appearance (was) strong and great'. In later sources, תקיף is used of God himself, as for example at Gen. 31.42 *Tg. Neof.*, where God is described as תקיפא דיצחק, 'the strong one of Isaac'.

In the Greek bible, תקיף is rendered with ἰσχυρός at 2 Esdras 4.20; Dan. 2.40 LXX Theod.; 2.42 LXX Theod.; 3.33 (100) Theod.; 7.7 Theod.; and with ἰσχύς at Dan. 7.7 LXX. Similarly, תקף is rendered with ἰσχύς at Dan. 4.30 LXX Theod. (MT 4.27); 11.17 Theod. These renderings properly indicate the overlap in semantic area on account of which the proposal that תקיפא ברא מני is the source of ὁ ἰσχυρότερός μου is an entirely plausible one.

John evidently felt that he was not God's final messenger to Israel, and the reason for this was not the presence of anyone else in Israel at the time. He may simply have felt that his own ministry, centred on a baptism of repentance and thus on bringing Jews back to God, did not measure up to Jewish expectations of the last days. He is also likely to have been influenced by particular passages of scripture. These surely included Mal. 3. In the first verse of this chapter, God promises to send his messenger, and it is reasonable to suppose that it is this figure who is described as האדון. It would therefore be reasonable for John to describe him as תקיפא מני, as this is exactly what he would be expecting. Malachi also says of this figure יבוא, of which ἔρχεται would be a literal translation, so it is natural that John should begin אתה תקיפא ברא מני בתרי. Mal. 3.19 also uses the image of the wicked as stubble who will be burnt up, just the kind of image to inspire the rest of John's prediction. This is more generally reminiscent of other Jewish pictures of judgement. For example, at Hos. 13.3, idolatrous Israelites will be like chaff from the threshing floor (cf. more generally e.g. Jer. 4.11–14; Ps. 50.3–4; 66.10-12; 1QS IV.20–2). Thus the threat to the wicked is clear: the winnowing shovel and burning of the chaff mean perdition for them. It is evident from Mark 6.18; 11.31–2; and Matt. 21.32 that conventional Jewish leaders were among the wicked, and the implication of John's preaching as a whole is that they would not be alone.

Equally, the gathering of the wheat into the barn implies the salvation of many of the crowds who flocked to John's baptism. This was also

110   An Aramaic Approach to Q

an essential part of traditional Jewish expectation. For example, at Isa. 27.12 the LORD will thresh out the grain and the people of Israel will be gathered, and at Mic. 2.12 God will gather Jacob, and the remnant of Israel. The dominant context in the Hebrew bible is one of return from exile, and John's imagery of gathering wheat into the barn has transmuted this beautifully for people who lived in Israel.

We can now see the basic rationale of the Jewish traditions from which John framed his expectation of another figure who was still to come. Within the varied expectations characteristic of the Judaism of this period, the precise form of his expectation was unique, and he did not give this figure a title. He had no need to do so. We must note particularly that, however important and final this figure was to be, there was no need for John to call him משיחא. The reason for this is that this title had still not crystallised out as a necessary term for a/the final redemptive figure.[3] We should also dismiss the view that John expected this figure to be God himself.[4] There is no positive indication of this in the primary sources, and it makes nonsense of John's question to Jesus.

It is accordingly this figure of his own predictions to whom John referred in his question to Jesus. Jesus had been baptised by John, and had begun a dramatic ministry to Israel. He was therefore a reasonable candidate for תקיפא. At the same time, however, his ministry had so far brought more repentance and less judgement than John had expected to follow his ministry of repentance. The question therefore has an excellent *Sitz im Leben* towards the end of John's ministry and during the ministry of Jesus. It does not make proper sense before the historic ministry of Jesus had begun. John could rely on Jesus to remember his prophecy. I have therefore suggested that the source of ὁ ἐρχόμενος at Matt. 11.3//Luke 7.19 was הוא אתה. This is not a title, and it is sufficient to refer back to John's prophecy of a future figure who was known to be coming, but who was without either name or title. Equally, the question has no *Sitz im Leben* in the early church. The term ὁ ἐρχόμενος was not a known term in the early church, nor did they have reason to invent the notion that John was uncertain as to whether Jesus was the figure whose coming John had predicted. The arrangement of the material in the earlier

---

[3] M. de Jonge, 'The Use of the Word "Anointed" in the Time of Jesus', *NT* 8, 1966, 132–48; M. de Jonge, 'The Earliest Christian Use of *Christos*. Some Suggestions', *NTS* 32, 1986, 321–43; Casey, *From Jewish Prophet to Gentile God*, pp. 41–4; M. Karrer, *Der Gesalbte. Die Grundlagen des Christustitels* (FRLANT 151. Göttingen, 1991).

[4] E.g. J. H. Hughes, 'John the Baptist: The Forerunner of God Himself', *NT* 14, 1972, 191–218.

passages of the synoptics has begun the process of rewriting John to give the impression that he really predicted the coming of Jesus: that process was carried through thoroughly in the Gospel attributed to John the evangelist.[5] We are fortunate that neither Q nor Matthew nor Luke rewrote John's question.

There is no problem with the word אחרן, which simply means 'another'. It can be used of another of two, but this is the function of some contexts, not of the meaning of the word, and by this time ἕτερος was often used to mean 'another', regardless of the number already in mind. We should nonetheless infer that Luke altered Q's ἕτερον to ἄλλον, since the opposite alteration by Matthew is improbable.

Luke 7.20–1 is fairly obviously redactional, and may reasonably be excluded from the source used by both evangelists.[6] It intensifies the reports of Jesus' healing ministry, and helps to give the impression that the messengers had personally seen this activity.

Verses 4–6 show very close verbal agreement between Matthew and Luke. This is our first clear evidence that this portion of Q reached both evangelists in the same Greek translation. I have omitted ὁ Ἰησοῦς from the source, as it is absent from Luke. Aramaic narratives do not mention the subject as often as Greek and English ones, and Matthew inserts Jesus' name at other such points (e.g. Matt. 12.1, cf. Mark 2.23). The tense of the verbs in Jesus' introduction to his summary account of his ministry is quite unclear. I have suggested that the source had narrative participles, that Q therefore used present tenses and modified them to second-person plural, and that Luke put past tenses to fit his added summary of what had just been happening. An equally strong argument could be made for second-person perfects in the Aramaic source, translated as so often with aorists by Q, left by Luke and changed to present tenses by Matthew for the effect of immediacy. At this level we have a lot of uncertainty. Fortunately, it does not matter much, but it should be recognised.

The summary itself refers to Jesus' successful healing ministry, and then to his preaching activity. This corresponds to the synoptic accounts of the ministry, and does not contain any Christological statement such as we might expect from the early church. We must therefore accept its substantial authenticity. The word λεπροί, and words such as מצרעין, are

[5] Casey, Is *John's Gospel True?*, ch. 4.

[6] Likewise e.g. W. G. Kümmel, *Jesu Antwort an Johannes den Täufer: Ein Beispiel zum Methodenproblem in der Jesusforschung* (Wiesbaden, 1974), p. 149; G. Häfner, *Der verheißene Vorläufer. Redaktionskritische Untersuchung zur Darstellung Johannes des Täufers im Matthäusevangelium* (SBB 27. Stuttgart, 1994), pp. 164–6.

often translated 'lepers', but this can be very misleading. The word 'leper' in normal English means a person suffering from Hansen's disease, a crippling and ultimately fatal disease, the cure of which would have been truly miraculous. The relevant biblical words, however, cover a variety of skin diseases in people and fungal growths in houses. Some of the skin diseases come within the range of what traditional healers can heal, a remarkable fact but not one that is miraculous in any strict sense. Hence my translation, 'people-with-skin-diseases'.

In addition to referring directly to Jesus' ministry, this summary is strongly reminiscent of certain prophetic passages, notably Isa. 29.18–19; 35.5–6; 61.1. Jesus seems to have claimed indirectly to be fulfilling the hopeful parts of the prophecy, but not adjacent comments on judgement. At Isa. 29.18–19, we read עיני עורים תראינה ...החרשים ההוא ביום ושמעו, and we are told of the joy of עניים and אביוני אדם. At Isa. 35.5–6, תפקחנה עיני אז ...פסח כאיל ידלג אז תפתחנה: חרשים ואזני עורים. Isa. 61.1 includes לבשר ענוים and פקחקוח. This is sufficiently extensive for us to infer that it was deliberate, and that John the Baptist could reasonably be expected to pick it up.

There has traditionally been a problem over Jesus' reference to the raising of the dead, and this at two levels. At one level it has been regarded as a miraculous event, so that scholars coming in from a critical perspective have not been prepared to believe that it happened.[7] Secondly, it is not to be found in the scriptural passages referred to, nor in any prediction of the works of the Messiah, as Matthew called them. These problems can now be solved. Firstly, we know from the careful collection of evidence by Derrett that many people who have been taken to be dead have revived.[8] In our period, this led to the ruling that the bereaved could visit the grave for up to three days (*b. Sem.* 8.1). Consequently, we should believe that stories such as Mark 5.22–4, 35–43 have a genuine historical kernel. Jesus will have possessed the remarkable but not strictly miraculous ability to know when he could cause an apparently dead person to live. From his point of view, this will have been a particularly good example of the power of God working through him, and therefore very suitable for isolating in his response to John the Baptist.

Secondly, we should release our study of Jewish expectation from that of the Davidic messiah, since this was an unusual form of expectation. The

[7] For general surveys, including references to previous scholarship and other stories of resurrections, see H. van der Loos, *The Miracles of Jesus* (NT.S 9. Leiden, 1965), pp. 559–89; J. P. Meier, *A Marginal Jew. Rethinking the Historical Jesus*, vol. II (ABRL. New York, 1994), pp. 773–873.

[8] J. D. M. Derrett, *The Anastasis: The Resurrection of Jesus as an Historical Event* (Shipston-on-Stour, 1982), ch. 5.

resurrection of the dead is now mentioned in 4Q521.[9] This fragmentary piece deals with the expectation of a future anointed figure, probably an eschatological prophet. Line 12 reads as follows:

אז ירפא חללים ומתים יחיה ענוים יבשׂר

> then he will heal the slain and resurrect the dead, he will preach good news to the poor

This has healing, raising the dead and evangelising the poor, all together. Moreover, raising the dead was something which Elijah and Elisha were both believed to have done (1 Kings 17.17–24; 2 Kings 4.18–37), so something which it was most appropriate for an eschatological prophet to do. We should infer that raising the dead is in an appropriate place among those aspects of Jesus' description of his ministry which were designed to persuade John to accept him.

Finally, we should notice that the climax of the description is ענין מבשׂרין, the preaching of the good news to the poor. Jesus was not *merely* an effective healer who could appeal to his healing ministry as if this must indicate the power of God. The centre of his ministry was to bring unfaithful Jews back to God. This was also the centre of John the Baptist's ministry of baptism and repentance. Morever, the good news preached by Jesus included his message that the kingdom of God was at hand, which fitted the eschatological outlook characteristic of John's preaching. This final item in Jesus' summary was thus designed to persuade John that his ministry was the fulfilment of the central points of John's expectation, and that was infinitely more important than the fact that he was not quite what John had expected.

We must also notice something which this summary does *not* say: it does not mention the kingdom of God. Davies and Allison comment that Matt. 11.5–6 'characteristically proclaims the presence of the kingdom'. Among the many New Testament scholars whom they could cite are Jeremias, who produced this passage to illustrate the 'really new element' in Jesus' 'proclamation of the *basileia*'.[10] We should be much more careful than this. The kingdom of God was an important element in Jesus' teaching. To describe it accurately, we must in the first place use only passages in which he used this term. When we do so, we find an

---

[9] For edition and discussion, E. Puech, 'Une Apocalypse messianique (4Q521)', *RQ* 15, 1992, 475–519; J. J. Collins, 'The Works of the Messiah', *DSD* 1, 1994, 98–112; C. A. Evans, *Jesus & His Contemporaries. Comparative Studies* (Leiden, 1995), pp. 127–9.

[10] Davies and Allison, *Matthew*, vol. II, p. 244; Jeremias, *New Testament Theology*, p. 103.

important metaphor which was frequently used in an eschatological sense, and not very often with clear reference to the present course of Jesus' ministry (Matt. 12.28//Luke 11.20).[11] We must therefore be especially careful not to import it into passages such as Matt. 11.5//Luke 7.22. Jesus could have used it here if he had wished to; we must respect the fact that our primary source does not represent him as doing so. It might have confused the issue. John expected an eschatological figure; for Jesus to send a brief message using the kingship of God with reference to the present rather than the future would surely not have been helpful.

The passage ends with a beatitude. For σκανδαλισθῇ, I have suggested לקת. This is now attested at 11QtgJob XXV.6 (Job 34.30), and it is used in later Jewish Aramaic, Samaritan Aramaic, Christian Palestinian Aramaic, and Syriac, so it is likely to be the word which Jesus used. If John were to decide that Jesus was not the figure whom he had predicted, he would stumble, considerable harm might accrue to the Jesus movement, and a man regarded by Jesus as a great prophet would no longer be on God's side. Hence Jesus' concern to give a convincing answer to his question, one which might persuade him without pretending that Jesus was exactly what he had expected. Since he has already spoken in terms of the prophecies of Isaiah, it is probable that he had Isa. 8.14–15 particularly in mind. Here there will be צור מכשול, a rock of stumbling (*Tg.* לכיף מתקל, *Pesh.* לטרנא דתוקלתא), and similar obstacles: וכשלו בם רבים, 'And many among them shall stumble', (*Tg.* ויתקלון בהון סגיאין, *Pesh.* ונתתקלון בהון סגיאא). Those who do not stumble and fall like this are blessed by Jesus, and this general statement in prophetic terms is obviously applied particularly to John.

We must therefore conclude that we have an authentic report of John's uncertain question to Jesus, and of Jesus' reply. The amount of verbal agreement means that this passage reached both evangelists in Greek. Since, however, both Jesus and the earliest disciples spoke Aramaic, the source is likely to have been in Aramaic. There are no problems in re-constructing this. In this it differs from Matthew's introduction, where משיחא, behind τοῦ Χριστοῦ would not mean enough to be useful, un-like Matthew's Greek. This is at least coherent. In this case, the literally accurate translation into Greek has not significantly distorted the meaning, and the reconstruction of the Aramaic source does not make a significant difference. The most important point is simply that it can be done, and that, as far as it goes, it confirms other reasons for believing that we have an authentic and accurate source. The reconstruction of John's original prediction was, however, essential, and has enabled us to understand it in its original cultural context. This will become all the more important when we reach verse 12.

Jesus' view of John

The next verses clearly form a separate piece. This piece is not addressed to the disciples of John who have just left, but to a large audience who have gone out to see John in the wilderness. Since Jesus clearly expects them to regard John as a prophet, this audience must have been followers of John who had gone out into the wilderness, had been baptised and had been impressed by his preaching. The extent of verbal agreement in verses 7–10 is again so high that we must infer a continuation of Greek Q. In the opening phrase, however, Matthew and Luke differ significantly from each other. Their common ἤρξατο is a literal translation of the Aramaic שׁרי, which is used in these circumstances so much more than in Greek or English that we regard it as redundant. This word must belong to the Aramaic source. It must be followed at least by למאמר, underlying λέγειν, which is also common to Matthew and Luke, with ὁ Ἰησοῦς inserted by Matthew only for clarity's sake. It is characteristic of Aramaic narratives that they proceed without repeating the subject, whereas editors in non-Semitic languages will feel a variable urge to add things here and there. I have suggested that the opening phrases are due to separate editing by the two evangelists, each of whom replaced a simple καί which translated ו. It is difficult to reconstruct anything longer and convincing for an Aramaic source. The reconstructed source is, however, a perfectly reasonable continuation for an Aramaic sayings collection, whereas the additional connections were needed by the authors of narrative Gospels. I have put τοῖς ὄχλοις περὶ Ἰωάννου into Q, because both evangelists have something like it, and I have attributed it to the author of the Greek Q rather than to his Aramaic source, for similar reasons – he would need it more. It will, however, be clear that judgements of this kind are no more than decent guesses.

I have reconstructed the source of verses 8–9 according to a structure which has become conventional. It is possible to end the questions after ἔρημον/למדבר and ἐξεληλύθατε/נפקתון, thus beginning the answers with θεάσασθαι/דתחזון and ἰδεῖν/למחזה: 'But why have you gone out? To see a man dressed in soft clothing?', and similarly with the other questions. This is perhaps less probable, since everyone knew that they went out in response to John the Baptist, but it is possible. I have reconstructed verse 7 in this way, because the Aramaic seems to run more naturally like this.

The Aramaic מה has sometimes been taken to be a simple interrogative without any other meaning, giving a smaller number of longer questions: 'Did you go out into the wilderness to see a reed shaking in the wind?', and similarly.[12] But this use of מה is not attested until the Aramaic of a later period, so it is best to suppose that it is a later development.

I have reconstructed Luke's perfect ἐξεληλύθατε rather than Matthew's aorist ἐξήλθατε, as Q's rendering of the perfect נפקתון. The perfect ἐξεληλύθατε should in the first place be regarded as the correct reading in Luke. It is attested by the majority of manuscripts, including Θ, with A W as well in verse 9. There is weighty attestation of ἐξήλθατε, but this should be regarded as an early correction assimilating to Matthew, made by a scribe who considered the aorist more appropriate for a single past event. Otherwise, we cannot reasonably explain the origin of the reading ἐξεληλύθατε. For the same reason, ἐξεληλύθατε must also be the original reading of Q. Matthew will have changed it to the aorist ἐξήλθατε because he thought that Jesus was describing a single past event, just as he altered ἐλήλυθεν at Mark 9.13 to the aorist ἦλθεν (Matt. 17.12).

It is the perspective of the Q translator which is the most interesting. He could have used either ἐξήλθατε or ἐξεληλύθατε as a translation of נפקתון. He must have been accustomed to translating Aramaic perfects with Greek aorists, for they are so often equivalent. Accordingly, his translation of נפקתון with the perfect ἐξεληλύθατε implies that he intended the classic meaning of the Greek perfect, which may be overliterally rendered 'What have you come/gone out and are still here to see?' He must therefore have imagined Jesus in the wilderness, not in Capernaum or going through the towns and villages of Galilee. The Aramaic source, of course, could mean this but need not have this connotation. However, the Q translator certainly knew Aramaic, and was certainly in possession of the perfectly accurate traditions which we now read in this passage. It follows that he may have been right. He may also have been translating quite separate pieces, so we should not necessarily follow the present ordering of separate pieces and imagine that this piece always belonged late enough in the ministry to follow the previous piece. It is accordingly probable that this piece does not belong during the later part of the ministry, but rather to the period when Jesus was in the wilderness being baptised and tempted by the devil, before the arrest of John the Baptist, or during a longer period of overlapping ministries than we know about from synoptic sources.

There is no serious difference between θεάσασθαι in verse 7, and ἰδεῖν in verses 8 and 9. It is difficult to imagine Q's Aramaic source having

[12] K. Beyer, *Semitische Syntax im Neuen Testament* (2nd edn, Göttingen, 1968), pp. 100–2, n. 7.

anything other than אוה three times. Translators do in fact change their rendering of a word if it occurs more than once (e.g. 2 Chron. 4.6–8),[13] and I have simply supposed that the same part of אוה was used all three times here. I have followed א B in omitting εἰσίν from Matthew. It should be regarded as an addition by Luke, and by scribes of Matthew. The Aramaic source is entirely satisfactory with no equivalent to it, and the translator translated literally. To monoglot Greeks, however, something of the sort is necessary, and an early scribe of Matthew may have followed Luke in the addition of εἰσίν.

It is fortunate that the serious question of what Jesus really meant does not hang on these details, some of which are very uncertain. Jesus began with rhetorical contrasts leading up to his assessment of John the Baptist. A 'reed shaken in the wind' is a very common sight in the wilderness beside the Jordan where John baptised, and in other places such as beside the sea of Galilee. The suggestion that people might have gone so far in such conditions to see something so ordinary is deliberately ridiculous. Equally, the wilderness is the wrong place for 'a man dressed in soft clothing'. John the Baptist's appearance and diet, on the other hand, were remarkable enough for the Gospel tradition to transmit them: 'And John was clothed in camel's hair and a leather belt round his waist, and he ate locusts and wild honey' (Mark 1.6, cf. Matt. 3.4). Jesus' second suggestion is as ridiculous as his first. Some of the audience may also have thought of Herod Antipas. He was dressed in soft clothing and lived in a palace, and was known as a king even though he was technically a tetrarch. He also issued coins portraying reeds.[14] Be that as it may, Jesus' dismissal of these two possibilities leads into the normal verdict of the majority of Jews who went out into the wilderness to be baptised by John: they believed they went to see a prophet.

Up to this point, there is a parallel in the *Gospel of Thomas*, saying 78.

> Jesus said: Why did/have you come out into the countryside? To see a reed stirred by the wind? And to see a man clothed in soft garments? [ ] and your magnates (μεγιστᾶνος) are clothed in soft [garments], and they [shall] not be able to know the truth.

Here the sayings have lost their original context altogether. The Coptic ϹⲰϢE need mean no more than 'countryside', so there is nothing to recall the original scene, and there is no mention of John at all. The actual

[13] Casey, *Aramaic Sources of Mark's Gospel*, p. 207.
[14] On Herod, H. W. Hoehner, *Herod Antipas* (SNTS. MS 17. Cambridge, 1972); on the reeds, G. Theissen, *The Gospels in Context. Social and Political History in the Synoptic Tradition* (1991. ET Edinburgh, 1992), pp. 26–42.

word 'truth' is not found in the teaching of Jesus. The addition of which it is part has, however, a perfectly good *Sitz im Leben* in the kind of gnostic environment from which the *Gospel of Thomas* emerged. Here poor ascetics did believe that they could know the truth, that it was to be found in sayings of Jesus rather than in anything to do with John the Baptist, and that magnates were excluded from it.[15]

Continuing in response to his original questions, as correctly reported in Q, Jesus first of all accepts the popular verdict on John. John was indeed a prophet. The words יתיר על נביא do not put John outside the company of the prophets, but rather define which prophet he was – the one predicted by Malachi. The scriptural quotation has caused a lot of trouble, because of its resemblance to Exod. 23.20 rather than Mal. 3.1. We should infer that Jesus deliberately referred to the prophecy of Malachi, and that his quotation may have been affected by subconscious knowledge of Exod. 23.20; we should not suppose a deliberate reference to Exod. 23.20. The decisive point is the content of these passages. The prophecy of Malachi ends by identifying the messenger as Elijah (Mal. 3.23–4). This could reasonably be interpreted of a contemporary figure, and we know from Mark 9.11–13 that Jesus interpreted Mal. 3 of John the Baptist as Elijah. Other scriptural passages which he used included Isa. 40 and Job 14, and he used Jer. 6–7 with reference to the current state of Israel too. This mesh of scriptural passages cannot be understood without the earlier part of Mal. 3.[16] This is accordingly the cultural context of the passage in front of us: it interprets Mal. 3.1 of John the Baptist. This is not the case with Exod. 23.20, taken to be a deliberate reference. This is an account of God sending an angel before the people of Israel during the Exodus. This is sufficiently analogous to have interfered with Jesus' memory of Mal. 3.1, and it makes Exod. 23.20 a suitable text for some kinds of midrashic combination with Mal. 3.1, but the content of these passages demands that Jesus' primary reference was to Mal. 3.1.

The matter would be different if the two texts were already associated in Judaism, but the alleged evidence is altogether unconvincing. It is unfortunate that Strack-Billerbeck translated into German part of *Exod. Rab.* XXXII (93d) with dots after the quotation of Exod. 23.20, followed by a short piece which quotes Mal. 3.1. Subsequent scholars have quoted

---

[15] The extraordinary attempts of some American scholars to argue for the priority of the Thomas version are too arbitrary to merit detailed discussion here. See R. Cameron, ' "What Have You Come Out to See?" Characterizations of John and Jesus in the Gospels', *Semeia* 49, 1990, 35–69; Patterson, *Gospel of Thomas and Jesus*, pp. 78–9; and pp. 32–7 above.

[16] For detailed discussion of Mark 9.11–13, see Casey, *Aramaic Sources of Mark's Gospel*, ch. 3.

this as if the two biblical texts were closely associated.[17] The passage itself, however, is a massive collection of midrashic comments loosely connected to the opening text of Exod. 23.20. The final one ends with Mal. 3.1, but after the last re-quotation of Exod. 23.20 it first quotes Gen. 24.7; 48.16; Exod. 3.2, 4, 9 and Judges 6.11–14. This shows that, centuries after the time of Jesus, Mal. 3.1 was one of umpteen texts which could be loosely tacked together, beginning from Exod. 23.20. The scholarly view that it shows these two texts particularly connected by the time of Jesus is accordingly inaccurate.

The details of the actual biblical texts must now be considered. In the LXX, the words Ἰδοὺ ἐγὼ ἀποστέλλω τὸν ἄγγελόν μου are identical in both Exod. 23.20 and Mal. 3.1. Jesus will not have used LXX, and if the translator consulted LXX, he would surely go for Mal. 3.1 rather than Exod. 23.20, for the kinds of reasons just given. It is therefore important that there is no equivalent of μου in the MT of Exod. 23.20, and consequently not in the Targums or Peshitta to this verse either. The Hebrew text does have מלאכי at Exod. 23.23. We must infer that the LXX translator of Exod. 23.20 was influenced by Exod. 23.23. It follows that this is the first detail in which Jesus' quotation agreed with Mal. 3.1, and not with Exod. 23.20. I have suggested that he actually said ארו שלח אנא מלאכי; this is unproblematical, and so is its translation into Greek.

The next phrase in Q is πρὸ προσώπου σου. There is no equivalent to this at Mal. 3.1. This exact phrase occurs at LXX Exod. 23.20, where it is a literal translation of לפניך. I have reconstructed Jesus' saying with קדם אנפיך. There is sufficient reason to believe that אנפין was in use in the Aramaic of our period. It had been in use both literally and metaphorically for centuries, with על אפי ארקה already at *Sefire* I.28. The expression על אנפי תבל is found in the Jewish Aramaic of our period at 11QtgJob XXIX.3, where it renders על פני תבל ארצה (Job 37.12). The expression באנפוהי, 'before him', is found at *Ahiqar* 201: באנפי יהודן 'in the presence of John' is found at Mur 72.1.6, and בנפי, 'in my presence', should probably be read in Mur 18.3, which is dated to the second year of Nero (55–6 CE). Another important scriptural passage at this point is Mal. 3.23. This has the word לכם, which is very similar in meaning to קדם אנפיך, in the more precise prophecy אנכי שלה לכם את אליה הנביא. Both the Peshitta and the Targum naturally have לכון, and the Aramaic take-up of this same

[17] H. L. Strack and P. Billerbeck, *Kommentar zum Neuen Testament aus Talmud und Midrasch*, vol. I (Munich, 1922), p. 597, followed e.g. by K. Stendahl, *The School of St Matthew and Its Use of the Old Testament* (Lund, 1954), p. 50; D. Verseput, *The Rejection of the Humble Messianic King. A Study of the Composition of Matthew 11–12* (Frankfurt am Main, 1986), pp. 84, 393 n. 95.

prophecy in 4Q558 has לכן before אשלח. We have already seen that Jesus interpreted this prophecy of John the Baptist/Elijah. The actual word פנים is also used, in the form לפני, further on in the part of Mal. 3.1 quoted by Jesus. We must infer that it was primarily the memory of Mal. 3.23 and the rest of Mal. 3.1 which caused him to say something like קדם אנפי in his Aramaic presentation of this part of Mal. 3.1. This conforming of the text to the needs of the current situation by means of the rest of this text and another closely related text is normative for the Judaism of the period, and all the more natural when Hebrew texts are being expounded in Aramaic. We should infer that any influence of Exod. 23.20 on Jesus was unconscious.

The next words in Q are ὃς κατασκευάσει. It is difficult to be sure what this rendered. It is certainly quite different from Exod. 23.20, and this is a very big difference, a decisive point in favour of Jesus' use of Mal. 3.1 rather than Exod. 23.20. The Greek κατασκευάσει is also quite different from LXX Mal. 3.1 ἐπιβλέψεται, another reason for us not to believe that Q was really using LXX. κατασκευάσει could be an interpretative rendering of יפנא. This is the verb used to render the Hebrew פנה at Mal. 3.1 *Tg.*, and פנו at Isa. 40.3 *Tg. Pesh.* It means 'turn', 'turn away', and hence its use of clearing away, and consequently 'make clear' at both Mal. 3.1 and Isa. 40.3. At Mal. 3.1, the Peshitta similarly uses שפא, which means to 'make plain', 'make even', of a road, rather than 'prepare'. It is thus possible that κατασκευάσει in Q is an interpretative rendering of יפנא, on the same lines as ἑτοιμάσατε at Isa. 40.3 LXX. It is, however, more probable that we owe this shift to Jesus himself, which is why I have reconstructed יתקן. The Syriac versions all use נתקן here, and the Haphel of תקן is similarly used, meaning 'prepare', in late Jewish Aramaic. This is a more suitable metaphor than 'clear away' for what John the Baptist's ministry did for that of Jesus, and we can see from the rest of this and other passages that Jesus took part in the normal cultural habit of making interpretative alterations to scriptural passages as he used them. This is why it most probable that it was Jesus who made the change. Bearing in mind that in biblical Hebrew the semantic area of תקן includes 'make straight' (Eccl. 1.15; 7.13), one might perceive also an echo of ישרו at Isa. 40.3. Finally, the occurrence of תקן at Dan. 4.33 confirms that the word was available in Aramaic for Jesus to use.

The Q quotation concludes τὴν ὁδόν σου ἔμπροσθέν σου. This has equivalent words to Mal. 3.1, דרך לפני, but with different pronouns, neither σου corresponding to anything in the Hebrew, and the second one obviously different from the first-person suffix of לפני. It is even more different from Exod. 23.20 בדרך. We must infer firstly that Jesus was not using Exod. 23.20, and secondly that he was adapting Mal. 3.1 to the situation in hand.

We must therefore infer that, from the point of view of our understanding of Jesus, Exod. 23.20 is a red herring. The small number of detailed coincidences with it are either due to the general similarity of these passages, or to purely unconscious influence. Jesus intended to represent Mal. 3.1 in Aramaic. His representation of it was somewhat Targumic, adapted to his interpretation of it in terms of John the Baptist/Elijah. His use of קדם אנפיך was due both to the presence of לכם in Mal. 3.23, and to his correct memory that פנים was used somewhere in the text. That he used אנפין in a slightly different place is the sort of change that is liable to happen when quoting orally in a different language. The two suffixes assist the process of adapting the text to the proposed interpretation in a manner quite typical of the Judaism of the period.

So far, there is no sign that John the Baptist has died. We shall see that subsequent sayings which do imply this seem to have nothing to do with this little group. Moreover, we know from Mark 9.11–13 what a serious problem John's death caused for Jesus' exegesis of Mal. 3. He had to search the scriptures and find general statements about human mortality, since there are no scriptural passages which may readily be interpreted to deal with the death of John in particular. This adds to the argument of cumulative weight for supposing that some of Jesus' comments on John the Baptist belong to the period before his death. While we should not take the Q introduction to verse 7 too literally, therefore, it is entirely probable that the incident of verses 2–6 and the sayings of verses 7–10 belonged together in Q because they were originally collected together by someone who was there at the time. Not only do they have an excellent *Sitz im Leben* in the life of Jesus before the death of John the Baptist, they do not have any *Sitz im Leben* in the early church. The church had no reason to produce the questions that lead up to the main point, and περισσότερον προφήτου is the kind of judgement which they would gradually come to avoid.

Finally, this passage, like Mark 9.11–13, provides extremely clear evidence that Jesus did in fact identify John the Baptist as the Elijah figure prophesied in Mal. 3. This puts in proper perspective his own role as the final harbinger of the kingdom of God, and makes sense only if he thought that the End really was at hand.

The next two sayings about John and the kingdom have proved to be stunningly difficult. In the first part of verse 11, the expression ἐν γεννητοῖς γυναικῶν is not natural Greek. It is, however, Semitic, being found both in later Aramaic and in the Hebrew bible. In *Aramaic Sources of Mark's Gospel*, I was able to go much further than this. In the light of the Aramaic source of Mark 9.11–13, I recovered the biblical exegesis with which Jesus sought to understand John the Baptist's death. I found that he did so by means of general statements about the death of people.[18] The passages on which he meditated included Job 14. The first verse of this chapter is the origin of Jesus' expression:

אדם ילוד אשה קצר ימים ושבע־רגז

Jesus applied this general statement to John the Baptist as he sought to understand John's untimely death at the hands of Herod Antipas. It is this which has prompted his use of בילידין דנשין of John the Baptist. This verdict will accordingly have been passed after John's death. This is also shown by the content of the second part. זעירא cannot be comparative or superlative in a grammatical sense, but it is often used of a person regarded as inferior in rank or status (hence the use of μικρότερος as a translation). That such a person in the kingdom of God is greater than John must mean that John is excluded from the kingdom. For this to make any sense in the light of Jesus' verdicts on John as we know them from other passages requires that John is dead, and that the kingdom is being understood in an eschatological sense. This implies the same content as Mark 9.1: some people will still be alive to see the kingdom of God come in power. John would not see this because he was dead. Accordingly, this saying does not imply any undervaluing of John. It does imply that the term 'kingdom of God' was used so often in an eschatological sense that it could be so used quite elliptically.

With these main points settled, I can fill in some details. I have put אמן in the source, and ἀμήν in Q. This is a solemn statement which no one may have expected Jesus to make, an authoritative declaration about both John and being in the kingdom. It is therefore the kind of context in which Jesus used אמן in his unusual and probably unique way. Luke retains it only six times: presumably he was not too keen on it because it is not a Greek word. We also know that he replaced it with ἀληθῶς at Luke 9.27 (Mark 9.1) and 21.3 (Mark 12.43), and that he never has it in a Q passage. We should probably therefore infer that he omitted it here. Arguments to the contrary sometimes make much of Matthew's insertion of ἀμήν at Matt. 19.23 (cf. Mark 10.23); 24.2 (cf. Mark 13.2),[19] but these are not comparable cases because Luke 7.28 confirms the presence of λέγω ὑμῖν in Q. I have also put קום, translated with Matthew's ἐγήγερται, for this too is a standard Semitic mode of expression for the appearance of prophets

---

[18] Casey, *Aramaic Sources of Mark's Gospel*, pp. 126–30.
[19] E.g. Häfner, *Vorläufer*, p. 196.

and other people. I have also kept μείζων in its Matthean position. This permits the restoration of the idiomatic רב מן יוחנן: the Lucan word order does not permit this, and this increases the probability that I am right about אמן and קום, since we have a consistent picture of Luke editing Q in a Gentile Greek direction.

The opposite is true of מלכותה דאלהא and τῇ βασιλείᾳ τοῦ θεοῦ. We know that Matthew usually alters this, because he lived in a Jewish environment where ἡ βασιλεία τῶν οὐρανῶν was the normal expression. There should therefore be no doubt that the Lucan form is the one from which we must reconstruct approximately the expression used by Jesus. I have also treated τοῦ βαπτιστοῦ as a Matthean gloss. We should not read it in Luke because the manuscripts from which it is absent include a very strong combination of the oldest and best ones (P^{75} א B D): the majority of manuscripts assimilate to Matthew, because of a perceived need for precise description. For a similar reason, we should not reconstruct it in Q: Luke is most unlikely to have omitted it, whereas Matthew might well feel also the need for precise description. Jesus will not have needed to use this epithet because it will have been obvious which John he was referring to, and the author of the Aramaic source will have felt the same. We should not read προφήτης even in Luke. It is absent from P^{75} א B and some other manuscripts. It will have been produced by a scribe who noticed that Jesus was born of a woman and who did not think of him as a prophet, but as the truly divine Son of God.

Finally, I have not reproduced Q's last word, ἐστιν in its Aramaic source, because it is unnecessary in Aramaic. It is therefore just the kind of thing that even a fairly literal translator would have to add.

This gives a coherent result. Jesus cannot have expected John's death. After it, he resorted to the scriptures to understand it. This saying reflects that understanding. John had played a fundamental role in calling the people of Israel back to God. Nonetheless, it was better to be still alive, ready for the imminent coming of the kingdom. The whole saying has accordingly an excellent *Sitz im Leben* in the teaching of Jesus. The first half of it has no *Sitz im Leben* in the early church, and they are most unlikely to have expressed themselves in the terminology of the second half. The genuineness of the whole saying should therefore be accepted.

This saying has a parallel in the *Gospel of Thomas*, saying 46:

> Jesus said: 'From Adam to John the Baptist, among those born of women, there is none more exalted than John the Baptist, so that his eyes should not be broken. But I have said that whoever among you becomes a little (one/child) shall know the kingdom and he shall be more exalted than John.'

It is unfortunate that something has gone wrong with the text of this saying at the end of the first sentence. It should, however, be clear that this is not the original version of the saying. The original ἐγήγερται has been lost, because it was no more congenial to the tradition which ended in the *Gospel of Thomas* than it was to Luke. Equally secondary is the direct application of the saying to the contemporary audience with the words 'whoever among you becomes...' It is closely associated with the expression 'know the kingdom', which is not found elsewhere in the teaching of Jesus, nor indeed in the rest of the New Testament. It has, however, an excellent *Sitz im Leben* in the Gnostic environment in which the saying was transmitted. The pervasive importance of knowledge in that environment is more important than the closest parallel in the Coptic *Epistle of James*. Here the Lord tells the disciples that if they do not receive the kingdom through knowledge (γνῶσις), they will not be able to find it (fIV^v, lines 26–7).

These changes have given the saying a quite new meaning. The original eschatological setting has been replaced with the view that the Christians in the Thomasine group will be more exalted than John. We should also note that entering the kingdom is associated with being little ones/children in saying 22, and in saying 4 one can ask a little child of seven days about the place of life, and thereby live. This goes far beyond synoptic sayings such as Mark 10.14–15//Matt. 19.14//Luke 18.16–17 (cf. Matt. 18.3), which also have a quite different context.[20] Thus saying 46 is well integrated in this document, and it cannot possibly be original to the historical Jesus. We must accordingly regard the Q version of the saying as the original one. Jesus excluded John from the kingdom simply because John was dead, and Jesus expected the kingdom to come soon.

At this point, Matthew and Luke part company. I start with Luke 7.29–30, which is not in Matthew. These verses should be regarded as Lucan, for they are the kind of clarifying addition which Luke loves to make occasionally, and they may safely be excluded from Q. Lucan expressions include πᾶς ὁ λαός (Luke 10, Acts 6), and βουλή (nine of the New Testament examples are in Luke–Acts, none in Matthew or Mark). The term νομικός should also be regarded as Lucan (Matthew, one; Mark, none; Luke, six). It always occurs in contexts where Luke seems to be editing, and this is more important than his fourteen uses of γραμματεύς, most of which were taken over from Mark.[21] On the other hand, it has

[20] H. C. Kee, ' "Becoming a Child" in the Gospel of Thomas', *JBL* 82, 1963, 307–14.
[21] G. D. Kilpatrick, 'Scribes, Lawyers and Lucan Origins', *JThS* 1, 1950, 56–60; A. R. C. Leaney, 'ΝΟΜΙΚΟΣ in St Luke's Gospel', *JThS* 2, 1951, 166–7.

been suggested that εἰς ἑαυτούς is an Aramaism, a kind of ethic dative.[22]
This suggestion should not be accepted. Luke uses ἑαυτοῦ some fifty-
seven times in his Gospel, and some twenty-two times in Acts, so it is
obviously a Lucan word. His examples include Luke 9.25, where Luke
has replaced Mark's τὴν ψυχὴν αὐτοῦ with the better Greek reflexive
ἑαυτόν; and Luke 12.1, where ἑαυτοῖς might reasonably be described
as an ethic dative, and is absent from both Matthew and Mark, so it is
probably editorial. At Luke 7.30, however, εἰς ἑαυτούς is normal Greek
and reflexive, not the equivalent of an ethic dative. The Pharisees and
lawyers 'set aside the will of God for themselves', but they were not
so wicked as to prevent the baptism of others. This example illustrates
again how careful we must be with suggestions about single words or
expressions. This one has been suggested in an inappropriate Lucan place,
as well as misunderstood.

Matthew alone has Matt. 11.12–15, of which Matt. 11.14–15 has no
parallel anywhere in Luke. I have put verse 15 in Q, and reconstructed
its source. Jesus must have said this occasionally, and no harm is done
by putting it after verse 14, but this kind of thing might have appealed
to Matthew too, and my judgement in this matter has only a 50 per cent
probability even in my own estimation. Matt. 11.14 would certainly not
appeal to Luke; I shall suggest that it probably did belong to Q.

Matt. 11.12–13 does have a Lucan parallel, but at Luke 16.16, not here.
What has happened? This is obviously another place to try out the kind
of hypothesis that emerged in chapter 3, that where there is no common
order there have been two translations, and the sayings were collected into
Matthew's version of Q but not into Luke's. However, I cannot account
for the two versions in this way. Moreover, it is not difficult to see why.
The Matthean and Lucan versions are so different from each other that
at least one of them must have been heavily edited. We shall see that the
Lucan version fits so well into Lucan theology that it must have been
heavily edited. What, then, can we make of the Matthean version? Verse
12 is very strange on the surface, and no satisfactory interpretation of it
has so far been forthcoming.[23] In particular, it has been pointed out that
βιάζεται, βιασταί and ἁρπάζουσιν should all be used in a hostile sense.[24]

[22] Black, *Aramaic Approach* (3rd edn, 1967), p. 103, following Wellhausen and Torrey.
[23] For a critically incisive *Forschungsbericht*, P. S. Cameron, *Violence and the Kingdom: The Interpretation of Matthew 11:12* (ANTJ 5. 2nd edn, Frankfurt am Main, 1988), especially pp. 147–58, where he discusses interpretations which employ Hebrew and/or Aramaic words; further, G. Häfner, 'Gewalt gegen die Basileia? Zum Problem der Auslegung des "Stürmerspruches" Mt 11,12', *ZNW* 83, 1992, 21–51; *Vorläufer*, pp. 197–208, 232–7.
[24] E.g. W. E. Moore, 'ΒΙΑΖΩ, 'ΑΡΠΑΖΩ and Cognates in Josephus', *NTS* 21, 1974–5, 519–43.

This, however, makes it very difficult to make sense of the saying at all. We can make better sense of it as the work of a translator in difficulties.

On the basis of usage in the Peshitta and Targums, Chilton revived the suggestion that תקף might lie behind βιάζεται, and refined it with further evidence.[25] I accept this suggestion, for the following reasons. The word תקף is attested in Aramaic from before the time of Jesus. Its semantic area includes 'grow strong', and I propose that this is the intended meaning here. It is difficult to translate, and βιάζεται overlaps sufficiently with its semantic area to be reasonable. The translator will have suffered from interference as he struggled with the translation, and it is this which has caused him not to notice that in monoglot Greek a hostile sense of βιάζεται would be likely to be perceived. If this is so, the same thing is likely to have caused him to write βιασταί. I have accordingly suggested תקיפין. This again means strong, powerful beings, but the sense in which they are so varies according to the context. For ἁρπάζουσιν, some form of אחד is an obvious possibility, because of the large overlap in semantic area. At the same time, however, אחד can be used of grasping anything, in a favourable sense. For example, at *Tg. Isa.* 41.10 God, in supporting his servant Israel, says אחדינך בימין קושטי, 'I will grasp you with the right hand of my righteousness/truth'. In a parallel comment at *Tg. Isa.* 41.13, he declares ארי אנא יהוה אלהך מתקיף ימינך, 'Look! I YHWH your God will strengthen your right hand'. This gives us favourable uses of אחד and תקף closely together. At *Tg. Isa.* 56.1, God's salvation is announced and at 56.2 a blessing is formulated on בר אנש דיתקף בה, 'the (son of) man who keeps it fast', in parallel with doing it, keeping the sabbath and not doing evil. This is a good parallel to תקף being used favourably of God's kingship, since this also refers to his revelation of his salvation.

I also suggest that ἕως ἄρτι is an editorial addition. We shall see that it does not have a particularly good *Sitz im Leben* in the original saying. It does, however, have a good *Sitz im Leben* when collected with verse 13, since it balances ἕως 'Ιωάννου . I have suggested that it was in Matthew's source. Equally, however, he might have seen fit to insert it when he was altering ἡ βασιλεία τού θεοῦ to ἡ βασιλεία τῶν οὐρανῶν.

We now have a saying which can be interpreted from within the framework of the life and teaching of Jesus. It is about the growing strength of the kingdom of God in the period before its consummation. Dating this from the ministry of John is entirely reasonable, because of the massive success of his popular ministry in making Jews return to God. Kingship

---

[25] Chilton, *GOD* in *STRENGTH*, pp. 226–30.

is a perfectly decent metaphor for this example, because it refers directly to God's power. The תקיפין are people like John himself, Jesus and the Twelve. They are strong people who have laid hold on God's kingly power by a ministry of baptism and preaching which brought people back to God, by exorcism and the like.

For the original point of the saying, we must return to John the Baptist's original prophecy of the coming of תקיפא. We have seen that this was based on Mal. 3.[26] Jesus, however, believed that the prophecy of Mal. 3 was fulfilled by John the Baptist himself. Accordingly, John the Baptist was in Jesus' view the first of the תקיפין of this passage, for he took God's kingly power in his hands in his prophetic ministry. John's prophecy of the coming of תקיפא was fulfilled in the ministry of Jesus, though Jesus was not the only one of the תקיפין who laid hold of the kingship of God in his ministry of exorcism, healing and preaching the good news. The Twelve conspicuously shared in this power when Jesus sent them out on mission. This further illuminates the indirectness of Jesus' answer to John the Baptist's question at the beginning of this passage. He drew attention to his mighty works, and thereby left John to conclude that he was indeed תקיפא. The present saying also makes sense only if it was spoken some time after John's death.

It follows that this verse jars with the previous verse, because these two sayings were originally separate. They were collected together in the same general place because they are both concerned with John the Baptist, and they were put next to each other because they contain the same key phrase, מלכותה דאלהא. The compiler was not concerned at the sharp disjunction in usage because he was collecting sayings of Jesus, in groups on the same subject. He will probably have known what they meant, and will certainly have expected them to be expounded by someone, not merely read out.

In Matthew's Greek text, verse 13 is connected to verse 12 with γάρ. I have suggested that this connection is secondary, and that in the Aramaic source this was a separate saying, collected with this one because it is also about John. Like some of the earlier sayings in this collection, and the next one, it is concerned with the fulfilment of prophecy. Jesus believed that many prophecies were fulfilled during his ministry. As we have seen, he also believed that John the Baptist fulfilled some prophecies, including Malachi 3. This saying defines the time of fulfilment. All the prophets, and the Law, prophesied in the period preceding John. The mention of the Law has often been found secondary, but it has an excellent *Sitz im Leben* in first-century Judaism, and a

[26] See pp. 108–10 above.

decreasingly good one the further we move away from there. It was generally believed that there were prophecies in the Pentateuch, and this was known as תורה, in Aramaic אוריתא and in Greek νόμος. We do not have sufficient evidence from the teaching of Jesus to know which passages he had in mind. They may, for example, have included the prophet like Moses of Deut. 18.15–19, apparently applied to Jesus by Peter in Acts 3.22–3, perhaps therefore because this is what Jesus had taught the Twelve: but like all other possibilities, this text is not mentioned in the teaching of Jesus as it has been transmitted to us in the Gospels.

We can now see why the Lucan version (Luke 16.16) is found some-where else: it was collected into a different group of sayings (Luke 16. 10–18). Its equivalents to verses 12 and 13 are in the opposite order. Luke has used ἀπὸ τότε as a summary of ἀπὸ δὲ τῶν ἡμερῶν Ἰωάννου because John has already been mentioned; we should infer that this expression is secondary. The term ἐπροφήτευσαν has been omitted: in a Gentile environment the concept of the Law prophesying will have been found too difficult to repeat. The resulting saying contrasts the period of the Law and the prophets with that of the kingdom. A significant shift in a Gentile direction has thereby taken place, as the resulting saying lends itself to the Gentile interpretation that the period of the Law and the prophets is over. The mode of expression still uses ἡ βασιλεία τοῦ θεοῦ because a saying has been rewritten, not created. The rest of it has been completely rewritten: βιάζεται with ἡ βασιλεία τοῦ θεοῦ has been re-placed with εὐαγγελίζεται. This gives Luke an acceptable description of the ministry of Jesus, seen as after the period of the Law and the prophets. The rest of it, πᾶς εἰς αὐτὴν βιάζεται, should be seen as an acceptable reinterpretation of βιασταὶ ἁρπάζουσιν αὐτήν It uses βιάζεται, surely not by coincidence, but because the word was in front of Luke or his predecessor as he rewrote the saying.

It follows that we should not imagine two separate translations of these sayings from an Aramaic original: it is something very like Matt. 11.12–13 which has been rewritten to form a saying which is sufficiently congenial to Luke. It is therefore entirely possible that Luke altered the order of the two sayings. Be that as it may, this is a case where the Q material does not have a common order. Luke 16.17 has a fairly close parallel at Matt. 5.18. Luke 16.15 has been placed where it is, with Lucan introduction at 16.14, because of Luke 16.13, which has such a close verbal parallel to Matt. 6.24 that here too only one Greek translation is to be inferred. Moreover, Luke 16.16 would follow very nicely after Luke 7.28. We should probably infer that Matt. 11.12–13 had not been collected into the Greek sayings collection which Luke edited to form Luke 7.18–35.

It may therefore be that Luke did not have to contemplate whether to put verses 14 and 15 into Luke 7. It has often been remarked that he would not have liked verse 14 anyway. The Aramaic reconstruction is, however, more than a little interesting. In Matthew's Greek, εἰ θέλετε δέξασθαι is very odd. Why should Jesus or Matthew make the identification of John the Baptist as Elijah dependent on whether people accepted it or not? The Aramaic source does not have to mean this. ואן תצבון למקבלה could equally mean 'and if you are willing to receive him'. This could be a genuine early saying of Jesus. There must have been a time when he meditated on the prophecies of Malachi and wondered whether John might be the fulfilment of them, or whether he was, or not. This saying could mean that if people accepted the ministry of John, he would fulfil the prophesied role of Elijah. That has a much better *Sitz im Leben* in the early stages of John's ministry than εἰ θέλετε δέξασθαι has in Matthew. We should probably therefore infer that it is genuine. It has been collected here to make a decent inclusio with verse 10.

This generation

Verses 16–19 are another piece, collected here because they too involve John the Baptist. Here again the level of verbal agreement in Greek is so high that we must infer a single Greek translation which reached both evangelists in approximately the form reconstructed above. The interpretation of these verses has caused endless trouble to modern scholars. It is easier to deal with some problems in Aramaic, but not all of them. It is, however, possible to unravel all the main threads, and to make some reasonable suggestions about the last sentence, which has proved quite intractable.

The first problem is not with the substance of the passage, but the nature of the opening comparison. In several details I have preferred the Matthean version as the more original. Jesus criticised his generation on other occasions, and thus stood in a Semitic tradition. Luke will have added τοὺς ἀνθρώπους, as he added τῶν ἀνδρῶν at 11.31, because Greeks preferred the more literal expression, especially before the following similitude. Even in the shorter original version, it should be clear that the generation are compared to the children; it is accordingly not John the Baptist and Jesus who are compared to the children. Matthew's Greek τοῖς ἑτέροις is surprising, and Luke's ἀλλήλοις must be interpreted as an improvement of Q's Greek. For the Aramaic source I have suggested אחריא. Here the definite state does not mean anything very much: אחריא are simply 'others'. Since the children are an image of the people of Jesus' generation, the 'others' are an image of John the Baptist and Jesus. This is a good image of them, since the whole point of the comparison is to present a conflict situation between John and Jesus on the one hand, and the rest of their generation on the other. As so often with slightly peculiar Gospel Greek, Matthew's τοῖς ἑτέροις results from literal translation. The word ἑτέροις is a perfectly reasonable rendering of the word אחרין, and the article τοῖς simply represents it in the definite state.

In spite of the very straightforward nature of the declarations in both Matthew and Luke that this generation, or the people of it, are compared to παιδίοις, the majority of scholars have imagined otherwise. Creed put the main point bluntly long ago: 'The comparison is not exactly expressed. It is John and Jesus – not this generation – who are the counterparts to the children who invite their fellows to joy or mourning – in each case without success.'[27] We should not accept this because it arbitrarily contradicts the text. We must rather seek to understand what the text says.

What sort of city Jesus envisaged the children in is not clear, because it is not the point. For ἐν ταῖς ἀγοραῖς (Matthew) and ἐν ἀγορᾳ (Luke) I have reconstructed בשוקא. The Aramaic word שוק is an old word, being derived from the Akkadian *sūqu*, and in its earliest occurrences it means 'street'. When Aramaic was spoken in large Hellenised cities, it became the equivalent of the Greek ἀγορά. There is a beautiful example of this in the bilingual Palmyrene inscription CIS ii 3932 line 5 (PAT 0278), dated to 242 CE, where the official רב שוק is called in Greek ἀγορανομ-ήσαντα. Moreover, some streets could be rather big. For example, the new Jerusalem was pictured with the middle street of Jerusalem some fifty yards wide (5Q15 1 i 3). Hence ἀγορά is used to render שוק three times in LXX, two examples being the Lucan ἐν ἀγορᾳ for the Hebrew בשוק (Eccl. 12.4–5).

Cotter has attempted to place this incident in a large Hellenistic city.[28] She suggests that προσφωνεῖν is used in a formal sense. She notes that the ἀγορά was the centre of public life, and consequently it is frequently employed in reference to courts. She selects part of the semantic area of κάθημαι as meaning 'sit in judgement'. She concludes that 'this genera-tion' is being compared to 'children sitting in judgement at the courts'. This approach is not legitimate. The Greek word προσφωνεῖν is more colourful than καλέω, but it is not necessarily as formal as Cotter claims.

---

[27] J. M. Creed, *The Gospel According to St Luke* (London, 1930), p. 108. More recently, e.g. D. Zeller, 'Die Bildlogik des Gleichnisses Mt 11:16f/Lk 7:31f', *ZNW* 68, 1977, 252–7.

[28] W. J. Cotter, 'The Parable of the Children in the Market-place, Q (Lk) 7:31–35: An Examination of the Parable's Image and Significance', *NT* 29, 1987, 289–304, esp. 295–302.

Luke uses it, rather than Mark's προσκαλεῖται, of Jesus calling his disciples together (Luke 6.13); of Jesus in the act of healing (Luke 13.12), of Pilate calling to the crowd, in place of Mark's mundane ἔλεγεν (Luke 23.20); and of Paul speaking to a crowd in Aramaic (Acts 21.40; 22.2). The Q passage fits well into this kind of area, a perfectly suitable word for children as an image of scribes and Pharisees calling to each other. The ἀγορά was used for more than law suits, and κάθημαι is an ordinary Greek word for 'sit', used some eighteen times by Matthew and thirteen times by Luke in his Gospel. What Cotter has done is to ignore the Jewish setting of the Gospels and the language spoken by Jesus, and with the wrong cultural setting in mind she has pushed the setting in a predetermined direction by selecting only the convenient part of the possible associations of Greek words. We must not proceed like this.

There are some problems with the words of verse 17, because this is not the kind of subject discussed in early Aramaic documents. For ηὐλήσαμεν, I have put זמרנא. There is no doubt that this is the right word in Syriac, and that is why the Syriac versions unanimously use it here. It is found in earlier Aramaic, but in extant texts it means 'sing', 'play' (a musical instrument). Hence the rendering of זמריא (Ezra 7.24) with ᾄδουσιν at 2 Esdras 7.24, and of זמרא with μουσικῶν by both LXX and Theodotion at Dan. 3.5, 7, 10, 15. I have supposed that the Syriac meaning was available earlier. For ὠρχήσασθε, I have put רקדתון. There is no doubt that this too is the right word in Syriac, and the versions unanimously use it here. It is also found in late Jewish Aramaic, and in Christian Palestinian Syriac. It is therefore a reasonable conjecture that it was the appropriate Aramaic word at an earlier date.

For ἐθρηνήσαμεν, I have reconstructed הולילנא. The Hiphil of ילל is well attested in biblical Hebrew, and rendered with θρηνέω seven times in LXX. The Haphel occurs in Aramaic, meaning 'lament', at *Ahiqar* 41. This is sufficient to establish it as an early Aramaic word, even though it is the only early Aramaic occurrence, and it is absent from the Dead Sea scrolls. It does occur in later Jewish Aramaic, Christian Palestinian Aramaic and Syriac. In his reconstruction, Jeremias put ‘ᵃlēnan, but he offered no justification for this, and I can see none.[29] The Syriac versions have אלין (with אלינ in the Harklean), but this is not attested in any early sources, nor is it common in later Jewish Aramaic. We should therefore prefer ילל. For ἐκόψασθε, I have reconstructed ספדתון. The word ספד is common in biblical Hebrew, and it is rendered with κόπτω no fewer

[29] Jeremias, *New Testament Theology*, p. 26.

than twenty-eight times in the LXX. It is also normal in later Jewish Aramaic, beginning with the Scroll of Fasting, so it was a normal Jewish Aramaic word by the second century. It is also found in Christian Palestinian Aramaic and in Samaritan Aramaic. Jeremias has *'arqēdtūn*, but he appears to have simply copied the Syriac versions of Matt. 11.17, for this use of the Aphel of רקד is as far as I know specific to Syriac.

It will be apparent that there is some uncertainty about the exact words used by Jesus in verse 17. This degree of uncertainty does not, however, affect any matters of exegetical importance, so I shall now proceed to interpret the contents of the verse. The piping is mentioned first, because it is aimed at criticism of John, and the image is presented in the same order as the reality. We know from elsewhere that chief priests did not accept John the Baptist (Mark 11.27–33), nor did scribes and Pharisees (cf. Matt. 21.32), nor did the Herod who had him put to death. This image reflects their refusal to accept John's ascetic ministry. The wailing and mourning is second, because it is aimed at critics of Jesus. We know that at this stage they were orthodox Jews, and we must infer that they had criticised Jesus' eating habits, as they do elsewhere (Mark 2.16, cf. 18). This is also a polemical description of them as miserable.

The use of אתה in verse 18 clearly refers to John arriving on the scene, and does not imply his pre-existence or the like. The word אתה has a very broad semantic area, so that this usage should not be regarded as problematical. I have suggested that the original translator put ἐλήλυθεν as a literal rendering of the Semitic perfect, and that Matthew altered this to ἦλθεν because he thought that both ministries were past events. Since this is the same translator as the one who put ἐξεληλύθατε in verse 7, 8 and 9, he is likely to have thought that this saying too was spoken while John the Baptist was still alive. This also makes excellent sense of the present tenses λέγουσιν and ἔχει. It is also to be noted that a translator of אתה put ἐλήλυθεν at Mark 9.13, only to have Matthew alter it to ἦλθεν.

I have supposed that Matthew's μήτε ἐσθίων μήτε πίνων reproduces his Greek source, which was a literal translation of לא אכל ולא שתא. Luke expanded this because it could not be true if interpreted too literally. This is entirely intelligible. The reverse process, in which decent Greek μὴ ἐσθίων ἄρτον μήτε πίνων οἶνον was shortened to a more semitic mode of expression, is not at all probable. The brief phrase is a perfectly good picture of John's ascetic life style. In that sense it is confirmed by Mark, who reports him eating a diet of locusts and wild honey (Mark 1.6). The accusation that John was possessed by a demon is not confirmed by other sources, which are, however, too meagre for this to cast doubt on the accuracy of Jesus' comment. His vigorous opponents firmly believed both in God and in the demonic world. They could hardly maintain the priesthood, the detailed observance of the Law, and their opposition to him, unless they took some such view. John was very unconventional. He lived in the wilderness, away from cities, as demoniacs sometimes did too. He dressed and ate unconventionally, less than his opponents. The accusation that he had a demon will have come as naturally to his opponents as it did to scribes and Pharisees who accused Jesus of casting out demons by the prince of demons.[30]

The statement about Jesus is put indirectly, using the general term בר (א)נשׁ(א). This term continues to be controversial, but I have recently set out the main Aramaic evidence elsewhere, so I make only some main points about the use of בר (א)נשׁ(א) before discussing this particular saying.[31] The basic semantic area of בר (א)נשׁ(א) remained effectively unchanged for centuries: it was always a general term for 'man'. The earliest example, from centuries before the time of Jesus, is already used in the same idiomatic way that lies behind verse 19: it is a general statement used because the speaker wants to make a point about himself, or himself and a group of other people.

1. *Sefire* III.14–17.

> והן יסק על לבבך ותשׂא על שׂפתיך להמתתי ויסק על לבב בר ברך וישׂא
> על שׂפתוה להמתת בר ברי או הן יסק על לבב עקרך וישׂא על שׂפתוה
> להמתת עקרי והן יסק על [ל]בב מלכי ארפד בכל מה זי ימות בר אנשׁ
> שׁקרתם לכל אלהי עדיא זי בספרא זנה.

And if you think of killing me and you put forward such a plan, and if your son's son thinks of killing my son's son and puts forward such a plan, or if your descendants think of killing my descendants and put forward such a plan, and if the kings of Arpad think of it, in any case that a son of man dies, you have been false to all the gods of the treaty which is in this inscription.

This example was written centuries before the time of Jesus, in the name of the king of Ktk. It uses בר אנשׁ in a general statement which refers to the king and his descendants. In view of the cultural context, it is most unlikely that it was intended to refer to the death of anyone other than people on the side of the king of Ktk, and it probably refers only to the king and his descendants.

All the examples of בר (א)נשׁ(א) extant from around the time of Jesus are of a general kind (1QapGen XXI.13; 11QtgJob IX.9 (Job 25.6); XXVI.3

---

[30] See pp. 158–61 below.
[31] Casey, *Aramaic Sources of Mark's Gospel*, esp. pp. 111–21.

(Job 35.8); cf. Dan. 7.13; and in the plural Dan. 2.38; 5.21; *1 En.* 7.3; 22.3; 77.3 (4Q Enastr^b 23); 1QapGen XIX.15; 4QGiants 426; 11QtgJob XXVIII.2 (Job 36.25)). Passage 2 is especially worthy of note:

2. 1QapGen XXI.13: MT אִישׁ (Gen. 13.16).

ואשגה זרעך כעפר ארעא די לא ישכח כול בר אנוש לממניה

And I will multiply your seed like the dust of the earth which no son of man can count...

Here the fact that בר אנוש has been chosen to represent the Hebrew אִישׁ must mean that it was felt to be especially suitable for a general statement. This would surely not be the case if (א)בר נש(א) also brought to mind a resplendent heavenly figure, the Son of man concept (Menschensohnsbegriff) beloved of too much scholarship.[32]

Later sources also have examples in which a speaker uses a general statement with particular reference to himself, or himself and one or more other people. These include passage 3:

3. *Gen. Rab.* LXXIX.6.

ציפור מבלעדי שמיא לא מיתצדא. חד כמן וכמן נפש דבר נש.

A bird is not caught without the will of heaven: how much less the soul of a son of man.

After saying this, R. Simeon emerged from his cave with his son. It follows that this is a general statement which applies particularly to the speaker and one other person.

It is clear from these examples that this idiom was in use for centuries before and after the time of Jesus. This is natural, because it consists of a simple application of general statements to fulfil a normal human need, that of speaking indirectly about oneself. If therefore sayings of Jesus emerge as examples of this idiom when straightforwardly reconstructed, we should accept them as examples of it.

When sources are sufficiently abundant, בר נש(א) has all the normal human experiences. In passage 4, these include eating and drinking:

4. Bardaisan, *The Book of the Laws of the Countries*, page 559, lines 11–14.[33]

---

[32] See further P. M. Casey, 'The Use of the Term "son of man" in the Similitudes of Enoch', *JSJ* VII, 1976, 11–29; *Son of Man. The Interpretation and Influence of Daniel 7* (London, 1980), pp. 99–141.

[33] For the text, Bardesanes, *Liber Legum Regiorum*, cuius textum syriacum vocalium signis instruxit, latine vertit F. Nau, annotationibus locupletavit Th. Nöldeke, in F. Graffin (ed.), *Patrologia Syriaca* vol. II (Paris, 1907), pp. 490–657.

כינה דברנשא הנו דנתיליד ונתרבא ודנקום באקמא ודנוליד ודנקש כד אכל וכד
שתא וכד דמך וכד מתתעיר ודנמות.

This is the nature of (the son of) man, that he should be born
and grow up and reach his peak and reproduce and grow old,
while eating and drinking and sleeping and waking, and that he
should die.

This is a very general statement about human beings. In the light of
scholarly discussion of בר (א)נש(א), it is important to note that it is by no
means true of everyone. When it was written, many children died before
they were grown up, some people had no children, and relatively few
grew old. This was not considered relevant to this general description of
human life.

I can now return to the interpretation of verse 19. The idiomatic use of
בר (א)נש(א) was due to Jesus being in the humiliating situation of being
falsely accused of what we shall see was a serious offence. The use of
this idiom in a general statement does not imply that the statement was
thought to be true of everyone. The first part of it is, however, true of
everyone:

אתה בר אנש אכל ושתה

Everyone does come eating and drinking, otherwise they die! It should
be clear that אתה has this very general level of meaning, as in the previous
sentence about John the Baptist; it does not refer to Jesus' pre-existence,
a piece of Christian doctrine which had not yet been produced. This
very general statement provides the cover for the more precise comments
which follow. These reflect the criticisms of Jesus made by his opponents.
Jesus has used the term בר (א)נש(א) because it was a normal Aramaic way of
saying something indirectly in humiliating circumstances. For the idiom
to be effective, it is necessary for the rest of the statement to be true of
more people than of Jesus, but not of everyone. This is the case.

The subject of the next verb is left open. This is commoner in Aramaic
than in Greek, German, English and the like. We must therefore reconstruct אמרין behind Matthew's λέγουσιν, and Luke's λέγετε must be regarded as an editorial alteration. The effect is to include anyone who
makes this kind of criticism, not just the opponents of Jesus, so a general level of meaning is maintained. The reconstruction of φάγος καὶ
οἰνοπότης is at first sight very difficult, since the nearest expression in
Aramaic is אכל ושתה, which we must reconstruct behind ἐσθίων καὶ πίνων.
This expression cannot be posited twice, since it would not make very
good sense either of the sentence or of the translator. I therefore suggest

that φάγος καὶ οἰνοπότης translates a quotation of the Hebrew זולל וסבא,
from Deut. 21.20.

The Hebrew words זולל וסבא conclude the description of the rebellious
son. Jesus' opponents were scribes and Pharisees, who will have read the
scriptures in Hebrew, as Jesus did himself. They could therefore use these
Hebrew words, and Jesus could reproduce them. Jesus' relationship with
his family was evidently difficult at times: on one occasion, they came out
to seize him, an incident which Mark associates with his being accused
of exorcising by the power of the devil (Mark 3.20–30), a very similar
accusation to that thrown at John the Baptist and recorded in the previous
verse.[34] This is the cultural background for Jesus' opponents to have
resorted to this passage of scripture. There is also criticism of Jesus for
feasting with the wrong people, and Mark represents Jesus' opponents
describing these people as τῶν τελωνῶν καὶ ἁμαρτωλῶν (Mark 2.16).
This too is the same criticism as we have here in Q. The criticism of
people for similar behaviour is also attested elsewhere. It is found in
scripture at Prov. 23.20–1. Some passages of literature from about the
time of Jesus take up this theme too (cf. *T. Judah* 14; Philo, *De Spec. Leg.*
IV.97–104; *De Ebr.* 206–24; Jos. *C. Ap.* II.195). It follows that people
who feasted will have been accustomed to criticism from stricter Jews. It
is that criticism which makes the general level of meaning of the son of
man statement plausible. It is a generalisation from his own experience
of being called a זולל וסבא, which will have struck a chord with people
sympathetic to him partly because strict Jews were liable to say it of some
of the people with whom he associated as well.

For φίλος I have suggested חבר, which is rendered with φίλος three
times by Theodotion (Dan. 2.13, 17, 18). The word is very well attested in
earlier and Qumran Aramaic. It means any sort of associate or companion.
In rabbinical literature, in both Aramaic and Hebrew, it is the word used
for groups of orthodox Jews who kept purity laws more strictly than
most people did. Since the halakhah of the orthodox was stricter in the
Second Temple period than it was later, it is probable that this sense of
the term was already in use. It makes a very sharp piece of polemic. It
presupposes that, as a significant Jewish teacher, Jesus should have been
a חבר to ספרין ופרישין. He is accused of being a חבר to quite the wrong sort
of people, מכסין וחטיין. The translator was faced with a problem, because
the customs involved in being an orthodox Jewish חבר were not general in
Judaism, and, as far as we know, had not been described in Greek. φίλος
is an entirely reasonable translation in the circumstances: its semantic

---

[34] See further pp. 150–61 below.

area includes both the equivalent of the English 'friend', and institutional usages when people such as kings had official 'friends', who were chosen because they acted as the king thought they should. It is therefore a better choice than the possible ἑταῖρος, which does not have these connotations, and the semantic area of which included the inappropriate 'pupil, disciple' (cf. Matt. 26.50). The variety of LXX renderings of חבר also show how a good translator would want to consider carefully the nuances of his translation.

The two groups of people with whom Jesus associated, מכסין וחטיין, have both become controversial for rather different reasons. The word מכסין is not a problem. It means 'tax-collectors', and has been properly translated with τελωνῶν. What has recently become controversial is the reason why Jesus' opponents felt that he should not have been associating with them. The τελωνῶν are obviously connected with ἁμαρτωλῶν, and here both the word and its associations are problematic. I have suggested חטיין, which is a somewhat Hebraising word used in Aramaic, properly corresponding to ἁμαρτωλῶν in its semantic area and corresponding also to the English term 'sinners'. Some scholars have suggested רשעים, 'the wicked', a view recently espoused with vigour by E. P. Sanders. This compounds the difficulty of seeing what Jesus was doing, though it may be thought easier to see why he was criticised for doing it.

The traditional view was straightforward. Its view of the Pharisees is clearly stated in the standard work of Schürer, Vermes and Millar.[35] The Pharisees separated themselves from the rest of Israel by careful observance of legal traditions which included much development of the unwritten traditions of the elders. A Pharisee is the same sort of person known in Mishnah as a חבר, 'one who punctiliously observed the law, particularly in respect of Levitical purity and priestly dues'. The opposite group to the חברים were 'the עם הארץ, of whom a strict observance of the law could not be expected'.[36] Careful observance of the traditions of the elders by Pharisees is clearly attested by Josephus (e.g. *A.J.* XIII.295–7; 408). That the Pharisees kept themselves apart from the people is held to be attested in Mishnah: 'The garments of the "*'am ha-arez*" are *midras* (unclean) for the Pharisees'. 'A *ḥaver* does not enter the house of an *'am ha-arez* and does not accept him as a guest if the latter wears his own garments.' Schürer, Vermes and Millar conclude: 'Thus the Gospel accounts of Pharisaic criticism of Jesus because of his free intercourse

[35] E. Schürer, rev. G. Vermes, F. Millar and M. Black, *The History of the Jewish People in the Age of Jesus Christ* (3 vols., Edinburgh, 1973–87), vol. II, ch. 26.
[36] *Ibid.*, p. 398.

with "publicans and sinners" (Mk. 2:14–17; Mt. 9:9–13; Lk. 5:27–32) correspond exactly to the viewpoint here described.'[37]

New Testament scholars have often gone further than this. The standard work of Jeremias describes the good news preached by Jesus as 'a slap in the face to all the religious feelings of the time'. To explain this, Jeremias declares, 'The supreme religious duty for contemporary Judaism was to keep away from sinners.' To explain the Pharisaic perspective, he quotes the equally standard work of Otto Betz: 'dealings with sinners put at risk the purity of the righteous and his membership within the realm of the holy and the divine'. Jeremias knew texts about the mercy and forgiveness of God. He commented, 'But his [sc. God's] help was for the righteous; judgement was the destiny of the sinner.'[38]

Some of this has been vigorously challenged by E. P. Sanders. He accepts that Pharisees were known for careful observance of the traditions of the elders. He is, however, careful of the identification of the Pharisees with חברים, suggesting cautiously that before 70 CE 'there was probably an appreciable overlap between Pharisees and *haberim*'.[39] This caution should be accepted. Equally, however, we should note that Jesus' opponents were not necessarily Pharisees. Those who asked why the disciples did not wash their hands before meals were 'some of the scribes who came from Jerusalem' as well as Pharisees (Mark 7.1), and those who accused him of casting out demons by the power of the devil are simply described as scribes from Jerusalem (Mark 3.22). The opponents in the present passage are anonymous: they must have been orthodox, but they were not necessarily Pharisees, and they were surely stricter than rabbis who legislated for all Israel after 70 CE.

Sanders objects very strongly to the identification of the עם הארץ with 'sinners'. He rejects not only the view that they *really were* sinners, but also Jeremias' reasonably nuanced view that two perspectives were involved, that of Jesus and that of his opponents.[40] He suggests that behind άμαρτωλοί 'stands, almost beyond question, the Hebrew word *resha'im* (or the Aramaic equivalent) . . . *Resha'im* is virtually a technical term. It is best translated "the wicked", and it refers to those who sinned wilfully

[37] *Ibid.*, p. 400, with their ET from *m. Hag.* 2.7 and *m. Dem.* 2.3.

[38] Jeremias, *New Testament Theology*, pp. 118–19, with a quotation from O. Betz, *What Do We Know about Jesus?* (London, 1968), p. 74.

[39] E. P. Sanders, *Jesus and Judaism* (London, 1985), p. 187.

[40] Sanders, *ibid.*, pp. 176–7, with p. 385 n. 14; and earlier, 'Jesus and the Sinners', *JSNT* 19, 1983, 5–36. For responses, D. C. Allison, 'Jesus and the Covenant: A Response to E. P. Sanders', *JSNT* 29, 1987, 57–78; B. D. Chilton, 'Jesus and the Repentance of E. P. Sanders', *TynB* 39, 1988, 1–18.

and heinously and who did not repent.'[41] This is technically inadequate,
for two reasons. Sanders should have specified the Aramaic word and
discussed its semantic area, and the use of a single Aramaic, let alone
Hebrew, word to alter the meaning of a text is always suspicious and
needs careful justification, which is lacking here. It follows that Sanders
cannot cope with the primary source material in the Gospels. Though he
thinks there is something in the charge of eating with sinners, he declares
that the story of Mark 2.13–17 'is obviously unrealistic'.[42] Thus Sanders
has gone too far. Without going back to ancient prejudices, we must try
again. I suggest that Jeremias was centrally right to perceive a main point
in different perspectives. We must begin with the word.

The word רשע was used in Aramaic as well as in Hebrew, and the two
occurrences in *Ahiqar* (168, 171) are sufficient to show that it had been in
use for centuries. Most occurrences in the Dead Sea scrolls are in rather
broken contexts, but there is sufficient indication that it refers to the really
wicked who rejected the Law. So, in the eighth of the ten weeks into which
human history is divided, a sword will be given to the righteous to exact a
righteous judgement מן כול רשיעין, 'from all the wicked' (*1 En.* 91.12). At
11QtgJob XI.3 רשיעין, translating רשע at Job 27.13 (LXX ἀσεβοῦς), are
basically those who have rejected God. They are those from whom the
psalmist prayed to be delivered (Ps. 17.8–14). We have the wrong group
of people for Jesus to be offering unconditional forgiveness to. He called
on people to repent, and רשיעין are people who did nothing of the kind.

We must therefore turn back to biassed use of חטיין. There should be
no doubt that חטיין was in use in the Aramaic of our period, and that it
is the real equivalent of ἁμαρτωλῶν. It is possible that Jesus' opponents
used the native Aramaic חיבין, and that it was translated fluently with
ἁμαρτωλῶν (rather than literally with ὀφειλέτων, cf. Matt. 6.12//Luke
11.4). This makes no significant difference. The reference of all these
words is to people who committed sins. It is at this point that more than
one perception of many people is possible. We must infer that this term
is a hostile description of people who were not fully observant. The word
מכסין is the next clue. There is nothing to indicate that the tax-collectors
stopped collecting taxes. The only approach to an exception is Zacchaeus,
who was at least rich enough to make reparations, so the story from
unsupported Luke (Luke 19.1–10) is untypical even if perchance it be true,
and even it does not say that Zacchaeus would stop being an ἀρχιτελώνης.
We should infer that, in general, tax-collectors who followed Jesus did

[41] Sanders, *Jesus and Judaism*, p. 177.   [42] *Ibid.*, p. 178.

not stop collecting taxes. If they had, Jesus would have become famous overnight for this too, and scribes and Pharisees would have had reason to honour his achievement, rather than criticise him. If they really stopped collecting taxes, they might soon become observant enough for anyone to eat with! Another clue comes from Jesus' saying at Matt. 21.31–2. Here tax-collectors are associated with prostitutes. We are first told that they will both precede 'you' into the kingdom of God. It follows that prostitutes will enter the kingdom of God. What happens in the meantime? Do they cease to be prostitutes? Surely not! The teaching of Jesus does not require that oppressed people shall starve because they abandon their only means of making a living. Moreover, the saying does not even make sense if applied to people who *used to be* tax-collectors and prostitutes. Whereas 'you' did not believe John the Baptist, 'the tax-collectors and prostitutes' did believe him. Even more striking is the accusation that 'you' did not repent when they saw this, and believe him. The whole situation does not make sense if the tax-collectors and prostitutes had ceased to be so.

It follows that tax-collectors and prostitutes repented in the manner represented by the Aramaic word חוב and the Hebrew שוב. They returned to the Lord. Like most faithful Jews, they will then have proceeded to keep the Law as best they could. *Being* a prostitute is not against the written Law, except for the daughters of priests, who are to be burnt alive if they become prostitutes (Lev. 21.9). Making one's daughter a prostitute is also forbidden (Lev. 19.29), as is adultery. It follows that prostitutes were likely to have neither father nor husband alive, and to have been economically desperate. It is this complex of conditions which explains why Jesus should accept them into the kingdom of God. It is equally unsurprising that strict Jews should regard them as sinners. They tempted men to sin (cf. Prov. 7; Sir. 9.3ff; 19.2–3)! Moreover, the general approach to prostitution in the Hebrew bible is one of vigorous rejection. This was originally at least partly because sacral prostitution entailed the worship of other gods. So sacral prostitution of either sex is forbidden (Deut. 23.17). So also is the bringing of money earned from prostitution of either sex into God's house in payment of a vow (Deut. 23.18), a prohibition which presupposes the continued practice of prostitution in the Jewish community. Vigorous rejection is evident in the attitude of Philo, who roundly declares that a prostitute should be stoned (*De Spec. Leg.* III.51). This is contrary to the written Law and to Jewish custom, and even more extreme than his condemnation of men who marry childless women (*De Spec. Leg.* III.34–6). It is illuminating, however, because it is such a natural orthodox extension of the written Law. Jesus' orthodox opponents will have felt similarly, and Jesus' acceptance of prostitutes into the kingdom of God will have increased their condemnation of him, regardless of how often real prostitutes were to be found in his entourage.

Collecting taxes is not against the written Law either. While evidence that tax-collectors were unfit to be witnesses or judges (*b. Sanh.* 25b) is much too late for the time of Jesus, it is likely that they were unpopular, as indicated by the way they are mentioned at Matt. 5.46, where *even* tax-collectors love each other. Those in Galilee would be employed by Herod Antipas, so claims that they were regarded as Gentiles are exaggerated too. They were seriously vulnerable to committing theft and violence in overenthusiastic collection of taxes, and a possible perspective on people who collected the sometimes heavy rate of taxation might be that they did not love their neighbours as themselves. They are not likely to have remitted all debts in the seventh year, and would certainly be tempted to lend money at interest. We should not try to dispose of them by playing tricks, especially not by going for a misunderstood Aramaic word *telane*, supposedly meaning 'playboy' or the like.[43] The Aramaic word טלני has been recorded only from late sources, and does not mean 'playboy' or the like even in them. Transliteration in place of translation does not occur elsewhere in Mark or in Q, except for words such as πάσχα which were already in use in Jewish Greek. This explanation requires both translators to have become stuck independently and transliterated to produce the same natural Greek word with the wrong meaning. This is altogether too improbable. Indeed, it is an error of method which we have met before. The text has been considered difficult, and instead of reconstructing it in Aramaic, a single word has been suggested as a means of altering the meaning of the text. We must not proceed like this.

Finally, from an orthodox perspective, followers of Jesus will have committed other sins too. They are not likely to have gone to Jerusalem for major festivals three times a year. Consequently, they are not likely to have offered the prescribed sacrifices every time they sinned. Many of them were poor: if they were offered employment by Gentiles, some may have worked on the sabbath.

We now have enough to understand these accusations against Jesus. At Mark 2.16 Pharisaic scribes merely ask why Jesus eats and drinks with tax-collectors and sinners. The description 'sinners' means that they did not keep the whole Law. Pharisees regarded themselves as guardians of the Law, and there is sufficient evidence that they did not eat with other people

---

[43] So recently W. O. Walker, 'Jesus and the Tax Collectors', *JBL* 97, 1978, 221–38, at 237, followed by R. A. Horsley, *Jesus and the Spiral of Violence* (Minneapolis, 1987), pp. 220–1.

if that could be achieved. They therefore merely asked the disciples why Jesus did so. They had every right to ask, since they might have expected that someone as plainly devoted to God as Jesus was would keep the Law in the same way as they did. The accusation at Matt. 11.19//Luke 7.34 is a more serious development of the same thing. Jesus has been described as a חבר of such people because he associated with them, and even ate with them. This is condemnation, not a question. It reflects the success of his ministry among Jews who were not fully observant, in circumstances where it was very difficult for them to be so.

These conclusions are a long way from both Jeremias and Sanders, but it will be appreciated that each of them got something very important right. We cannot make sense of this situation without the double perspective which Jeremias sought to describe, and Sanders has found something important with the realisation that Jesus did not require restitution as that might be normally understood. Equally, however, restitution cannot have been a main issue because our sources do not mention it. This is simply because not observing the whole Law was a great deal more common than scholars have generally realised.

We must therefore conclude that, faced with condemnation by his opponents, Jesus defended himself by associating himself with John the Baptist, as he was to do when he had cleansed the Temple (Mark 11. 27–33). In this case, he portrayed their opponents with an unfavourable image, and retailed their accusations as if to show that they were obviously foolish. In his own case, he also resorted to the idiomatic use of a general statement with בר (א)נש(א). One of the major situations in which this idiom was used was in humiliating situations, of which this is obviously one.

The final verse has proved extremely difficult to understand. Attempts have been made to derive Matthew's τῶν ἔργων and Luke's τῶν τέκνων from the Aramaic עבדיא, but this does not make good sense of the passage as a whole, since the level of verbal agreement is too high for us to believe in two translations of an Aramaic source. Moreover, עבד means 'servant', 'slave', and would be much more likely to give rise to παίδων rather than τέκνων, as so often in the LXX (e.g. Dan 2.4, 7, LXX and Theod). This is a nineteenth-century suggestion, which we should stop repeating.[44] I have suggested a single Aramaic reconstruction of the source of Q: זכת חכמה מן עובדה. It is probable that זכת underlies ἐδικαιώθη, because of the overlap in semantic area, and I propose that better sense than usual can be made of the passage if we try this. δικαιοῦμαι does mean to 'be set

---

[44] For decisive criticism, see already J. Wellhausen, *Das Evangelium Matthaei* (Berlin, 1904), p. 55.

free, made pure'. There is also an overlap of semantic area between צדק, which is usually rendered with δικαιόω in the LXX, and זכי, which is used to render it at 11QtgJob XXXIV.4 (Job 40.8). The Greek ἀπό is obviously מן. Wellhausen, followed by Jeremias, suggested *min q^{e}dham*, 'in view of',[45] but the absence of any equivalent for קדם must cause concern when the translator has just been rather literal, and the resulting sense is not particularly good. The Aramaic עב(ו)בד can be used collectively of all a person's deeds. For example, at *Ahiqar* 21, we find [עבידתך הו יעבד [לי 'he will do your work for me': here the older equivalent עבידתך, 'your work', means everything done by this person. At *1 En.* 2.2 in 4QEn^c, עובד is used with reference to the earth's works, so everything created on this planet. In 4QEn^a this is not written plene, and a scribe has added ה at the end to give עבדה. The Greek has τῶν ἔργων τῶν ἐν αὐτῇ γενομένων, so a similar understanding of עב(ו)דה to that which I am proposing here. When the third-person singular suffix to this singular noun is written down, it is simply ה, whichever the gender. I suggest trouble on this front.

Jesus' whole comment repeats the end of his opponents' criticism. By עובדה they meant the whole of his ministry, all of his deeds. Having referred to him as a rebellious son, and one who was a חבר to tax-collectors and sinners when he should have been associating with scribes and Pharisees, they also declared that Wisdom was not responsible for anything he had done. The figure of Wisdom is in Judaism not quite a separate entity, but she was much developed by wise men as a symbol of their own identity. Jesus' opponents were orthodox Jews, men who were wise in their own eyes, genuinely learned in the minutiae of the Torah, and doubtless in other things too. The use of this figure therefore fits very well at the end of these criticisms of him for doing things which were quite out of keeping with what was expected of a wise man, a Jewish teacher.

This meaning is not only clear, it is quite out of line with what a Christian translator would be expecting. The next two passages of Matthew are quite different in content, and have their parallel way ahead in Luke 10, where there are also contextual reasons for placing them. We should infer that there was a time when Matt. 11.19//Luke 7.35 ended a collection of sayings which were being translated from Aramaic into Greek. The Aramaic collector simply collected them – he was not concerned about the fact that his sayings ended with a criticism of Jesus, because he was simply collecting and may well have expected to add some others sometime anyway. It did not occur to him that a change of subject might be interposed. The Greek translator was, however, ending

---

[45] *Ibid.*, followed by J. Jeremias, *The Parables of Jesus* (2nd ET, London, 1963), p. 162.

a piece, and will not have expected it to end with a criticism, but rather with a comment by Jesus. He was so accustomed to Aramaic sayings that he did not expect that a change of subject would necessarily be marked. He rendered זכה with ἐδικαιώθη because that seems reasonable in light of the semantic area of these words. The suffix of עובדה did not tell him whether the reference was to Wisdom or to Jesus. If the saying is a saying of Jesus, however, rather than a criticism by his opponents, he has to go for the suffix being a reference to Wisdom. Hence αὐτῆς. This means that עובדה must be taken as a collective reference to the deeds of Wisdom. Hence the translator opted for the plural, τῶν ἔργων. The result is rather forced, as is the exegesis of every interpreter whom I have read. Matthew will have associated it with τὰ ἔργα τοῦ Χριστοῦ in his opening verse 2. Luke did not like it, which was reasonable of him. He tried altering τῶν ἔργων to πάντων τῶν τέκνων. This gives a contrast between the children of the parable, and people like John the Baptist, Jesus and his disciples who are children of wisdom. It also aligns John the Baptist and Jesus with πᾶς ὁ λαός and οἱ τελῶναι who were justifying God at Luke 7.29. This is perhaps a little better.

It may be argued that this is very conjectural. That criticism has to be accepted. I claim in this instance only to have told a very plausible story. Why? Because one item in it is almost certainly right: at some stage, secondary editing has made the saying something other than a literal translation of the Aramaic source of Q. That is all that is necessary to make reconstructing the source very hazardous.

Conclusions

The following conclusions may therefore be suggested. In these passages, the accounts of Matthew and Luke go back in part to a common source, which was written in Greek. We know this because of the high level of verbal agreement. This Greek source was, for the most part, a literal translation of an Aramaic source. Consequently, we can reconstruct most of it with a high degree of probability. When we do so, we find that the material in it has an excellent *Sitz im Leben* in the life of Jesus, and none at all in the early church. One part of it, verses 16–19a, requires an Aramaic reconstruction for its original sense to be recovered. The rest of it has not undergone significant change.

Some other parts of these passages have not been translated at all, but are due to the vigorous editorial activity of Matthew and Luke. The very opening, with τοῦ Χριστοῦ in Matthew and τὸν κύριον in Luke, illustrates especially well how both of them edited in accordance with the needs of

Christian communities. Matthew and Luke also edited the details of their sources some of the time. This has made it very difficult to reconstruct some of the original sources and sayings of Jesus, and some of the above suggestions are highly conjectural. One important saying (v. 12) and those after the end of the passages studied in detail are not in the same order in Matthew and Luke. This supports a somewhat chaotic model of Q, and we saw that this makes a nice hypothesis about the translation of the very end of the passage. Once again, however, the editorial work of the translator and the evangelists has made it impossible to maintain this hypothesis with certainty.

It is therefore very important to note that the conjectural nature of what can be recovered from some parts of these passages in no way casts doubt on the accuracy of the conclusions reached in others. Most of this passage consists of sayings which Jesus certainly spoke, and which illustrate the very high regard in which he held John the Baptist. He believed that John was greater than the prophets before him, and that he fulfilled the prophecy of Mal. 3 that God would send Elijah before the Day of the Lord. We also know with certainty that John the Baptist sent disciples to Jesus to ask him whether he would fulfil John's own prophecy that one stronger than he was coming. I have also put forward a very strong argument of cumulative weight for supposing that the ministries of John the Baptist and Jesus overlapped, and that this is where some of Jesus' sayings belonged.

Finally, this is quite different from the material studied in chapter 3. Before reflecting further on what models of Q can still be deemed possible, I must consider a major incident which gave rise to sayings in both Mark and Q.

5

EXORCISM AND OVERLAPPING SOURCES:
MARK 3.20–30; MATTHEW 12.22–32;
LUKE 11.14–23; 12.10

Introduction

Exorcism was central to the ministry of Jesus.[1] There are numerous incidents of exorcism recorded, which have many features of primitive tradition. For example, in the first exorcism recorded by Mark (Mark 1.23–7), the description ἄνθρωπος ἐν πνεύματι ἀκαθάρτῳ is Aramaic (אנש ברוח טמה) rather than Greek. The man's reference to himself in the plural as well as the singular is evidence of a drastically disturbed state of mind. His description of Jesus as ὁ ἅγιος τοῦ θεοῦ, so קדישה די אלהא, is the recoil of someone who has accepted the classification of himself as a man with an unclean spirit, and it is not the kind of Christological title which might be produced by the early church. There are other signs of primitive tradition in the following context too. In the first place, there was no objection to this exorcism or the following healing (Mark 1.30–1) being performed on the sabbath. Nonetheless, people brought other sick people, including demoniacs, to Jesus only 'when it was evening, when the sun had set' (1.32), that is when the sabbath was over. The story assumes that we all know that carrying burdens on the sabbath is forbidden (Jer. 17.21–2), and that sick people are so obviously heavy as to constitute burdens. Such evidence of primitive tradition marks other exorcism narratives too.

The importance of exorcism in Jesus' ministry is further shown by its importance in the work of his disciples. When the Twelve were chosen, Mark gives as one reason that they should be with him, so that we have the deliberate choice of an inner group to symbolise the twelve tribes of Israel; and as a second reason, ἵνα ἀποστέλλῃ αὐτοὺς κηρύσσειν καὶ ἔχειν ἐξουσίαν ἐκβάλλειν τὰ δαιμόνια· (Mark 3.14–15). In the story of them being sent out in twos, Mark duly records καὶ ἐδίδου αὐτοῖς ἐξουσίαν τῶν πνευμάτων τῶν ἀκαθάρτων, and that δαιμόνια πολλὰ ἐξέβαλλον

---

[1] For recent general discussion, see especially G. H. Twelftree, *Jesus the Exorcist* (WUNT II.54. Tübingen, 1993).

(Mark 6.7, 13). Luke found an additional saying of Jesus, which appears to refer to an associated vision and which has nothing about it characteristic of the early church:

'Εθεώρουν τὸν Σατανᾶν ὡς ἀστραπὴν ἐκ τοῦ οὐρανοῦ
πεσόντα.   (Luke 10.18)

This illustrates the kind of battle in which Jesus thought that he and his disciples were involved.

There is evidence of a quite different kind that Jesus was exceptionally famous as an exorcist. Mark reports that his disciples found a man exorcising in Jesus' name, even though he was not a member of the Jesus movement (Mark 9.38). The disciples stopped him, but Jesus told them to let him continue. Jesus must have been an exceptionally effective exorcist himself for an exorcist who did not belong to his group to exorcise in his name. Jesus' own attitude is also very noteworthy: he accepted the validity of this man's exorcisms. At the same time, Jesus was the most outstanding exorcist of all.

This highly successful ministry of exorcism put Jesus' opponents in a quandary. The result was a ferocious dispute, in which Jesus was accused of casting out demons by the power of Satan himself. This dispute is attested in both Mark and Q. It is quite notorious that some passages of Q overlap with some passages of Mark. Many scholars have considered this to be a serious objection to the priority of Mark, the existence of Q, or both. The purpose of this chapter is to offer an Aramaic reconstruction of the overlapping passages, in order to determine how far this helps us to establish the authenticity of the sayings and the history of their transmission. I also reflect on the importance of this for our understanding of the priority of Mark and the nature of Q.

The recovery of Aramaic sources is especially complex in a case of this kind. I begin by reconstructing a possible Aramaic source of the Marcan narrative, and then of the Q material. I then proceed to a critical discussion of all of it. In the first passage, I retain the Marcan verse numbering for convenience.

Reconstructed sources

20 ועללין בבי. ואתכנשת תובא כנשא, ולא יכלו למאכל לחם.
21 ושמעו אחוהי ונפקו למאחדה. ואמרו דשנא.
22 וספריא דנחתו מן ירושלם אמרין דיש בעל זבול לה, ובשר שדים הוציא את־השדים.
23 ואמר, היכה יכל שטן לאנפקה שטן?
24 ומלכו הן אתפלגת על נפשה, לא כהלה למקם מלכותא דך.

25 ובי הן אתחפלג על נפשה, לא יכל למקם ביתא דך.

26 והן שטנא קום על נפשה, אתחפלג ולא יכל למקם אלא סוף לה.

27 לא כהל כל אנש למעל לבית חסינא ולמבז מאנוהי הן לא לקדמין אסר חסינא,
ובאדין יבז ביתה.

28 אמן אמר אנה לכון דכל די ימלל מלה לבר אנשא ישתביק לה,

29 ומן דמלל מלה על רוחא קדישתא לא ישתביק לה לעלמין.

[20] And they entered a house. And a gathering assembled again, and they could not eat bread. [21] And his brothers/kinsfolk heard, and came out to seize him. And they said, 'He is out of his mind.'

[22] And (the) scribes who came down from Jerusalem said, 'He has *Ba'al Zebūl*' and 'By the prince of the demons he casts out the demons.' [23] And he said, 'How can Satan cast out Satan? [24] And if a kingdom is divided against itself, that kingdom cannot stand. [25] And if a house is divided against itself, that house cannot stand. [26] And if Satan rises up against himself, he is divided and cannot stand but comes to an end. [27] No man can enter a/the strong one's house and plunder his vessels unless he first binds the strong one, and then he will plunder his house. [28] Amen I say to you, everyone who speaks a word against a/the (son of) man, it shall be forgiven him, [29] and whoever speaks/has spoken a word against the spirit of holiness, it shall not be forgiven him for ever.

I now offer a reconstruction from some of the Q material. I have renumbered the verses, because of the confusion which follows from trying to use the numeration of either evangelist, neither of whom followed his Q source with any semblance of consistency.

1 והוה מפק שיד והוא חרש ונפק שיד ומלל חרשא.

2 ותמהו ואמרו בשליטא בשידין מפק שידיא.

3 ואמר להון, כל מלכו על נפשה דאתחפלגת חריבה, וכל בי דאתחפלג על נפשה לא יקום.

4 והן שטנא על נפשה אתחפלג, מה תקום מלכותה?

5 והן אנה בבעל זבול מפק שידיא, בניכון במן מפיקין? כלקבל דנה אנון להון דיניכון.

6 והן באצבע אלהא אנה מפק שידיא, מטאת עליכון מלכותה דאלהא.

7 כדי חסינא מזינא נטר דרתה, בשלם נכסוהי. וכדי חסין מנה אזל תקף לה, שקל זינה
דהימן בה וחלק בזתה.

8 מן דלא עמי לקבלי הוא ומן דלא כנש עמי בדרני.

9 וכל די ימלל מלה לבר אנשא ישתביק לה, ומן דמלל מלה על רוחא קדישתא לא
ישתביק לה לעלמין.

[1] And he was casting out a demon, and it was dumb, and the demon came out and the dumb person spoke. [2] And (people) were amazed. And (people) said, 'By the ruler of the demons he casts out demons.'

³And he said to them, 'Every kingdom which is divided against itself is laid waste, and every house which is divided against itself will not stand. ⁴And if Satan is divided against himself, how will his kingdom stand? ⁵And if I cast out demons by *'Ba'al Zebūl'*, by whom do your sons cast them out? Accordingly, they will be your judges! ⁶And if I cast out demons by the finger of God, the kingdom of God has come upon you. ⁷When a/the strong man is armed and guards his courtyard, his possessions are safe. And when one stronger than he comes and overpowers him, he takes away his armaments in which he trusted and divides the spoils. ⁸Whoever is not with me is against me, and whoever does not gather with me scatters me. ⁹And everyone who speaks a word against a/the (son of) man, it shall be forgiven him, and whoever speaks/has spoken a word against the spirit of holiness, it shall not be forgiven him forever.

The extent of verbal identity between Matthew and Luke is so high through most of these verses that we should infer a single Greek translation. In the first two verses, however, the Matthean version has been very heavily edited, and a more original version is found at Matt. 9.32–3. The passage may be reconstructed as follows:

1 καὶ ἦν ἐκβάλλων δαιμόνιον, καὶ αὐτὸ ἦν κωφόν· καὶ τοῦ δαιμονίου ἐξελθόντος ἐλάλησεν ὁ κωφός.

2 καὶ ἐθαύμασαν οἱ ὄχλοι. καὶ ἔλεγον, ἐν τῷ ἄρχοντι τῶν δαιμονίων ἐκβάλλει τὰ δαιμόνια.

3 εἰδὼς δὲ τὰς ἐνθυμήσεις αὐτῶν εἶπεν αὐτοῖς, Πᾶσα βασιλεία μερισθεῖσα καθ᾽ ἑαυτῆς ἐρημοῦται, καὶ πᾶσα οἰκία μερισθεῖσα καθ᾽ ἑαυτῆς οὐ σταθήσεται.

4 καὶ εἰ ὁ Σατανᾶς ἐφ᾽ ἑαυτὸν ἐμερίσθη, πῶς σταθήσεται ἡ βασιλεία αὐτοῦ;

5 καὶ εἰ ἐγὼ ἐν Βαγαλ ζαβυλ[??] ἐκβάλλω τὰ δαιμόνια, οἱ υἱοὶ ὑμῶν ἐν τίνι ἐκβάλλουσιν; διὰ τοῦτο αὐτοὶ κριταὶ ἔσονται ὑμῶν.

6 εἰ δὲ ἐν δακτύλῳ θεοῦ ἐγὼ ἐκβάλλω τὰ δαιμόνια, ἄρα ἔφθασεν ἐφ᾽ ὑμᾶς ἡ βασιλεία τοῦ θεοῦ.

7 ὅταν ὁ ἰσχυρὸς καθωπλισμένος φυλάσσῃ τὴν ἑαυτοῦ αὐλήν, ἐν εἰρήνῃ ἐστὶν τὰ ὑπάρχοντα αὐτοῦ· ἐπὰν δὲ ἰσχυρότερος αὐτοῦ ἐπελθὼν νικήσῃ αὐτόν, τὴν πανοπλίαν αὐτοῦ αἴρει ἐφ᾽ ᾗ ἐπεποίθει, καὶ τὰ σκῦλα αὐτοῦ διαδίδωσιν.

8 ὁ μὴ ὢν μετ᾽ ἐμοῦ κατ᾽ ἐμοῦ ἐστιν, καὶ ὁ μὴ συνάγων μετ᾽ ἐμοῦ σκορπίζει με.

9 καὶ ὃς ἐὰν εἴπῃ λόγον κατὰ τοῦ υἱοῦ τοῦ ἀνθρώπου, ἀφεθήσεται αὐτῷ· ὃς δ᾽ ἂν εἴπῃ κατὰ τοῦ πνεύματος τοῦ ἁγίου, οὐκ ἀφεθήσεται αὐτῷ οὔτε ἐν τούτῳ τῷ αἰῶνι οὔτε ἐν τῷ μέλλοντι.

Out of his mind

Mark 3.20–1 is unique to Mark. That neither Matthew nor Luke copied it indicates how uncomfortable so serious a dispute between Jesus and his family was to them. These verses form an obvious Marcan sandwich with Mark 3.31–5 as the other piece of bread, and the Beelzeboul incident as the filling. We shall see that the Q account of this incident had a different introduction. We should probably infer that Mark was himself responsible for bringing the two incidents together.

The success of Jesus' ministry, and his absolute centrality in it, is well indicated by the presence of the thronging crowd. For the frequent Marcan ὄχλος, I have suggested כנשה. The verb כנש occurs frequently enough with the meaning 'assemble'. Despite the fragmentary nature of 4Q530 ii 5, it is evident that בכנשת means 'in the assembly of', and at 4Q530 6 i 8 כנשתא גבריא means 'the assembly of the giants'. The noun כנישתא means 'gathering', 'assembly' as well as 'synagogue' in later Jewish Aramaic, Christian Palestinian Aramaic and Samaritan Aramaic, and כנשא means 'gathering', 'multitude', 'assembly' in Syriac. Hence the Syriac versions use it abundantly to render ὄχλος, as sin pesh hark do here. Moreover, I cannot see any reasonable alternative.

Two expressions in Mark 3.21 have caused difficulty to scholars: οἱ παρ' αὐτοῦ and ἐξέστη. The expression οἱ παρ' αὐτοῦ in Koine Greek refers to those closely connected with someone, such as their family and/or relatives. For the Aramaic source, I have suggested אחוהי, of which the same is true: it means 'brothers', but then extended family and associates. At first sight, we might expect the translator to have rendered it with οἱ ἀδελφοὶ αὐτοῦ; on careful consideration, however, we should rather infer that he knew the rest of the sandwich. Jesus' mother is mentioned with his natural brothers in the narrative at Mark 3.31, which is sufficiently emphatic to suggest that they have indeed come to seize him. She is placed first (for we should surely follow the reading of א B C D and other mss), and this emphasises her importance. She is mentioned with his brothers again in the information given to Jesus by some people at Mark 3.33, and in Jesus' question, Τίς ἐστιν ἡ μήτηρ μου ἢ οἱ ἀδελφοί; This is the more difficult reading, and a natural rendering of

מן היא אמא לי, או אחיא?

or of

מן איתי לי אמא או אחיא?

The other readings can then be seen as corrections to more natural Greek, mostly assimilating to verse 34.

An Aramaic source like this is the only reasonable explanation of the original Greek text of Mark. It is, however, different from it in one respect: the position of אמא is more emphatic. This is natural in the context, since אחיא has the broader range anyway, so it is אמא which prepares for the more dramatic metaphor in the following verse. Here Jesus looks around the crowd and sees in them his mother and brothers. His explanation of this in verse 35 is, however, notably different. In this general statement which identifies his relatives as anyone who does the will of God, Jesus uses the more natural metaphors of brother and sister first, and puts the less natural metaphor of mother at the end. There is only one possible explanation for the prominent position of 'mother' at the beginning and through most of the passage, with her less prominent position at the end. She was really there, and she was very important. That is why she is mentioned first both in the narrative, and in Jesus' first attempt to interpret relatives metaphorically. Mark's translator will have known this, and this made him quite rightly reluctant to use οἱ ἀδελφοὶ αὐτοῦ for אחוהי in verse 21, as this might be taken to mean his brothers only. The Greek expression οἱ παρ' αὐτοῦ provided him with an entirely reasonable alternative. This moreover gives us the correct interpretation of אחוהי. Like the translator, we must take Mark 3.31–5 into account when we consider this, and infer that the group who came to seize Jesus was led by his mother: that was why she was so prominent in the other outer part. We must infer a significant rift between Jesus and his family.

The other word which has caused a lot of problems is ἐξέστη. The semantic area of ἐξίστημι includes 'go out of one's mind', 'go mad', 'be out of one's senses'. This part of the semantic area of ἐξίστημι makes excellent sense here, and is the only meaning of this word to make sense. I have accordingly suggested that it is a translation of the Aramaic שנא. This is basically the equivalent of the English 'change'. Already in Akkadian, however, *šanê ṭemi* meant 'madness'. At Dan. 4.13, where Nebuchadnezzar goes mad, his heart is changed from that of a man: ישנון לבבה מן־אנושא. At 1QapGen II.17, where Lamech becomes concerned that he is not really Noah's father, Bitenosh asks why his face has changed upon him: למא אנפך כדנא עליך שנא. The Syriac שנא has 'go mad' as part of its semantic area, and it is quite common with this meaning. The Harklean version of Mark 3.21, faced with the unSyriac translation of ἐξέστη as הונה נפק, put שנא instead, presumably therefore regarding this as a more literally correct equivalent. We should infer from all this evidence that שנא was already in use at the time of Jesus with the meaning 'go out of one's mind', 'go mad', 'be out of one's senses'. This is the word which our source will have used here.

To understand why Jesus' family were so worried about his behaviour, we have to delve into the Marcan context. It is obvious from the Marcan sandwich that Mark believed that Jesus' exorcisms were the cause of his family's concern. Exorcism is also to be found in the immediately preceding context. The Marcan summary at 3.11–12 gives a quite dramatic impression of the behavioural patterns found on these occasions. It has the demoniacs fall down and shout; what they shout would be in Aramaic something very like אנתה הוא ברה די אלהא, a recognition of Jesus' access to divine power paralleled by קדישה די אלהא from the demoniac at 1.24, and the confidence of the man with a skin disease, אן תצבא תכל תדכיני (1.40); and it has Jesus rebuke them greatly, apparently after he was supposed to have cast the demons out. Since the demoniacs were shouting, Jesus would have had to shout in order to rebuke them too, and it is difficult to see what ἐπετίμα could represent in any Aramaic source except for גער, which has a considerable semantic area, including 'shout' and even 'roar'.[2] The overlap between Jesus' behaviour and that of the demoniacs might therefore appear uncomfortable. This summary account is followed by the appointment of the Twelve, who are also given power to cast out demons (Mark 3.14–15). While we cannot confirm the order of events in the Marcan narrative, we should infer the accuracy of this association: Jesus' family thought he was out of his mind at least partly because of his dramatic and unusual behaviour as an exorcist.

We can glean further light from an incident which Mark places later in his narrative, a visit by Jesus to Nazareth (Mark 6.1–6). Here people were severely critical of him, and he could not do much healing. There is also the valuable observation that he was amazed by people's unbelief, which puts his role as a faith-healer elsewhere in a fruitful perspective. It is evident that he did no exorcisms at all. People did, however, remember him perfectly well: they remembered him as a craftsman, and they remembered his family, citing Mary his mother and Jacob and other brothers by name. We must infer that Jesus had not exorcised and healed when he lived in Nazareth. He must have lived a relatively quiet life as an observant Jew and a craftsman. From his family's point of view, therefore, Jesus had changed drastically since he had left home. Unlike the Jesus whom they had known at home, he had become involved with people who were possessed with the devil. If they had heard of the appointment of the Twelve to symbolise the twelve tribes of Israel, and of his migratory ministry, that would have confirmed it: שנא!

---

[2] See especially H. C. Kee, 'The Terminology of Mark's Exorcism Stories', *NTS* 14, 1967–8, 232–46; J. M. Kennedy, 'The Root G'R in the Light of Semantic Analysis', *JBL* 106, 1987, 47–64; Twelftree, *Jesus the Exorcist*, pp. 44–6.

We can now see how right Mark was to place this incident with the following accusation that Jesus had Beelzeboul. In the culture of Jesus and his family, a man could not make himself go out of his mind; he could only do so under the influence of a supernatural agency. His mother and brothers were therefore concerned that Jesus was behaving in an extraordinary manner because he was possessed of the devil. This means that, despite the absence of Mark 3.20–1 from both Matthew and Luke, we have a very strong cultural agreement between Mark and Q, since the behaviour of Jesus' family was in fact effectively a result of a perception very similar to the notion that he cast out demons by the prince of demons.

These results have been difficult to achieve, and some steps in the argument may appear less than certain. The view which I have taken is also extremely unwelcome to people with mild respect, let alone total adoration, for the Holy Family. In this combination of circumstances, vigorous attempts to ensure that the text means something else are to be expected. This is already visible in the manuscript tradition, and some of the points made by modern scholars are of sufficient methodological importance to require discussion here. From a Catholic perspective, Dom Wansborough argued that οἱ παρ' αὐτοῦ refers to Jesus' followers. He took αὐτόν to be the crowd, and argued that Jesus' followers went out 'to calm it down', this being his interpretation of κρατῆσαι. The followers then continue as the subject of ἔλεγον, and ἐξέστη is their comment on the crowd: '... they said that it was out of control with enthusiasm'.[3]

This proposal has three major faults of an entirely traditional kind. Firstly, κρατῆσαι does not mean 'calm down', and ἐξέστη does not mean 'was out of control with enthusiasm'. Wansborough was wholly unable to justify these novel meanings of Greek words with any reasoned discussion of the semantic areas of these words.[4] Secondly, these quite incorrect proposals were fuelled by the hidden agenda of protecting the Holy Family. This ideological control of scholars remains a major factor in scholarship to the present day, and drastically inhibits our ability to correctly interpret our ancient sources. Thirdly, Wansborough's proposal suffers from the conventional fault of ignoring the Aramaic level of the tradition altogether. This shows yet again how completely this suggestion has its *Sitz im Leben* in Dom Wansborough's church life, and can barely be considered to belong to historical research at all.

[3] H. Wansborough, 'Mark iii.21 – Was Jesus Out of His Mind?', *NTS* 18, 1971–2, 233–5.
[4] See already D. Wenham, 'The Meaning of Mark iii.21', *NTS* 21, 1974–5, 295–300, at 295–6; E. Best, *Disciples and Discipleship. Studies in the Gospel according to Mark* (Edinburgh, 1986), pp. 53–4.

The suggestion that οἱ παρ' αὐτοῦ might refer to Jesus' disciples, especially the Twelve who have just been called in the immediate context (Mark 3.13–19), is, however, altogether more reasonable. A number of scholars have followed this suggestion, and it has recently been taken up by Painter.[5] Painter notes that the family home in Nazareth is some twenty-five miles as the crow flies from Capernaum, where this incident is usually placed. He sees this as a problem for the conventional identification of οἱ παρ' αὐτου with the family, because the reference to them going out in 3.21 does not suggest them setting out from so far away. He regards this as one of the 'serious *unsignalled* gaps in the narrative' created by the conventional reading of 3.20–35. He also considers it significant that nothing in Mark 3.31–5 suggests that Jesus' mother and brothers have been introduced previously, 'nor is there any indication of their hostility to Jesus'.[6]

These points are based on an unsatisfactory view of the Gospel of Mark. Painter belongs to a tradition of redaction criticism which attributes to Mark a degree of care and intentionality absent from much of the document which we now have. This is partly because some of it is unrevised translation of Aramaic sources.[7] Painter has the conventional fault of never discussing possible Aramaic sources, nor does he consider what οἱ παρ' αὐτοῦ and similar expressions might represent. The unsatisfactory nature of this approach to Mark is especially clear in this passage, where there really are serious unsignalled gaps in the narrative on any hypothesis. We are not told which mountain Jesus went up with the Twelve at 3.13. Only the conventional translation of οἶκον as 'home', added to conventional assumptions as to where that was, explains the conventional view that 3.20–35 took place in Capernaum. We are supposed to know that 'the sea' (3.7; 4.1) was the lake of Galilee, and we are not told on which part of the shore we should envisage the crowd, with Jesus in a boat.

Painter's interpretation of οἱ παρ' αὐτοῦ as the Twelve also makes nonsense of their behaviour. Their intention to seize Jesus is unmotivated, and there are no recorded consequences of their intention. Painter takes the subject of ἔλεγον (3.21) to be the crowd, but the crowd at 3.20–1 and 3.31–5 are surely intended to be favourable to Jesus rather than hostile. Painter's interpretation would be easier with the reading ἔρχεται at 3.20, where the plural is read by all Greek manuscripts except ℵ^c B W Γ.

[5] J. Painter, 'When Is a House Not Home? Disciples and Family in Mark 3.13–35', *NTS* 45, 1999, 498–513.
[6] *Ibid.*, 502, 504, 510.   [7] Casey, *Aramaic Sources of Mark's Gospel.*

Recognizing however that αὐτούς (3.20) and the context imply the presence of the disciples in the house, Painter has ἐξῆλθον mean that they went
out of the house to seize Jesus.[8] This means that Jesus must be outside
the house by 3.21, which contradicts the flow of the text. It is clear from
Painter's comments that the driving force of his interpretation is again
conventional redaction-critical treatment of Mark. This is the frame of
reference which enables the twelve to be seen as so irrationally hostile
to Jesus straight after their call. In Painter's argument, this follows from
the mention of the one who betrayed Jesus at 3.19, and is associated with
every criticism of them by Jesus in Mark, ending with their flight and
Peter's denial.

Painter also takes up the notion that 3.20–1 was composed by Mark,
citing especially the view that 'Marcan redaction is often introduced by
participles (ἀκούσαντες)' and that ἐξέρχεσθαι and κρατεῖν 'are characteristic Marcan terms'.[9] None of this is convincing. Participles are one of the
commonest features of the Greek language. Mark's use of ἐξέρχεσθαι and
κρατεῖν is perfectly consistent with his use of them in translation. This
is another of the basic faults of *Redaktionsgeschichte*. Features characteristic of a document are never sufficient to show that its author(s) was
writing freely rather than translating, because translators tend to translate
into their own idiolect. In addition to such features, therefore, we must
look for other features which help us to locate the original *Sitz im Leben*
of an account. In this case, the three features mentioned by Painter are too
common to function as indicators of creative writing, and the fitting of
the passage into recent redaction criticism of Mark should be regarded as
a forced and unconvincing placement of the passage into an execrescence
of modern criticism. The original piece has an excellent *Sitz im Leben* in
the life of Jesus, and the sandwich has an excellent *Sitz im Leben* in the
editorial habits of Mark. We should therefore conclude that we are dealing
with genuine historical material, but that the arrangement of Mark 3.20–1
and 3.31–5 on each side of 3.20–30 was the work of the Gospel writer.
This is further shown by the fact that Q had a different introduction to
this dispute, to which I shall turn next.

An exorcism in Q

We must place this exorcism in Q because it is in common order, and
sufficiently near in content to be recognisable as the same incident which
has been edited twice. We shall see that some of the succeeding sayings

[8] Painter, 'Disciples and Family', 508–9.   [9] *Ibid.*, 507, 509–10 with n. 26.

have such a high level of verbal agreement that we must suppose that this section of Q was transmitted in Greek. There is nothing about the actual account of the exorcism to make us think that it was translated twice, and some differences, such as that the Matthean demoniac is blind as well as dumb, could not possibly be due to different translations of an Aramaic source. We must infer that this incident was transmitted in Greek too.

Moreover, there is a doublet at Matt. 9.32–3 which is verbally much closer to the Lucan version of this incident, whereas the Matthean variants at Matt. 12.22–4 show several features which are characteristic of Matthew. One is the substantive insertion that people were wondering whether Jesus was the son of David (Matt. 12.23). Matthew has this term 'son of David' eight times, whereas it is rare in the rest of the synoptic tradition. While the son of Timaeus may have used it as a form of address (Mark 10.47–8), its *Sitz im Leben* is in the theology of Matthew, who must be seen to have invented this reaction to the exorcisms. At a linguistic level, Matthew was particularly fond of τότε, προσφέρω, δαιμονίζομαι and τυφλός (c. ninety, thirteen, six and seventeen times respectively). We must therefore use Matt. 9.32–3//Luke 11.14 to reconstruct the original Q version, as I have done above. This tells us that the demoniac was dumb, not also blind. Matthew has endeavoured to intensify Jesus' achievement, and to ensure that his readers would regard it as miraculous.

The account of the exorcism itself is very brief, and leads directly to the accusation that Jesus cast out demons by the prince of demons. It is to be noted that βεελζεβουλ is not found at Matt. 9.34, where Matthew follows Q most closely. It is moreover very unlikely that two transliterators would independently arrive at it. It is not probable that both would agree on two εs for the vowels of בעל, omit the ע, and put ου for ו. None of these decisions is beyond the pale of what is normal, but each has at least one alternative. We should therefore infer that βεελζεβουλ was not part of the Q account. Matthew and Luke both inserted it because they read it at Mark 3.22: Matthew inserted it at 12.24 when he was reading Mark 3.22, but not at 9.32–4 when he was reading Q. We shall see that it may be thought to have a somewhat better *Sitz im Leben* among Jesus' opponents mentioned by Mark, rather than those presupposed by Q. Mark and Q still have the very strong agreement that Jesus was accused of casting out demons by the prince of demons.

Matthew and Luke do not agree as to who made this accusation. Matthew has the Pharisees both at 9.34 and 12.24, but he does like them to be the opponents and Luke had little reason to remove them if they were there in his text. Luke has τινὲς δὲ ἐξ αὐτῶν, which is linguistically normal Greek in accordance with Lucan habits. It has the very interesting effect of locating the accusation as coming from members of the crowds. Luke is not likely to have made that up, so he must be interpreting his source in a manner which he found inevitable. We must surely infer that the Greek Q had no subject at this point, which is entirely intelligible if it was a literal translation of an Aramaic source, since Aramaic narratives are frequently written like this. Luke's interpretation of this vague subject is perfectly correct. This reaction must have come from among the crowds, but a vague subject in an Aramaic narrative does not mean everyone, and Jesus' ministry would not have been a success in any sense if everyone had reacted against him like this.

Now that this reaction has been located as coming from some members of the crowds, we can understand it better. Jesus was a dramatic and successful exorcist. In this case, he is not likely to have been shouting loudly. The man was dumb and then spoke, so he will have been a case of somatised-illness behaviour.[10] Jesus evidently treated the man as if the dumbness were external to him, and by going through some kind of exorcism procedure encouraged him to speak again. Three groups of people were liable to react against this process. One was those who had maltreated the man and thereby caused him to take refuge in refusing to speak. These must necessarily have included some of those closest to him, who were likely to have been there at the time. A second group was simply the superstitious: confronted with an extreme and remarkable event, they may have inferred that Jesus was working with the devil because they could not understand how else such demons could be cast out. A third group was more explicit in Mark's account, as we shall see. Faithful Jews who had other reasons to disapprove of the Jesus movement, such as because it was not halakhically strict enough, or undermined the authority of scribes and Pharisees, would find it difficult to see the power of God working in the exorcisms. They could, however, take the same route as the other two groups and Jesus' family, and see the power of the devil himself. The popular nature of this opposition may explain a facet of the following arguments: some of them are by no means learned, but proceed rather by homely analogies. These may be thought to have an excellent *Sitz im Leben* among ordinary rather than learned people. In any case, while some of this material may have been secondarily collected together, it is culturally connected at a profound level. It follows that its basic *Sitz im Leben* is where Q has put it, and that the accusation was a

---

[10] For general discussion, in the light of cross-cultural study of healing, see Casey, *Aramaic Sources of Mark's Gospel*, pp. 176–80.

genuine reaction to perceiving real exorcisms. We shall see that the next sayings were real attempts at an answer.

I have not included in Q the request by 'others' for a sign from heaven, which is found at Luke 11.16 alone. This is evidently intended to anticipate Jesus' refusal of a sign, other than that of Jonah, at Luke 11.29–30. Matthew, on the other hand, immediately precedes the parallel Matt. 12.39–40 with the request for a sign by 'some of the scribes and Pharisees' at Matt. 12.38. Luke may have remembered the request for a sign at Mark 8.11, which belongs to his great omission. We should infer that Luke inserted Luke 11.16 himself.

Casting out demons by Beelzeboul

We have seen that, following summary accounts of Jesus' exorcisms, Mark records that Jesus' family believed he was out of his mind. We have seen that this must effectively mean that he had been affected by demonic power himself, and that Q records ordinary Jews supposing that he cast out demons by the ruler of the demons. Mark's next accusation is put in the mouth of 'scribes who came down from Jerusalem', and it is similar to the others, though the form of one word has caused much difficulty: ἔλεγον ὅτι Βεελζεβοὺλ ἔχει, καὶ ὅτι ἐν τῷ ἄρχοντι τῶν δαιμονίων ἐκβάλλει τὰ δαιμόνια. Here Βεελ must represent the old term בעל, which was in standard usage for some foreign deities, or means 'Lord'. The term is nonetheless read βεεζεβούλ by אB at every example except this one, where only B has it. This should be regarded as a regrettable Alexandrian mistake. Βεελζεβούλ is supported by intrinsic probability, since the transliterator will have had ל in front of him, and unlike some letters, ל and λ are exactly alike. The transliterator could therefore hardly fail to put λ. Weight of attestation is also in favour of Βεελζεβούλ, since it is read by all the oldest manuscripts except for אB in the other examples, and all the oldest manuscripts except B here. Transcriptional probability is also in favour of Βεελζεβούλ. If it is the original reading, a monoglot Greek scribe in Alexandria might get it wrong. If, however, the original reading were βεεζεβούλ, it is very difficult to see how scribes would uniformly accept a correction to one possible transliteration of בעל.

It is the letters ζεβουλ which have caused endless trouble to scholars, to the point where I do not repeat all the proposals of the older scholarship. I note only that Beelzebub is too weakly attested to be taken seriously, having no Greek manuscripts in its favour – it is due to copyists who did not understand Βεελζεβούλ and who did know Beelzebub from 2 Kings 1.2, 3, 6, 16. Considerable interest of a novel kind was caused by the discovery of Ugaritic source material, in which we find the expression *zbl b'l*, which apparently means 'Prince Baal', or 'Exalted Baal'.[11] There is also a more common expression, *zbl b'l arz*, 'Exalted Lord of the Earth'. These expressions are, however, not the same as Βεελζεβούλ, to the point where they do not help us to form an adequate explanation of it. We must therefore remember that Ugaritic is the wrong language, and the sources are more than a millennium too early.

Moreover, זבול is a Hebrew word. It occurs five times in the Hebrew bible (1 Kings 8.13; Isa. 63.15; Hab. 3.11; Ps. 49.15; 2 Chron. 6.2). It also occurs several times in the Hebrew Dead Sea scrolls, which should become the decisive piece of new evidence. In the majority of cases it certainly means 'dwelling place', and is used with reference to the abode of deities or demons: this may well be true of all examples.[12] For example, at 1 Kings 8.13 בת זבל is the Temple which Solomon has just had built. At Isa. 63.15, זבל קדשך is where God is in heaven, parallel to שמים. The meaning 'dwelling-place' is explicit in some of the ancient versions. Some use a form of מדור (*Tg. Isa.* 63.15; *Tg. Hab.* 3.11; *Tg. Ps.* 49.15), or מדיר (*Pesh. Isa.* 63.15; *Pesh. Hab.* 3.11); also בית מעמרא (*Pesh. 1 Kings* 8.13), τοῦ οἴκου (LXX Isa. 63.15), and κατοικητήριου (mss of LXX 1 Kings 8.13 which include the verse). This understanding is also reflected in the use of οἰκοδεσπότης with βεελζεβούλ at Matt. 10.25, and in the use of οἰκία at Mark 3.25. It is remarkable that all the evangelists transliterate this term and none of them translates it. They must all have regarded it as a name, an alternative to Satan, rather than as a word whose meaning they needed to pass on.

More of the necessary cultural background is provided by 1QM XII.1–2. Here we are told that צבאות מלאכים בזבול קדשכה, 'the hosts of angels are in the abode of thy holiness'. This is obviously a right and proper זבול, where God dwells with his good spirits, angels. In the next column, the priests and Levites curse Belial, the commonest term for the devil in the Qumran documents, ואת כול רוחי גורלו, 'all the spirits of his lot' (1QM XIII.2). This gives us the opposition to God as the devil in charge of his spirits. Israel are supported by שר מאור, a 'prince of light' (1QM XIII.10). Michael is already השר הגדול who stands up for Israel at Dan. 12.1. The Hebrew word זבול continued to be used of God's dwelling in the rabbinical period. For example, at *b. Ḥag.* 12b, 1 Kings 8.13 is used to show that it is the Temple, complete with the altar where Michael the great prince

---

[11] I regret that I do not read Ugaritic, and have consequently relied on the *opinio communis* of colleagues who do.

[12] See now D. J. A. Clines (ed.), *The Dictionary of Classical Hebrew*, vol. III (Sheffield, 1996), p. 81.

(הַשֹּׁר הַגָּדוֹל) sacrifices, and Isa. 63.15 is used to identify it as the heavenly rather than the earthly Temple.

We must also bear in mind traditional Jewish rejection of foreign deities. Some of these were simply called הבעל (e.g. 2 Kings 10.18–28). They could also be described with an additional term, so that בעל has no article because it is in the construct. Such beings included בעל זבוב, 'Lord of flies', perhaps a deliberately rude description of the God of Eqron at 1 Kings 1.2, 3, 6, 16. With בעל in the construct state, בעל זבול will have been an equally definite description of a particular being, the same being as is described as τῷ ἄρχοντι τῶν δαιμονίων. We might translate it as 'The Lord of an Abode'. It is, however, pretty clear that the Hebrew זבול would call to mind heaven, where God was and the prince of demons conspicuously was not. That would necessarily call up also בעל שמים, the widely worshipped Semitic deity. The equation of foreign deities with demons is already found in the Hebrew bible (Deut. 32.17; Ps. 106.37), and continued in the Dead Sea scrolls (4Q243 13 2; 4Q244 12 2). This gives reasonable meaning to the scribes' first accusation, which is more precise than that of Jesus' family and of people from among the crowds. They suggest that he is actually possessed by בעל זבול. It is because he is possessed by בעל זבול that Jesus can cast out demons by his power: he is effectively supposed to be manipulating his own minions, presumably so as to deceive faithful Jews into imagining that Jesus is acting with divine power, and that therefore his preaching should be believed.

In view of all this, we should believe Mark's information that this accusation was made by scribes from Jerusalem. It is they who had reason to use a Hebrew word, because they will in fact have spoken Hebrew.[13] Moreover, their opposition to Jesus' ministry fits very well into the general opposition which came from orthodox Jews. Jesus was on the prophetic rather than the orthodox wing of Judaism. His whole ministry was a threat to the authority of orthodox scribes and Pharisees, who could be completely undermined by the prophetic spirit, and we have already seen how serious was the breach between these two sides which developed as the ministry progressed.

The scribes' second accusation, that Jesus cast out demons by the prince of demons, is effectively the same as that recorded in Q as an accusation of people from among the crowds. Whether it was in Hebrew or Aramaic makes no serious difference to the meaning, but it does make some difference to the *Sitz im Leben*. The scribes expressed themselves in a learned manner in Hebrew, and then, still in Hebrew, they said what

---

[13] For further discussion, see Casey, *Aramaic Sources of Mark's Gospel*, pp. 79–81.

they really meant. The Aramaic version of the accusation does not make learned and obscure reference to בעל זבול, it makes the main point in Aramaic which normal Jews could understand and repeat. We should probably infer that scribes from Jerusalem told people what they meant in normal Aramaic, but that they fired the longer and more learned version at Jesus in Hebrew, because they knew that he would understand both their language and the cultural ramifications of בעל זבול.

Like the crowds, the scribes could not deny Jesus' exceptional effectiveness as an exorcist. They were therefore faced with a stark choice. They could believe that Jesus worked through the power of God, which would validate his whole ministry, including his criticisms of them; or they could accuse Jesus of being in league with the devil himself. They chose this latter option, the only one consistent with their retaining their power as the supreme interpreters of the Law. That the same accusation should be found in both Mark and in Q means that it is exceptionally well attested. The motivation has in common hostility, and the inability of some people to cope with Jesus' outstanding ability as an exorcist. The power structure is, however, likely to have been different. The scribes would have their own position quite undermined if they admitted that Jesus' exorcisms were a display of the power of God. This is more severe than the probable effects on people from among the crowds. It follows that the opposition from the scribes was always likely to harden and escalate.

The kingdoms of God and of Satan

Both Mark and Q turn at this point to a group of sayings of Jesus. Both groups have an analogy with a divided kingdom and a divided house, and use these analogies to argue that Satan cannot be working against himself, so that Jesus cannot be casting out demons by means of the prince of demons. That these sayings are so closely related means once again that this kind of response by Jesus is very strongly attested. Argument by homely analogy from kingdoms may be felt to be especially appropriate to the Q situation, where the accusation was made by people from the crowds. Jesus may nonetheless have fired this at scribes as well. I have suggested that, in the original sayings collections, the introduction was simply ואמר, this being a natural Aramaic way of carrying on from the respective accounts of what went immediately beforehand. This makes the present introductions secondary. I have supposed that Mark himself added καὶ προσκαλεσάμενος αὐτοὺς ἐν παραβολαῖς: compare Mark 4.2, 10–13, 33–4; 7.14, 17; 8.1, 34; 10.42; 12.1, 12, 43. I have equally supposed that Q added εἰδὼς δὲ τὰς ἐνθυμήσεις αὐτῶν, and Luke altered this to αὐτὸς δὲ εἰδὼς αὐτῶν τὰ διανοήματα. The details of this process must be regarded as uncertain, and this must not be allowed to obscure the perfectly certain deductions as to the editorial process itself. Whether the proposed details are precisely correct or not, there should be no doubt that Mark, Q, Matthew and Luke give us edited versions of authentic sayings on the same subject.

There should be no doubt about the authenticity of both groups of sayings. The early church had no interest in making up the dispute itself, nor the analogous sayings, and the more direct sayings could not stand on their own without the dispute. Every saying has an excellent *Sitz im Leben* in the teaching of Jesus, and in this actual dispute. Of course, perfect transmission and *ipsissima verba* cannot be guaranteed, and the differences between Mark and Q illustrate this well. Moreover, it is quite clear that the differences between Mark and Q cannot be accounted for as differences in two translations of a single underlying Aramaic text. The two Aramaic reconstructions offered above correctly represent the real situation: either Jesus said similar things on different occasions, or his words have been reworded in transmission by one or both sources, or both.

Some of the details, notably those in common between Mark and Q, require further discussion. Satan is a biblical being, but in the Hebrew bible he is one of the sons of heaven, who incites God to test people, as notably in Job 1–2. By the New Testament period, however, he has become what we usually call the devil, a wholly evil figure who leads the forces of evil opposed to God. In texts which survive in Hebrew and Aramaic, he is generally known as בליעל, שׂטן being certainly used only of one of many demons (e.g. 4Q213 1 i 17). At 11Q5 xix 15, however, he can be read as a single being, as he must be in texts which survive only in Ge'ez at *Jub.* 10.11; *1 En.* 54.6. We must infer without hesitation that סמנא was one of the names of the devil in Second Temple Judaism, and ascribe the virtual absence of this name from texts surviving in Hebrew and Aramaic from the Second Temple period as simply due to the vagaries of transmission. βελιαρ or the like occurs in the New Testament only at 2 Cor. 6.15, whereas Σατανᾶς is used in Greek by several other New Testament authors, including Paul (e.g. 1 Cor. 5.5) and John the Divine (e.g. Rev. 2.9, 13), both of whom were Jews who knew Aramaic and Hebrew as well as Greek. We must next infer from Mark and Q that סמנא was Jesus' normal term for him (see also Mark 8.33; Luke 10.18; 13.16). The definite state of the Aramaic סמנא is reflected in the α used at the end of the Greek form ὁ Σατανᾶς, which has then been declined.

The Marcan sayings begin with the centre of Jesus' experience, expressed in a way which did not appeal to either Matthew or Luke:

היכה יכל שׂטן לאנפקה שׂטן?

We should take this absolutely seriously, and almost literally. It is based on Jesus' own personal experience of being an exorcist. He had felt the power of God working through him on the dramatic occasions when he cast out demons which he felt to be evil. The notion that the devil could and would muster this power which he had felt working through him seemed to him to be ludicrous to the point of being inconsistent. This is accordingly the main point, and Mark is consequently quite right to begin with it. The next two sayings are analogies which seemed relevant because of this basic point.

In the first of these two sayings Jesus uses the term מלכו, 'kingdom', both in an argument by analogy and in direct reference to Satan's rule. This reflects standard belief among Second Temple Jews, but it is couched in Jesus' favourite terminology. For example, 1QS III has the angel of darkness (מלאך חושׁך) lead all the children of righteousness astray, referring to his dominion (ממשׁלתו), and 4Q544 ii 5 has Melkiresha' rule (משׁלט) over darkness. The nearest we get to Jesus' terminology is at 4Q510, where we find the rule of wickedness (ממשׁל[ת] רשׁעה), together with demons, Lilith and the like, where מלכות is used of God's kingship. Jesus' use of the term 'kingdom' is a different way of referring to Satanic power. מלכו was one of his favourite words for the rule of God, both in the universe in general and in people's lives. It was therefore natural that he should use it to refer to the opposing power of the devil. This reflects his vigorous concept of the devil's power. This was not a merely abstract concept. As Jesus performed exorcisms, he will have felt the power of God working through him to subdue the kingship of Satan (cf. Q v. 6, Matt. 12.28//Luke 11.20). His description of a kingdom divided is obvious at an analogical level, and reflects Jesus' experience of the difference between the action of God and the power of Satan being so strong that for Satan to try to exercise it would be an exercise so damaging to him that he could not and would not do any such thing.

The next saying returns to the זבול in בעל זבול and uses the image of a house. This is not of course a building. It was in common usage for a much extended family, slaves included, as for example at 1QapGen. XX.16–17, where God sent an evil spirit (רוח באישׁה) to afflict Pharaoh וכול אנשׁ בותה. Equally, it could refer to a whole nation, as for example בית ישׂראל (e.g. Exod. 16.31). Thus a house is an alternative analogy to a kingdom. At the analogical level, it is obvious that a divided house will fall, and this second analogy fills out Jesus' conviction that Satan could not possibly be attacking the beings of his own dominion. Mark 3.26 ends this part of the argument. It concludes from the two analogies that Satan would not rise up against himself, for that would be the end of him. I have followed the reading of א* C* al., ἐμερίσθη καί, which D surely sought to clarify, because this makes excellent sense of Jesus' argument. This draws together the comments on the house and kingdom being divided by making the substantive point that if Satan rises up against himself he is in fact divided. Jesus' opponents assumed otherwise in their criticism of him. The tendency of the scribes is also shown by א^c C^c, who made corrections in accordance with the conventional view that Satan being divided was an assumption, rather than a substantive point. It was moreover obvious that Satan had not come to an end. I have reconstructed the whole verse, though we cannot exclude the possibility that ἀλλὰ τέλος ἔχει is a Marcan gloss. Either way, it should now be possible to see that Mark 3.23–6 is not a random collection of sayings, but a logically constructed argument.

We have seen that the Q version of this incident began with an exorcism, and I shall discuss verses 5 and 6 which are in the Q version alone. The agreements between Matt. 12.25–6 and Luke 11.17–18 are so great that I must reconstruct a Q version of these verses too, as I have done in verses 3 and 4 above. The end of Luke 11.18 is an explanatory gloss, which I have therefore excluded from Q. Matthew's πόλις is also a gloss, to make sense of οἰκία when the direct reference to זבול was no longer noticeable. Luke has also shortened the 'house' saying to make it a mere illustration of what happens when a kingdom is divided. We can now compare Q with Mark. In the first place, it has no equivalent to Mark 3.23, which is unfortunate, because this verse contains Jesus' central conviction that Satan cannot cast out Satan. Accordingly, Q begins Jesus' response to the allegation made against him with the first analogical argument from a divided kingdom. After this, Q has all three points in the correct order. They are expressed slightly differently, but they are obviously the same three points – analogical arguments from a kingdom and a house, and the conclusion. This does not imply any literary relationship between Mark and Q, since the sayings are certainly genuine and the Marcan beginning enables us to see the logic of Jesus' whole argument. That is to say, these sayings are in common order because this is the original order. This is exceptionally strong attestation for the originality of an argument which the early church had no reason to produce.

The next Q saying (v. 5, Matt. 12.27//Luke 11.19) is a different kind of response altogether. Here Jesus aligns himself with other Jewish exorcists. He knew that the evidence, successful exorcisms, was basically similar in several cases. This gave him a very useful argument. If people inferred from his successful exorcisms that he was in league with the devil, they ought to make the same inference in the case of other people of whom they approved. This is another argument by down-to-earth yet entirely reasonable analogy, perhaps more likely as a response to an accusation coming from people in general than criticism from specifically legalistic Pharisees. On the other hand, the use of בעל זבול implies the more learned group described by Mark as οἱ γραμματεῖς οἱ ἀπὸ Ἱεροσολύμων καταβάντες (Mark 3.22). The transliteration in Q is unlikely to have been the same as in Mark. I have written βαγαλ ζαβυλ in Q, not because one knows what stood in Q, but to make clearly the point that a different transliteration was probable, so it is most probable that it was Matthew and Luke who were responsible for ensuring consistent following of the Marcan form.

Jesus described the other successful exorcists as בניכון. The term בניכון is significantly broader than the English 'sons', and need not necessarily mean that his critics were related to the other exorcists. His critics must, however, have been closely associated with other exorcists, since this is what makes Jesus' argument feasible. Some trouble has been caused by taking literally the Matthean setting, which would imply that these exorcists were especially associated with the Pharisees, but the setting is secondary, and in Q the accusation came from unmentioned people. This makes much better sense, since the Pharisees were not especially associated with exorcism, whereas we know that there were other exorcists in Israel at the time. Such exorcists were perhaps more likely to be associated with the scribes from Jerusalem, who would be more likely to use the term בעל זבול. Much more trouble has been caused by those scholars who have been unable to imagine that Jesus took a positive view of the ministry of other Jewish exorcists. For example, Harvey suggests that their treatment was not very successful, a view for which there is no evidence at all; Gundry suggests that the argument of verse 5 'does not necessarily imply Jesus' acceptance of the exorcisms practised by his antagonists' followers', which is contrary to Jesus' whole approach to this subject.[14]

This kind of approach has been carried even further by Shirock, who has revived the patristic view that by 'your sons' Jesus was actually referring to his own disciples.[15] This contradicts the text, in which the Greek

[14] A. E. Harvey, *Jesus and the Constraints of History* (BaL 1980. London, 1982), p. 109; R. H. Gundry, *Matthew. A Commentary on His Literary and Theological Art* (Grand Rapids, 1982), p. 235.
[15] R. Shirock, 'Whose Exorcists Are They?: The Referents of οἱ υἱοὶ ὑμῶν at Matthew 12.27/Luke 11.19', *JSNT* 46, 1992, 41–51.

οἱ υἱοὶ ὑμῶν, and the underlying בניכון, uniformly and unambiguously refer to associates of Jesus' critics, not his disciples. Shirock brings forward other examples of ὑμῶν and claims they are similar to his proposed interpretation, when they are in fact quite different.[16] For example, he cites Luke 15.30, where the brother of the 'prodigal son', speaking to their father, refers to his brother as ὁ υἱός σου. But the prodigal son *was* his father's son, whereas Jesus' disciples were not in any reasonable sense the sons/disciples/associates of his most vicious oppponents. Shirock also cites τῷ νόμῳ δὲ τῷ ὑμετέρῳ from John 8.17, but this is quite different again. Here Jesus is falsely represented as distancing himself from the Torah because the Johannine community was rewriting history during its ferocious quarrel with the Jewish community.[17] In verse 5 of this Q passage, the historical Jesus is associating his most serious opponents with exorcists who really were associated with them, because he expected those exorcists to support his view of the nature of exorcism. Moreover, Shirock reveals his not-too-hidden agenda when he prefers the disciples to other Jews as successful exorcists, and objects to the possibility that Jesus might have taken a positive view of other exorcists by declaring that 'he would have been endorsing and comparing his own Spirit-led work to the work of Jewish magicians'.[18] Accordingly, his whole argument must be characterised as dogmatic bias: anyone interested in what happened during the ministry of Jesus should prefer historical research.

The end of the verse has also cause considerable trouble to exegetes. In the first place, considering κριταί . . . ὑμῶν in the light of English and German translations as they are naturally understood in our culture, interpreters generally suppose that they are judges who will judge Jesus' opponents. This is not, however, the most probable interpretation of דיניכון in this first-century Jewish sentence. In extant texts, judges generally belong to a place or to an authoritative person. So, for example, דיני מדינתא are the judges of the district (Cowley, *Papyri*, 16.7), and דיני מלכא are the royal judges because they belong to the king (Cowley, 1.3). A different usage is not impossible, as for example in Hebrew at Ps. 68.6, where God is a judge of widows (דין אלמנות) because he protects them. Here, however, the former kind of usage is surely more probable. Jesus suggested that exorcists associated with his opponents should replace his opponents as their judges of him. This was because they had successful experience of the power of God at work in exorcism, so they were bound to vindicate him.

[16] *Ibid.*, 49–50.   [17] Casey, *Is John's Gospel True?*, esp. pp. 111–27.
[18] Shirock, 'Whose Exorcists?', 48–9, 46.

They would moreover vindicate him in the here and now, which would bring the dispute to an end with a victory for Jesus. Scholars have a pronounced tendency to set the end of the verse at the eschatological assize,[19] but this should not be accepted. The reference is so brief that the shift from this world to the final judgement would be so unlikely to be picked up that it is not likely to have been intended. Rather, Jesus' response to people's accusation is to claim support from other exorcists. They would tell everyone in the here and now that they did not cast out demons by the power of the devil, and that the way they cast them out was not evidence that they did so. In that sense, they would be unfavourable judges of those who had accused Jesus.

Finally, problems have been found in the relationship between verses 5 and 6, but I cannot discuss these until I have settled the interpretation of verse 6. Verse 6 (Matt. 12.28//Luke 11.20) has moreover elicited massive scholarly discussion, on account of its importance for our understanding of Jesus' concept of the kingdom of God. I must settle the detailed wording before I consider this central point. The saying is almost verbally identical in the two Greek versions, but Matthew has πνεύματι where Luke has δακτύλῳ. Most scholars consider the Lucan version original, and I have followed the majority view, reconstructing δακτύλῳ in the Greek Q as a translation of אצבע. This gives excellent sense in the saying of Jesus, for 'finger of God' is a relatively rare metaphor for God in action. There is a particularly striking example of it at Exod. 8.15, where Egyptian magicians could not reproduce Aaron's miraculous turning of dust into gnats, and explained their failure with the declaration 'this is the finger of God' (אצבע אלהים הוא). T. W. Manson drew attention to the even closer parallel at *Exod. Rab.*X.7, where the magicians recognise that the plagues are 'the work of God and not the work of demons'[20] (מעשׂה אלהים ולא מעשׂה השׂדים). This source is much too late in date to have influenced Jesus, but it does properly indicate the same cultural nexus. In Judaism throughout the centuries these were the only alternatives. Jesus has already argued that he has not cast out demons by the power of the devil. He now turns to the only alternative, that he has cast out demons by the power of God.

The decisive argument for the originality of אצבע, translated δακτύλῳ, is the redaction-critical one. The word δάκτυλος occurs only twice else-where in Luke–Acts (Luke 11.46; 16.24), in neither case as a metaphor for the action of God. The term πνεῦμα, however, occurs thirty-six times

---

[19] E.g. Davies and Allison, *Matthew*, p. 338; J. A. Fitzmyer, *The Gospel according to Luke* (2 vols., AB 28–28A. New York, 1981–5), vol. II, pp. 916, 922.

[20] Manson, *The Teaching of Jesus*, pp. 82–3.

in Luke and seventy times in Acts, frequently of God in action. It follows that Luke is most unlikely to have altered πνεῦμα to δάκτυλος. Matthew, however, has πνεῦμα nineteen times, including the obviously redactional quotation of Isa. 42.1–4 in the immediately preceding passage 12.18–21, with the words θήσω τὸ πνεῦμα μου ἐπ' αὐτόν. It follows that πνεύματι is Matthew's redactional alteration of δακτύλῳ, which stood in Q and was retained by Luke. Matthew will not have felt that he was altering the meaning of the saying, but rather clarifying the fulfilment of scripture in the ministry of Jesus.

This settles the wording of the saying in Greek, and there should not be any serious doubt about the rest of the proposed reconstruction. In particular, מטא is the obvious source of ἔφθασεν, which is used to translate it by Theodotion at Dan. 4.11, 20, 22, 24, 28 (MT 4.8, 17, 19, 21, 25); 6.25; 7.13, 22. Both words correspond approximately to the English 'come upon', and Jesus, Q and both evangelists must have meant that the kingship of God in some sense came upon those people to whom he was talking. To see what that meant, I now turn to the metaphor of the kingdom/kingship of God.

The word מלכות is rare in the Hebrew bible, but the general notion of God's kingship is not rare, it is merely expressed with מלך rather than מלכות. It indicates the divine status of superiority, and divine functions of power and rule. For example, at Ps. 47.3 we are told that יהוה עליון is a great king (מלך) over all the earth. This evidently celebrates the present and permanent kingship of God, and says nothing about a future and final establishment of his rule. It was part of the sacred text at the time of Jesus. Dan. 4.31 is an especially striking passage which does use the Aramaic word מלכו. Here Nebuchadnezzar repents and praises God, being healed of a serious illness. He says of the Most High (עליא) that his sovereignty is everlasting, and that his kingdom/kingship is from generation to generation (שלטנה שלטן עלם ומלכותה עם דר ודר). Despite being written during the Maccabean persecution, this uses the term מלכו in praising the present and permanent kingship of God. It does so in a book which, taken as a whole, does expect the final establishment of God's kingdom soon (Dan. 2.44; 7.14, 18, 22, 27), but that is not what Dan. 4.31 refers to. It refers to God's present and permanent kingship, and could have been written, like Ps. 47.3, in a text which did not have eschatological expectations whose fulfilment was expected in the near future. It is therefore a particularly close parallel to the teaching of Jesus in verse 6 (Matt. 12.28//Luke 11.20). Here the kingship of God is displayed in the victorious healing activity of Jesus in casting out demons in the present time. Here too, the kingship of God is a powerful metaphor which need not have eschatological overtones, even though it is used by a teacher who also expected the final establishment of God's kingship in the near future.

In a few documents of our period, מלכות is also used in descriptions of heavenly events which are repeated, not eschatological, and which therefore also means that God has such mighty power in the present time that he could display it in the present time if he chose to do so. The most striking is found in 4Q405, which describes the service of the mightiest angels in the heavenly sanctuary.

> These are the chiefs of those wonderfully dressed for service, the chiefs of the kingdom/realm (ממלכות), the kingdom (ממלכות) of the holy ones of the King of holiness in all the heights of the sanctuaries of the kingdom (מלכות) of his glory. The princes in charge of offerings have tongues of knowledge, [and] they bless the God of knowledge with all His glorious works...
>
> 4Q405 (*Songs for the Holocaust of the Sabbath*) 23 ii 10–12.

Here God is himself called king, and מלכות is used to refer to the heavenly realm in which he has present, permanent and complete power.

It does not matter that this text was probably transmitted by the same people as transmitted 4Q246, in which מלכו is used with reference to God's final establishment of the kingdom of the people of God. Like Dan. 7.14, 18, 22, 27, 4Q246 does not mean that the word מלכו on its own has taken on eschatological connotations. Rather, it can be used with an eschatological reference when this is made clear in the context, whether the general cultural context within which a person is speaking, or the immediate literary context. If, however, the context implies a present reference, that is what everyone would take it to have. Equally, passages such as Dan. 4.31 and 4Q405 cannot possibly mean that the expectation of the final establishment of God's kingdom has been, or is being, fulfilled. God is king of the universe now and for always. If an author or preacher is to get across the message that eschatological expectations are being fulfilled, he has to say something to get that message across. If he merely says that God is king, or that his מלכו lasts for ever, that is what he will be taken to mean.

I can now return to the interpretation of verse 6 (Matt. 12.28//Luke 11.20). What does מטאת עליכון מלכותה דאלהא really mean? It should be noted, in the first place, that there is no sign of eschatological reference in the immediate context, apart from the forward reference of לעלמין in Mark 3.29 and Q verse 9, and, secondly, that there is abundant reference to the recent past. The situation arose out of Jesus' successful ministry of exorcism, which he has already placed within the context of exorcism by other people too. The first part of Q verse 6 refers to this successful ministry with quite unambiguous clarity. We must infer that מטאת עליכון מלכותה דאלהא refers to the powerful display of God's kingship in this ministry of exorcism, and not to anything else. It does not imply that the end is at hand, nor that eschatological expectations are being fulfilled. It is of especial importance that the the the term מלכו is sufficiently broad and overarching for Jesus not to be guilty in any way of inconsistency if he is found to have used it elsewhere with eschatological reference. We must not push עליכון too hard either. For example, Sanders, working from the Greek text, poses this puzzle: 'has the kingdom of God "come upon" Jesus' opponents and not upon those whom he healed?'[21] Certainly not! The one thing that Jesus and his opponents agreed about was that his exorcisms appeared very successful, and all Jesus' disciples accepted his view that this was the power of God working through him. This may have been a way in which he told them so. The saying may have been secondarily collected here, so we do not know who the original referents of עליכון were. If the reference is to his opponents, however, the saying still makes excellent sense. The point of מטאת עליכון is then to say that God's kingly power has been demonstrated so openly that his opponents have not been able to avoid its real effects, and should therefore confess its real nature as the power of God, not of the devil.

All this also means that verse 6 sits very comfortably with verse 5, which now becomes easy to integrate into the overall context. Jesus must have believed that the kingship of God was displayed in other people's exorcisms too. This is a necessary consequence of his analogical arguments about the kingdom of Satan not being divided. These are so generalised that they must be applied to other people's exorcisms too, and it follows merely from this that other people also exorcised demons by the power of God. Jesus' comment on the effect of his own exorcisms, מטאת עליכון מלכותה דאלהא, is a metaphorical way of saying this. There is no question of other people's exorcisms being signs of the End, or the fulfilment of eschatological expectations either. In other words, once we have seen Jesus' powerful metaphor for what it is, there is no reason to deny the obvious implication that it applied to other people as well.

There are no peculiarities in the Greek translation which both evangelists inherited as part of Q. Matthew's ἡ βασιλεία τοῦ θεοῦ is, however, remarkable, because he almost always alters τοῦ θεοῦ in this expression to τῶν οὐρανῶν. All his few exceptions, however, may be interpreted as

---

[21] Sanders, *Jesus and Judaism*, p. 134.

references to the kingship of God down here in the present time or the very near future (Matt. 19.24; 21.31, 43: cf. also 6.33, where τοῦ θεοῦ should probably not be read). This is also the case here, as we have seen. Moreover, in this passage ἡ βασιλεία τοῦ θεοῦ forms a good contrast with ἡ βασιλεία αὐτοῦ, that is, Satan's present and permanent kingdom, in verse 4, and a good follow through from ἐν δακτύλῳ/πνεύματι θεοῦ in this same verse. We must infer that Matthew was well aware that Jesus intended a deliberate reference to a mighty display in the present time of the kingship which God always had possessed and still did possess at the time. He did not confuse this with the final establishment of God's rule in the last days.

All this is contrary to most scholarly interpretation, and some views are so widespread that they must be discussed. Weiss argued that φθάνω and ἐγγίζω are alternative translations of the Aramaic מטא, and that the saying meant that the kingdom is very near, and already present only in a limited sense. K. W. Clark accepted this conclusion, and tried to show that φθάνω means 'just reach', so that the saying in its present form would also mean that the kingdom 'has just reached you', rather than that it has already come.[22] We must be more careful than this. The Greek φθάνω is the equivalent of the Aramaic מטא, whereas ἐγγίζω is the equivalent of קרב, which genuinely means 'come near' rather than 'arrive'. We must not dispute this by noting the rendering of מטא with ἐγγίζω at LXX Dan. 4.9, 19.[23] The translator of LXX Daniel is not a good model, and in these two passages he has rendered interpretatively, so that the tree reached up to heaven but did not quite get there. In this, as in much else, LXX was corrected by Theodotion. Examples like this should never be used to equate the semantic areas of different words in the same or in different languages. Equally, we must be careful of the rendering of ἔφθασεν with the Syriac קרב at Matt. 12.28 cur pesh and Luke 11.20 sin cur pesh. These renderings are also interpretative, and were properly corrected to the more literally accurate מטא in the Harklean revision.

Kümmel recognised the meaning of φθάνω representing מטא, and argued that 'it is the person of Jesus whose activities provoke the eschatological consummation'.[24] Here the final coming of the kingdom is

[22] J. Weiß, *Die Predigt Jesu vom Reiche Gottes* (Göttingen, 1892), pp. 12–13; (2nd edn, 1897), pp. 69–73; ET *Jesus' Proclamation of the Kingdom of God* (with introduction by R. H. Hiers and L. Holland. London and Philadelphia, 1971), pp. 65–7; K. W. Clark, 'Realized Eschatology', *JBL* 59, 1940, 367–83, at 374ff.

[23] C. H. Dodd, ' "The Kingdom of God Has Come" ', *ET* 48, 1936–7, 138–42, at 140–1; see further Casey, *Aramaic Sources of Mark's Gospel*, pp. 26–7.

[24] W. G. Kümmel, *Verheißung und Erfüllung* (AThANT 6. Basel, 1945; 2nd edn, Zurich, 1953), 98–101; ET *Promise and Fulfilment* (SBT 23. London, 1957), pp. 106–8.

seen to be already present in the historic ministry of Jesus. This creates problems with the previous verse, as it would at first sight seem to follow that the final coming of the kingdom was also seen by Jesus as coming in the ministry of other Jewish exorcists. Kümmel accordingly followed the scholarly tradition of seeing here detached sayings, which therefore did not have to be interpreted together.[25] Schnackenburg, despite operating with a more sophisticated concept of the reign of God, declares all the more dogmatically that however much Jewish exorcists may have expelled demons, this was in no sense for Jesus a sign of the reign of God.[26] Here the lack of sympathy shown by Christian scholars towards Judaism is a determinative factor. Verse 5 alone should be sufficient to show that Jesus took an entirely positive attitude towards other successful exorcists. It is this which makes the metaphor of the kingship of God appropriate. Kümmel suffered from too dogmatic a notion of what this meant, and the view that these sayings are so detached that these two need not be taken together illustrates how slicing passages into pieces enables them to be interpreted not just separately from each other, but separately from Jesus' cultural context altogether. It is only when we have seen that, however important it was to Jesus, מלכו was a metaphor for God's power at any time, that we can see how appropriate it was for him to see the kingship of God displayed in his own ministry, as it was necessarily displayed also by any other faithful Jew who cast out demons from people and thereby brought the power of God to them.

These traditional scholarly trends should therefore be set aside. Confronted by opponents who declared that his successful ministry of exorcism was due to the power of the devil, Jesus affirmed that it was the power of God in action. This is the main point of verse 6. This also enabled him to argue from the successful exorcisms of other faithful Jews, which he understood as a demonstration of God's power, and which he used in argument because he knew that his opponents accepted this. Whether verses 5 and 6 were actually spoken on the same occasion is quite another matter, into which we can gain little insight. Both verses are absent from Mark, but he may not have liked the end of verse 5 nor the present use of the term מלכותה דאלהא in verse 6. Alternatively, they may have been spoken on a different occasion, and collected here because everyone knew that they were responses to the same charge. The important point is therefore the general cultural one. All these sayings are genuine and significant responses to

---

[25] Kümmel, *Promise and Fulfilment*, pp. 105–6.

[26] R. Schnackenburg, *Gottes Herrschaft und Reich* (Herder, 1963); ET *God's Rule and Kingdom* (2nd edn, London and New York, 1968), p. 124.

the serious accusation made by Jesus' opponents. They have an excellent *Sitz im Leben* in the teaching of Jesus and none in the early church, who had no more interest in producing verses 5 and 6 than the rest of the controversy. We must therefore accept the authenticity of both verses, and keep the interpretation of them within their original cultural context.

Verse 7 is similar to Mark 3.27. Matthew follows Mark. We should infer that verse 7 stood in Q, even though it is found only at Luke 11.21–2. It is in common order in Matthew and Luke, since Matthew takes an equivalent verse from Mark to place in between verses 6 and 8 of Q. Secondly, we know that in general Luke prefers to keep going with Q in significant chunks, whereas Matthew often conflates Mark and Q, as I suggest he is doing here. Thirdly, the Marcan version is straightforward enough. If the Lucan version of the saying did not stand in Luke's Q, he had no reason to leave Mark and turn to a separate source, whereas to keep going with Q would be typical of him. It has inevitably been suggested that Luke was himself responsible for his revision of Mark, or (less often) Matthew. This should not be accepted. For example, Légasse suggests that this view is probable because the language is so solidly Lucan.[27] For example, he notes that ἐν εἰρήνῃ is septuagintal, 'au sens de "securité"'. This is true, but it in no way shows that it is not a translation of בשלם, which makes excellent sense and could well be translated ἐν εἰρήνῃ by someone familiar with the Septuagint. Again, Légasse notes that πανοπλία 'recouvre une notion non sémitique'. This is also true. However, it occurs only here in Luke, so it does not fit the overall argument that the language of this piece is specifically Lucan. Moreover, translators normally translate into their first language, and sometimes translate freely into it precisely in such a way as to produce features of the target language which cannot readily be paralleled in the source language. Consequently, there is nothing wrong with the hypothesis that πανοπλία is a good Greek rendering of זינה. Thirdly, Légasse notes that trust in one's riches is a theme dear to Luke. So it is, but it probably goes back to Jesus and this man is trusting in force, not merely in riches. All these arguments are faulty in method. They uniformly presuppose that translators cannot produce a translation which is in accordance with the needs of the target culture, and the idiolect of an author whom they partly are, not merely serve. This is not, however, the case.

Fleddermann has recently carried Légasse's arguments further, but they are no more convincing in this more extreme form.[28] Fleddermann lists no

---

[27] S. Légasse, 'L' "homme fort" de Luc xi 21–22', *NT* 5 (1962), 5–9, followed e.g. by J. Nolland, *Luke 9:21–18:34* (WBC 35B. Dallas, 1993), p. 641.
[28] H. T. Fleddermann, *Mark and Q. A Study of the Overlap Texts* (BEThL 122. Leuven, 1995), pp. 52–5.

fewer than six words from this short passage which are found only in Luke among the synoptic writers. There are two things wrong with this. Firstly, no fewer than four of them, καθωπλισμένος, σκῦλα, πανοπλία and νικάω occur only here in Luke. They therefore do not support Fleddermann's view that 'much of the vocabulary is Lucan'. Secondly, νικάω, ἐπέρχομαι and διαδίδωμι are being judged on much too narrow a base of comparison. All three are normal Greek words, used only once, three times and twice, respectively, in Luke's Gospel; they do not become more common in Luke merely because they are absent from Matthew and Mark. Fleddermann's next point is that 'φυλάσσω, ἑαυτοῦ, εἰρήνη and ὑπάρχω are all Lucan characteristic expressions, and ἐπάν and αὐλή, though not characteristically Lucan, surface elsewhere in Luke'.[29] Here again there are two faults of method. Firstly, ἐπάν and αὐλή occur only once more each in Luke, so the important point is that they are indeed 'not characteristically Lucan'. The methodological point in regard to the other four words is more interesting, for while they are all common Greek words, nonetheless they really are by any reasonable standard of judgement 'Lucan characteristic expressions' for they occur some six, fifty-seven, fourteen, and fifteen times respectively in this Gospel. It is consequently important that even such common words do not show that Luke himself made the passage up. At points like this, synoptic critics in general have not properly taken the force of two well-known facts: translators use words which are common in their idiolect even when translating fairly literally a source in their second, third, or whatever language, and editors like Matthew and Luke may be editing rather than inventing material when they use words characteristic of themselves. It follows that none of these arguments demonstrate that Luke himself produced verse 7 by creatively editing Mark.

It is nonetheless true that Jesus' little images may have been elaborated, simplified and otherwise altered in transmission. The important fact is that both Mark and Q testify to a saying of this kind, with the strong man as an image of Satan, and a stronger person as an image of Jesus overcoming Satan. This multiple attestation at the same point in both Mark and Q is decisive evidence that Jesus did use this kind of image too in refuting the charge of his opponents that he used the power of Satan himself to cast out the demons. The Marcan version fits best in its present position. We have seen that after the question formulating his basic premise that Satan cannot cast out Satan, Jesus proceeded with two analogical arguments from a kingdom and a house. He inferred that Satan would be finished if he rose up against himself, from which it follows that Satan cannot

---

[29] *Ibid.*, 52–3.

have done any such thing. His next argument is another analogy, seen this time from his own perspective. At the analogical level, it is obvious that no strong man will let you plunder his house, whereas people were often tied up to render them powerless. Many people who were tied up subsequently escaped, or were released, so that binding the strong man is an image of rendering him powerless temporarily, not permanently. This image is therefore different from passages such as Tob. 8.3, where a demon is bound and the effect is permanent, but only one demon is bound and Satan is unaffected: *1 En.* 10–16, where Asael and other beings are bound until the final judgement, but evil spirits from the giants are not bound; and *T. Levi* 18.12, where Beliar is bound by the new priest in the last times. Jesus' image is of a single exorcism where the devil is bound temporarily for the exorcism to take place, but the power of evil continues in the world, both in other demoniacs and in Jesus' opponents.

In considering the saying at the level of reality, we must note that, unlike conventional translations into English, the Aramaic original and Greek translation have no word for 'man', with the result that the real level of meaning is more readily available than in English. At this level, the strong being is Satan. Binding him is a very strong metaphor for the degree of control over Satan experienced by Jesus when he prepared to exorcise a person. In extreme cases, this might include a direct and immediate need for prayer and fasting (Mark 9.29). The plundering of the strong man's vessels is a metaphor for the actual exorcism, taken up again at the end with the metaphor of plundering his house. This is the same metaphor as in the analogy at Mark 3.25, and we have seen that this picks up זבול from the original accusation made by the scribes from Jerusalem. While Mark 3.27 is parabolically expressed, it is thus an integral part of this series of consistent, partly analogical arguments. Moreover, like the opening question and all the other arguments, it is firmly based in Jesus' own personal experience. We must therefore conclude that Mark 3.27 is part of Jesus' original response to the accusation of the scribes from Jerusalem, and that it is placed with the preceding verses because that is where it originally belonged.

Verse 7 of Q has significant points of contact with Mark 3.27, but it is a much more elaborated little tale. Like so many of Jesus' parables, it makes perfectly good sense as a story on its own, and if one treats it in isolation from its context, one is simply puzzled as to why he should have told it. In context, the strong one is still clearly the devil, and the stronger one is Jesus. The detailed reflection of the context characteristic of Mark 3.27 is, however, absent from this elaboration. We should infer that the elaborated version is secondary. Given the story nature of so many parables attributed to Jesus, it does not necessarily follow that he never told the elaborated version himself. We should not, however, see it as part of his original argument, and we have to keep an open mind as to whether the elaboration was done by him or his followers, in Aramaic or in Greek.

There is yet another version of this saying in the *Gospel of Thomas*, saying 35:

> Jesus said: 'It is impossible for one to go into the house of the strong (one) and take him/it by force unless (εἰ μή τι) one binds his hands. Then (τότε) one will remove (the contents of) his house.'

Deprived of its context, this saying is pointless. The first saying of this Gospel declares that he who finds the interpretation of these sayings will not taste death. Saying 35 illustrates as well as any of them the need for an exegetical tradition because it is so pointless without one. It is therefore profoundly secondary, even though it is clearly the original version of Jesus' saying which it is secondary to, not the Lucan version. If we had only this version of the saying, we could not possibly recover Jesus' interpretation of it. It illustrates the profoundly late and secondary nature of the tradition in this document.

Verse 8 was evidently in Q at this point, since it is found in both Matthew and Luke, but not in Mark. The saying at Mark 9.40 should be regarded as a different one, suitable for the less hostile situation presupposed by the sayings which immediately precede and follow it in Mark. This Q saying is especially well suited to the serious dispute in which it is found in Q. The Beelzeboul controversy was about the centre of Jesus' ministry, and it was so serious that anyone who did not go on Jesus' side and accept that he cast out demons by means of the Holy Spirit was necessarily on the side of his enemies. The metaphor of gathering and scattering is more graphic. It suits especially well the gathering of sheep in a flock, from which they should not be scattered (e.g. Jer. 23.1–4). It could also bring to mind the harvest, when the wheat is gathered into barns and other things may be scattered rather than burnt (e.g. Matt. 3.12//Luke 3.17). One word favours the former image, and scholars have found it impossible to understand. This is με read after σκορπίζει at Matt. 12.30 by א 1382* 33 Or et al., and at Luke 11.23 by א*.2 C² L Θ Ψ 33 579 et al. Despite this considerable attestation, Metzger comments bluntly on the Lucan text, 'The addition of με after σκορπίζει, which is so difficult as to be almost meaningless, must be a scribal blunder.' His comments on the Matthean variant are equally uncomprehending, but recent scholars have tended to follow him or leave it out.[30] We must turn to the Aramaic sentence which Jesus spoke.

The Aramaic equivalent of σκορπίζει is בדר. This is used at Dan. 4.11 of the violent scattering of the fruit of a tree (LXX omits, Theod. 4.14 διασκορπίσατε), and in the Babata archive of scattered trees (Beyer, *Ergänzungsband*, nV 7, 13.50). Thus it is attested in the right period. In the bilingual inscription from Sardis from the fourth or fifth century BCE it is used with a singular suffix, albeit with a following noun added; this calls upon Artemis to do something drastic to anyone who damages the stele or the like, and even if it is to scatter him and his seed (יבדרונה וירתה), בדר is something one can do to the wicked individual. At *Tg. Sam.* 14.3, the derived part בדוריה is used with reference to a single banished person (rendering the Hebrew נדח, of Absalom). In a directly relevant metaphor, the Hebrew פזר is used of a single sheep, שה פזורה, so a sheep which has been scattered like others and hence was driven off and is isolated (Jer. 50.17, LXX 27.17 understandably πλανώμενον). We must surely infer that Jesus used the Aramaic בדר with reference to himself in a similar metaphorical way. People who joined the Jesus movement helped him to gather in Israel, as a shepherd gathers his flock. In practical terms, the Beelzeboul controversy marked such a crisis point in the ministry that those who did not join the Jesus movement could be seen as treating him as if he were not merely a lost sheep, but as someone cast out from Israel. Jesus' opponents could especially be seen like this, since the accusation that he cast out demons by Beelzeboul meant that he was quite driven out from Israel, a position in which some scribes and Pharisees would very much have liked to see him. It follows that this saying has an excellent *Sitz im Leben* in the situation where we find it in Q. Equally, it has no *Sitz im Leben* either in Greek or in the early church. It follows that this is a genuine saying of Jesus, and it adds further cumulative weight to the arguments for regarding this part of Mark and Q as literally accurate tradition.

The unforgivable sin

The next saying is one of the most remarkable in the whole synoptic tradition. We have seen that where we have alternative versions of a saying

---

[30] B. M. Metzger, *A Textual Commentary on the Greek New Testament* (3rd edn, Swindon, 1971), p. 158, cf. p. 32, followed e.g. by I. H. Marshall, *The Gospel of Luke: A Commentary on the Greek Text* (NIGTC. Exeter, 1978), p. 478: omitted e.g. by Fitzmyer, *Luke*, pp. 919, 923; catalogued with no significant comment e.g. by Davies and Allison, *Matthew*, vol. II, p. 343 n. 51.

in Mark and in Q, we cannot regard them as alternative translations of a single Aramaic underlay. In this case, however, we have good reason to do so. Moreover, the Matthean version continues in this place, as though Q had the saying in the same order as Mark. The Lucan version, however, is in a quite different place, quite out of common order, and may reasonably be treated as a third translation of the same Aramaic saying. This saying accordingly takes a lot of unravelling.

I begin with the common Aramaic underlay to Matt. 12.32 and Luke 12.10, neither translation of which has been as heavily edited as Mark 3.28–9.

וכל די ימלל מלה לבר אנשא ישתביק לה, ומן דמלל מלה על רוחא קדישתא
לא ישתביק לה לעלמין.

This saying has an excellent *Sitz im Leben* in the context in which it now occurs in Matthew, the same context as the different translation of it now found in Mark. The first part of it is a general statement decreeing forgiveness to people who oppose or even slander other people, the kind of view to be expected in the teaching of Jesus. The use of בר (א)נש(א), however, is the particular idiom whereby the statement refers particularly to Jesus himself.[31] The saying therefore appears at first sight to grant forgiveness to Jesus' opponents. The sting is in the second half. The Holy Spirit is a metaphor for God in action. Nowhere is the action of God to be seen more vigorously and obviously than in Jesus' exorcisms. The accusation that he cast out demons by Beelzeboul is accordingly an unforgivable sin. What Jesus seems to concede in the first part of the saying is thus quite removed in the second part. This polemic, like the content of the saying, accordingly has an excellent *Sitz im Leben* where the Matthean and Marcan sayings are now to be found, in this dispute over Jesus' exorcisms. The idiom is also specifically Aramaic. Once again, we certainly have a genuine word of Jesus.

The Matthean translation of this saying is reasonably clear and straight-forward. ὃς ἐάν for כל די will have been done with ὃς δ' ἄν for ומן ד already in mind: it gives an excellent balance to both language and meaning in the resulting piece, and it is not beyond the parameters of what an ancient translator might do. The words εἴπῃ λόγον, with Luke's alternative ἐρεῖ λόγον, establish the original wording ימלל מלה ל, which we shall see lies behind Mark's highly explicitative rendering, and which is also essential for establishing the original wording of the opening of the second half of

---

[31] See Casey, *Aramaic Sources of Mark's Gospel*, esp. pp. 111–21; pp. 133–5 above.

the saying. The potentially ambiguous לעלמין at the end has been translated explicitatively with οὔτε ἐν τούτῳ τῷ αἰῶνι οὔτε ἐν τῷ μέλλοντι. This makes it quite clear that Jesus' opponents will not be forgiven in this life or in the next, a point which was simply beyond the purview of Jesus' original polemic.

Luke 12.10 is equally comprehensible as an alternative translation. Luke's πᾶς ὅς is more literal than Matthew's ὅς ἐάν, with ἐρεῖ as literal as possible for ימלל. The preposition εἰς is an obvious possible alternative to Matthew's κατά with the genitive. In the second half of the saying, Luke's τῷ βλασφημήσαντι is a particularly interesting difference from Matthew's ὅς δ' ἂν εἴπη, which presupposes λόγον from the first half. It must surely be an alternative rendering of מלל מלה על. This is the same basic clarification as used by Mark's translator, and an entirely appropriate one when it is the Holy Spirit which is being spoken against, since this is a metaphor for God himself in action. The potentially ambiguous לעלמין at the end has been omitted rather than expanded. The Lucan context is one of collected sayings which are not in common order and which provide other evidence of more than one translation of an Aramaic original. This is notably true with the replacement of בר (א)נשׁ(א) by ἐγώ at Matt. 10.32–3, the Matthean parallels to Luke 12.8–9. This is a reasonable solution to the difficulties of translating the Aramaic idiom into Greek, but not a probable editorial alteration in a Gospel writer who uses ὁ υἱὸς τοῦ ἀνθρώπου no fewer than thirty times as a term for Jesus. Many other small differences may also be understood as translation variants. Moreover, if Luke met his version of this saying in its place in Q material, he might well leave it there, as he leaves other collected sayings in their places. He might well have accepted an exegesis which he could derive from its context there, where he could, for example, have associated it with objecting to the words spoken by persecuted disciples under the influence of the Holy Spirit, as in the following saying. In contrast, he might have regarded speaking against the Son of man as something that many Christians had done before their conversion, and consequently to be forgiven, even though it had been very wrong. Luke may well have preferred such an exegesis of Luke 12.10 to anything he could think of as an interpretation of a similar saying placed between Luke 11.23 and 11.24. He may, for example, have regarded Mark 3.28 as untrue, and speaking against the Son of man in the previously related incident as unforgivable. All this is necessarily rather conjectural. It is, however, sufficient for us to conclude that what is now Luke 12.10 was collected with the sayings which surround it on the catchword principle, and that this caused the original meaning of Jesus' saying to be lost.

The Marcan version has been independently translated by a translator who was worried about the sense. This is shown by his use of τοῖς υἱοῖς τῶν ἀνθρώπων, the only use of the plural of ὁ υἱὸς τοῦ ἀνθρώπου in the whole of the Gospels. This diverges from the detectable strategy of translating (א)נש(א) בר with ὁ υἱὸς τοῦ ἀνθρώπου when it refers to Jesus, and with something else when it does not, including when it is plural.[32] It is also a good explanation of his explicitative additions. We must infer that he did not believe that speaking against Jesus was forgivable. This is entirely reasonable for someone who lived in the early church, who knew Jesus' polemic against his opponents and who periodically suffered damage from the outside world which included vilification of Jesus. It is also an entirely reasonable interpretation of the immediate context. Speaking against the Holy Spirit is said to be unforgivable, and Mark locates this correctly in its original context by interpreting it with reference to the accusation that Jesus had an unclean spirit. The translator was therefore certain that לבר אנשא could not follow immediately after יאמר מלה. Accordingly, he took לבר אנשא closely with ישתביק לה, and regarded לה as simply picking up לבר אנשא before the verb. He also took בר אנשא as a collective term for people in general, and, like לה, it told him who would be forgiven – everyone in general, which fits the teaching of Jesus perfectly well.

The translator now took כל to mean everything, and the object rather than the subject of the verb of saying. The term מלה, no longer controlled by its context, is altogether too general a term – it means any thing, not only a word. The Greek term λόγος must surely have occurred to the translator, but he must have felt that it was not specific enough. Taking כל...מלה to mean everything except blasphemy against the Holy Spirit, he has therefore translated explicitatively. His addition, τὰ ἁμαρτήματα καὶ αἱ βλασφημίαι ὅσα ἐὰν βλασφημήσωσιν is phrased in such a way as to make clear that what very sinful people usually do is forgivable, a sentiment in accordance with the teaching of Jesus and the needs of formerly sinful converts in the early church.

In the second half of the saying, ὃς δ᾽ ἂν βλασφημήσῃ εἰς is a perfectly reasonable rendering of ומן דמלל מלה על, with the verb βλασφημέω being a particularly natural choice in view of the wording which he had just thought of for his explicitative addition to the first half of the saying. Here Mark ends with a very determined piece of explicitation. Verse 30 declares the connection between the accusation and the incident, which

---

[32] Casey, 'Idiom and Translation', 164–82; *Aramaic Sources of Mark's Gospel*, pp. 130–2; pp. 55, 133–6 above.

Mark evidently felt might get lost if it were not explicitly stated. Equally, he has clarified the refusal of forgiveness for ever by adding ἀλλὰ ἔνοχός ἐστιν αἰωνίου ἁμαρτήματος. This ensures that לעלמין cannot be regarded as just a metaphor. Mark may also have used εἰς τὸν αἰῶνα as a relatively conventional rendering of לעלמין, or it may have been added by a scribe, for it is absent from D W Θ 565 569 and other manuscripts. Fortunately this does not affect the exegesis of the original saying nor appreciation of the behaviour of the translator, who was determinedly explicitative, whether or not he added εἰς τὸν αἰῶνα.

It might be suggested that the saying was expanded in Aramaic rather than in Greek. This cannot quite be excluded, especially not if the translator was in close touch with the actual recording of this material before he translated it. It is not, however, the most probable hypothesis, precisely because the explicitative expansions make such excellent sense within the editorial habits of Mark. If we simply need Jewish assumptions to understand a piece, Mark assumes that they will be filled in. This is not such a case. Jewish assumptions would tell those who heard a literal translation only that the sin against the Holy Spirit was speaking against God in action. This enabled Luke to interpret the saying in a new context specific to Christians who were persecuted, and the saying in that form has enabled many tormented Christian souls over a period of centuries to imagine that they have committed this sin. Mark was aware that a literal translation could be drastically misconstrued, and he was in touch with the original interpretation, which required more than Jewish assumptions – it required true tradition about the circumstances in which the saying was originally composed and its exact exegesis. This is another argument for the early date of Mark, who was so clearly in touch with authentic written material from the time of the ministry.

There is another version of this saying in the *Gospel of Thomas*, saying 44:

> Jesus said: 'Whoever speaks blasphemy against the Father, it shall be forgiven him, and whoever speaks blasphemy against the Son it shall be forgiven him, but (δέ) whoever speaks blasphemy against the Holy Spirit (πνεῦμα), it shall not be forgiven him, either (οὔτε) on earth or (οὔτε) in heaven.'

This is a completely secondary form of the saying. In the first place, it has lost its context, so that the blasphemy against the Holy Spirit no longer has any connection with the false accusation made by Jesus' most serious opponents during the historic ministry. Secondly, the idiomatic use of the Aramaic בר (א)נש(א) has been replaced by the Christian theological term 'the Son', which reflects later Christian doctrine. Thirdly, the addition of the first line in which blasphemy against the Father is forgivable is remarkable in itself. Taken with the replacement of 'son of man' by 'the Son', it shows that this form of the saying is dependent on the later Christian doctrine of the Trinity. Finally, a Jewish expression about the coming age has been replaced with a reference to earth and heaven. It is clearly not the Lucan version on which this late formulation is ultimately dependent. The blasphemy against the Father and the Son is a more precise version of the reference in Matthew and Mark to the forgiveness of all blasphemies. Quite how the collectors of the saying into the *Gospel of Thomas* understood it is difficult to determine. Valantasis may be on the right lines in associating blasphemy against the Holy Spirit with denigrating the voice of the living Jesus as found in this collection of sayings.[33]

We can now see the original saying in its original context. I have already shown the logical progression of the other Marcan sayings, and that, after the question formulating his basic premise that Satan cannot cast out Satan, Jesus proceeded with two analogical arguments from a kingdom and a house. He inferred that Satan would be finished if he rose up against himself, from which it follows that Satan cannot have done any such thing. His next argument was another analogy, referring to the real experience of conflict with the devil before an exorcism. Having thus made absolutely clear that his exorcisms were done by the power of God, Jesus finally accused his opponents of the unforgivable sin of opposing the power of God. That completes a logical progression of arguments, provided that the final argument is read in Aramaic and all the arguments are seen in their original cultural context. This is surely not coincidental. I have uncovered a series of arguments which belong together in the same dispute, and which are very likely to be a partial record of a single occasion.

The next incident in Mark is that of the arrival of Jesus' family, a separate though connected incident. The next saying in Q appears to have been the parabolic warning about what happens if a demoniac who has been exorcised is not then looked after (Matt. 12.43–5//Luke 11.24–6). Here too Matthew and Luke have a very high degree of agreement in wording. It follows that Q in a single Greek translation continued after the end of the Beelzeboul incident, and that this parabolic warning was collected here because of its general relevance to exorcism. We have therefore reached the end of this important overlap.

---

[33] R. Valantasis, *The Gospel of Thomas* (London, 1997), p. 121.

Conclusions

The reconstruction and interpretation of the Aramaic originals of both
Mark and Q show that the question as to whether Mark used Q, or Q
used Mark, or the agreements between Matthew and Luke are due to an
Ur-Markus, should now be made out of date. Despite some uncertainties
in detail, I have been able to reconstruct two sets of original material.
Despite some explicitative translation, some editing and some moving
of material from one context to another, we have seen that most of the
material from this controversy is derived from genuine controversy which
took place during the ministry of Jesus. Some variation in wording in the
Aramaic tradition emerges from the process of reconstructing these two
early sources. This may be due to Jesus repeating himself with variations,
or it may be due to alterations in wording during transmission. For this
reason, and on general grounds, therefore, I am not suggesting that I have
recovered the *ipsissima verba* of Jesus. I am suggesting that we should
be altogether certain that we now have before us a close approximation
to what he and his opponents said to each other during this fierce controversy. We have also seen that Mark 3.23–9 forms a logically constructed
argument, so much so that it may well be a record of what was said on a
single occasion.

This controversy was a very important aspect of Jesus' ministry, and
we may infer from it a great deal about Jesus, his view of his mission,
and his conflict with his opponents. Firstly, Jesus himself. Everyone in
Jesus' culture believed that some people were possessed by demons,
who were the servants of the devil. A successful exorcist, therefore, was
bound to believe that he was acting by the power of God. It is clear from
Gospel narratives, as we have seen, that exorcisms were dramatic events.
It follows that Jesus felt the power of God acting through him. This is
quite sufficient to make him an important servant of God, and a man
who had no doubts at all that God worked mightily through him. Hence
the saying about the kingship of God coming upon people – from Jesus'
perspective, people could see and feel the action of God himself through
him in his ministry.

Secondly, we have seen that it is implicit in one of Jesus' arguments
that he believed that the power of God was also exercised by other successful Jewish exorcists. This is less difficult and more important than
traditional scholarship has supposed. Jewish dualism was quite simple –
demoniacs were inspired by the devil, and given Jesus' other arguments,
he was left with no alternative but to suppose that people who cast demons
out were inspired by God. We then have to ask who was the most able

exorcist of Jesus' time. Our primary sources should leave us with no doubt about that – Jesus himself is reported to have exorcised far more often and dramatically than anyone else, to the extent that other people are said to have tried exorcising in his name (Mark 9.38–40; Acts 19.13–17, cf. 16.18). This is important because it follows that Jesus must have been sharply aware of the power of God working through him more abundantly than through other people to whom God had given the same gift.

This also increases our insight into Jesus' view of his mission. If God himself inspired so dramatic and vigorous a defeat of the devil through Jesus, there could be no doubt that the mission itself was inspired by God. This view could only be reinforced by Jesus' conflict with his opponents. We have seen how serious this was. The accusation that Jesus cast out demons by the power of the devil is a drastic rejection of the ministry. Jesus not only declared that the kingship of God was displayed in the exorcisms, but correctly supposing that this criticism of him would make him an outcast from Israel, he declared it to be an unforgivable sin. This means that there was a very serious polarisation of position between Jesus and his opponents, to the point of further conflict being altogether inevitable. In this conflict, Jesus used no Christological title, and supposed without doubt that God was on his side. So strong were his convictions of divine inspiration that he continued to exorcise, to teach others, and to find criticism of him beyond the pale.

The categories of prophet and teacher are the natural ones for such a figure at the time. Neither prophet nor teacher was a fixed category with a rigid definition. When we look over the phenomenon of Jewish prophecy as a whole, we can see that significant prophets had two major features in common – they proclaimed the word of God and acted upon it. The exorcisms of Jesus were, from the perspective of himself and his disciples, mighty acts of God. He and his disciples were bound to accept the verdict which Luke put in the mouth of Cleopas and his companion: ἀνὴρ προφήτης δυνατὸς ἐν ἔργῳ καὶ λόγῳ ἐναντίον τοῦ θεοῦ καὶ παντὸς τοῦ λαοῦ (Luke 24.19). Moreover, such mighty acts could only reinforce the Jewish identity of the disciples, as they witnessed these mighty acts done in deliberate opposition to Jews who did not belong to the Jesus movement. It follows that this conflict was a significant part of the total ministry which not only was important for Judaism at the time, but also made Christological development inevitable after Jesus' death. Accordingly, it fits perfectly into the picture of the early development of Christianity which I have begun to describe elsewhere.[34]

---

[34] See especially Casey, *From Jewish Prophet to Gentile God.*

6

CONCLUSIONS

In surveying the history of previous scholarship in chapter 1, I showed that the Aramaic dimension of Q has never been properly treated, and is conventionally omitted. This is a remarkable fact. Most people have noticed that language is a significant part of culture, but the study of Q, like the study of Jesus in general, has proceeded as if this were not the case. I also showed in chapter 1 that the whole notion that Q was a single document written in Greek has never been satisfactorily demonstrated. The omission of the Aramaic dimension is one significant aspect of this, since it has prevented a proper critical assessment of those passages in which the material was transmitted in Aramaic, of which Matthew and Luke used or made different translations. It is not, however, the only significant defect in scholarship. The predication of a Q community, and attempts to portray Jesus as a Cynic philosopher are among other major problems. All these problems are related at a profound level. The omission of Aramaic is one aspect of a general failure to see the Q material within the culture in which it was produced. This general failure is behind most of the other serious problems. This failure is due to the presence of scholarly investigators in their own part of the modern world, and their strong tendency to repeat each other reflects the fact that a scholar's membership of our vast academic bureaucracies is in some ways as important as ideological orientation.

In spite of this, there are some interesting suggestions scattered over the older scholarship, and Aramaic source material is an obvious possible explanation of the origins of passages where Matthew and Luke are similar to each other in content, but have a relatively low level of verbal agreement. In *Aramaic Sources of Mark's Gospel*, I showed that the publication of the Aramaic Dead Sea scrolls has opened up all sorts of possibilities. In particular, I demonstrated the fruitfulness of reconstructing Aramaic sources from passages of Mark's Gospel which show clear signs of literal translation from Aramaic into Greek. An attempt to see what could be done with the possibility of Aramaic sources of Q required a further discussion of method, followed by a close examination of passages of three kinds.

In the first place, I examined Matt. 23.23–36//Luke 11.39–51. This is a passage where Matthew and Luke are similar to each other in content, and have a significant amount of verbal overlap, but a lot of verbal differences too. The passage does not belong in common order either. Despite some problems due to heavy editing, especially by Luke, it proved possible to produce a reconstruction of a common Aramaic source. It was possible to demonstrate that this was a very old source, containing authentic material from the historic ministry of Jesus. This reconstructed source contains very fierce polemic directed by Jesus at his orthodox opponents. The conflict to which this polemic belonged was an important element in the situation which led to Jesus' death, and subsequently to the origins of Christianity.

The first saying showed Jesus in dispute with his orthodox opponents, who had expanded the tithing laws to cover herbs and spices. Without objecting to such tithing, Jesus accused them of not practising the main points of the Law, which he defined as justice, mercy and trust. The precise nature of the dispute can be seen much more clearly when we have the most important words in Aramaic, because this enables us to link up this dispute more clearly with other discussions of similar matters. The second dispute showed orthodox opponents who had expanded the purity laws, and were accused by Jesus of robbery and excess. We saw that there was a link with the previous saying in that they supported the extraction of tithes from the poor by rich priests, a link not made on the surface of the text. The same underlying charge of hypocrisy continued with opponents who broadened their phylacteries and loved important seats in synagogues. It became more serious when Jesus likened them to whitewashed tombs, an exceptionally polemical way of announcing that their overt concern for purity advertised their wickedness. In the next saying, I was able to uncover the quite lethal nature of this dispute. Orthodox opponents were involved in building the tombs of the prophets, who were generally believed to have been put to death. Jesus accused his opponents of being the genuine descendants of those who killed the prophets because they had rejected the message of John the Baptist, who was murdered by Herod Antipas, and they were now plotting the death of Jesus. Hence he threatened the judgement of God upon them soon. Throughout this passage, the careful study of the Aramaic words of Q made it possible to place this dispute very carefully in the life of Jesus, and to understand better its cultural ramifications.

It follows that this passage does not provide evidence about a Q community, though it does show that Jesus' disputes with his orthodox opponents were of continuing interest to the early church. I also reconstructed the way in which Luke edited the source for the benefit of Gentile churches, and showed repeatedly that the Matthean version of these sayings is the more original. I reinforced the traditional view of a minority of scholars that Luke occasionally misread his Aramaic source, and showed that he did so in line with his overall editorial habits, not merely by mistake. Here too the careful study of Aramaic words was essential, and enabled me to explain far more of the differences between Matthew and Luke than the more partial studies done by the earlier scholarship. It follows that in this lengthy passage, Luke did not use Matthew, and that this part of Q was not part of a Greek document used by both evangelists. This proves that Q was not a single Greek document.

The second passage examined was Matt. 11.2–19//Luke 7.18–35, a passage in which Matthew and Luke used a single Greek translation. I reconstructed the Aramaic source of this Greek translation as far as was possible. This helped to demonstrate the authenticity of several sayings in this passage, and was necessary for the interpretation of the end of the passage. Some details were, however, quite conjectural. This appeared to be due not only to having to work from one Greek translation rather than two, but also to very heavy editing by the evangelists. Reasons were given for supposing that this collection of sayings originally ended at the end of this passage, so adding to the arguments for a chaotic model of Q.

Detailed study of this source cast an interesting light on a period when the ministries of John the Baptist and Jesus overlapped. This was an unexpected result, which could hardly be obtained without careful study of the Aramaic source. The source turned out to be almost entirely historically accurate. It adds to the evidence that Jesus saw John the Baptist as Elijah. I also argued that further light can be cast on Matt. 11.12//Luke 16.16 by reconstructing a common and separate Aramaic source, and by reconstructing John the Baptist's prediction of a stronger one than himself. Jesus believed not only that he fulfilled this prediction, but also that he himself and the Twelve were strong ones who were taking hold of the kingship of God in his ministry. This further adds to the value of doing Aramaic reconstructions from this material. It is also further evidence that a more complex and rather chaotic model of Q is the only kind of model that could be right.

Thirdly, I examined a group of passages in which we find one of the overlaps between Mark and Q: Mark 3.20–30; Matt. 12.22–32; Luke

11.14–23; 12.10. Here I inferred two separate accounts of an incident which was once very important in the life of Jesus. Like the first passage, these accounts revealed a major conflict with very severe polemic: in this case, the conflict included at least a temporary conflict with Jesus' family and people in general, as well as a full-blown quarrel with scribes from Jerusalem. The scribes were not even the only people to accuse Jesus of collusion with the devil in his ministry of exorcism, and his family made a very similar accusation. The Aramaic reconstructions clarified the nature of two sources similar in content but different in wording, rather than evidence that Luke used Matthew, or Mark used Q, or Q used Mark. They helped greatly with the interpretation of a number of sayings. In particular, it was possible to show that the sayings in the source of Mark 3.23–9 form so consistent a set of images and arguments that they are likely to have been said on the same occasion. An Aramaic reconstruction was also helpful in seeing Matt. 12.28//Luke 11.20 in its original cultural context, in which Jesus saw his exorcisms as a demonstration of God's mighty power in the present and immediately past events of his ministry. It was then possible to defend the view that Matt. 12.27//Luke 11.19 shows Jesus taking an entirely positive view of the work of other Jewish exorcists, the only view which makes sense of his arguments as a whole.

An Aramaic reconstruction was also the only way to find the original interpretation of Matt. 12.30//Luke 11.23. We can now make sense of the minority reading with με. The reconstructed saying shows that Jesus was rejecting his opponents' accusation by pointing out that acceptance of it would put him outside Israel. The saying is not a general statement, but a precise one with a *Sitz im Leben* in this particular conflict. An Aramaic reconstruction was also decisive in recovering the meaning and cultural context of Jesus' view that his opponents had committed an unforgivable sin. This was their accusation that he had cast out demons by means of Beelzeboul, as Mark knew very well. In the case of this saying, and this one only, I found good reason to posit no fewer than three Greek translations which were derived ultimately from a single Aramaic original, a very helpful aid to reconstructing the original text and meaning of a very primitive source. The position of one of these translations in Luke 12.10 also contributes to a chaotic model of Q, since it was evidently collected quite separately from the incident to which it originally belonged.

We must therefore conclude that reconstructing Aramaic originals from passages in the synoptic Gospels is one essential tool in the quest to recover the Jesus of history. It helps to recover early and normally authentic sources, especially where the Gospels present us with a literal translation of such a source. The study of Aramaic should not, however, be used on its own. It is rather a part of a whole process of recovering the original meaning of Jesus' sayings in their original contexts. Moreover, it cannot always help. When Matthew and Luke have edited too heavily for us to recover an original source, we are stuck, a situation liable to be exacerbated at any particular point by the limitations of our knowledge of the Aramaic of the period. This book has, however, shown that massive progress is possible some of the time.

It follows that a more complete investigation than can be offered in a single monograph would be profitable. An attempt should be made to reconstruct the whole of the Q material, as well as associated and promising passages in Matthew and Luke. I have worked tentatively with a rather chaotic model of Q, about which we can now be a little more precise. We must conclude that the only viable models for Q are those proposed by Barrett and Taylor[1] many years ago, and that in recent years most scholarship has been working with an impossible model. With the results of the present investigation in mind, including the *Forschungsberichte* in chapter 1, one might propose the following model of Q.

1. A Greek Q including the preaching of John the Baptist, which caused Matthew and Luke to put this material where Mark has his main account of John the Baptist's ministry.
2. A Greek Q which included the Beelzeboul controversy, which caused Matthew and Luke to line it up with Mark's account of the Beelzeboul controversy. This Greek Q was a translation of the Aramaic source which I uncovered and discussed in detail in chapter 4.
3. A Greek Q which ended with some passion material, which caused Matthew and Luke to put it towards the close of the ministry. At this point it is especially evident that Q material cannot be marked off clearly from special Lucan material, which includes at least one authentic saying translated from Aramaic (Luke 22.48).
4. A Greek multi-Q, some material in Greek which is not in common order and never was. This may have included sayings which were transmitted orally. Further investigation might show how much of this material is authentic, and how much of it was once translated from Aramaic.
5. An Aramaic Q, which included material from Luke 11 and Matthew 23.

---

[1] See pp. 9, 12–13 above.

This model may be too simple, but a model of this kind surely merits investigation. It presupposes material handed down among different Christian communities and written down on wax tablets and the like. The process of writing it down may have begun during the historic ministry. It contains a very high proportion of originally authentic material, and a significant part of the Gospel writers' editing can be determined because of their differences from each other. It follows that a detailed investigation of every piece of this source material is an essential task for those of us who wish to end the quest of the historical Jesus by finding him. Like the Aramaic sources of Mark's Gospel which I uncovered in a previous book, the uncovering of the Aramaic dimension of Q enables us to see a more Jewish Jesus than is conventional. In particular, he was more immersed in Judaism than Christian pictures of him have generally supposed. Some of the passages studied in this book also enable us to understand with much greater precision the conflicts between him and his orthodox opponents, conflicts which were severe enough to be leading to his death even before he cleansed the Temple. This element is likely to prove crucial not only for our understanding of Jesus, but also in our attempts to uncover the underlying causes of the later split between Judaism and Christianity.

SELECT BIBLIOGRAPHY

Aramaic texts and tools of study

Bar Bahlūl, Ḥ, ed. R. Duval, *Lexicon Syriacum auctore Hassano bar Bahlule, voces Syriacas Graecasque cum glossis Syriacis et Arabacis complectens* (3 vols., Paris, 1888–1901).

Beyer, K., *Semitische Syntax im Neuen Testament* (2nd edn, Göttingen, 1968).

Die aramäischen Texte vom Toten Meer (Göttingen, 1984).

Die aramäischen Texte vom Toten Meer. Ergänzungsband (Göttingen, 1994).

Boer, P. A. H. de et al., *The Old Testament in Syriac according to the Peshitta Version*, edited on behalf of the International Organization for the Study of the Old Testament by the Peshiṭta Institute, Leiden (many vols., Leiden, 1966–).

Bokser, B. M., 'An Annotated Bibliographical Guide to the Study of the Palestinian Talmud', *ANRW* II.19.2 (1979), pp. 139–256.

Brockelmann, C., *Lexicon Syriacum* (Berlin, 1894–5; 2nd edn, Halis Saxonum, 1928).

Brooke, G. et al. (eds.), *Qumran Cave 4*, vol. XVII: *Parabiblical Texts, Part 3* (DJD XXII. Oxford, 1996).

Brown, F., Driver, S. R. and Briggs, C. A., *A Hebrew and English Lexicon of the Old Testament* (Oxford, 1906).

Chyutin, M., *The New Jerusalem Scroll from Qumran. A Comprehensive Reconstruction* (JSP.S 25. Sheffield, 1997).

Clarke, E. G., with Aufrecht, W. E., Hurd, J. C. and Spitzer, F., *Targum Pseudo-Jonathan of the Pentateuch: Text and Concordance* (Hoboken, 1984).

Corpus Scriptorum Christianorum Orientalium. Series Syriaca (many vols., Leuven, 1903–).

Cotton, H. M. and Yardeni, A., *Aramaic, Hebrew and Greek Documentary Texts from Naḥal Ḥever and Other Sites* (DJD XXVII. Oxford, 1997).

Cowley, A., *Aramaic Papyri of the Fifth Century B.C.* (Oxford, 1923).

Dalman, G., *Grammatik des jüdisch-palästinischen Aramäisch nach den Idiomen des palästinischen Talmud, des Onkelostargum und Prophetentargum und der jerusalemischen Targume* (2nd edn, Leipzig, 1905).

Díez Macho, A., *Neophyti 1. Targum Palastinense Ms de la Biblioteca Vaticana* (6 vols., Madrid, 1968–79).

Dirksen, P. B., *An Annotated Bibliography of the Peshiṭta of the Old Testament* (Leiden, 1989).

'Appendix: Supplement to *An Annotated Bibliography*, 1989', in P. B. Dirksen and A. Van der Kooij (eds.), *The Peshitta as a Translation* (MPIL 8. Leiden, 1995), pp. 221–36.

Donner, H. and Röllig, W., *Kanaanäische und Aramäische Inschriften* (Wiesbaden, 1962).

Epstein, I. (ed.), תלמוד בבלי *Hebrew–English Edition of the Babylonian Talmud* (32 vols., London, 1952–90).

Fitzmyer, J. A., *The Genesis Apocryphon of Qumran Cave I: A Commentary* (BibOr 18. Rome, 1966; 2nd edn, BibOr 18A, 1971).

The Aramaic Inscriptions of Sefire (BibOr 19. Rome, 1967. Rev. edn, BibOr 19A, 1995).

Fitzmyer, J. A. (ed.), 'A.Tobit', in M. Broshi et al. (eds.), *Qumran Cave 4*, vol. XIV: *Parabiblical Texts, Part 2* (DJD XIX. Oxford, 1995).

Fitzmyer, J. A. and Harrington, D. J. (eds.), *A Manual of Palestinian Aramaic Texts* (BibOr 34. Rome, 1978).

Fitzmyer, J. A. and Kaufman, S. A., *An Aramaic Bibliography*, part I: *Old, Official, and Biblical Aramaic* (Baltimore and London, 1992).

García Martínez, F., Tigchelaar, E. J. C. and Woude, A. S. van der, *Qumran Cave 11*, vol. II: *11Q2–18, 11Q20–31* (DJD XXIII. Oxford, 1998).

Graffin, R. (ed.), *Patrologia Syriaca: Pars Prima. Ab Initiis usque ad Annum 350* (3 vols., Paris, 1894–1926).

Grossfeld, B., *A Bibliography of Targum Literature* (3 vols., Cincinnatti and New York, 1972–90).

Hillers, D. R. and Cussini, E., *Palmyrene Aramaic Texts* (Baltimore, 1996).

Hoftijzer, J. and Jongeling, K., *Dictionary of the North-West Semitic Inscriptions* (2 vols., Leiden, 1995).

Jastrow, M., *A Dictionary of the Targumim, the Talmud Babli and Yerushalmi, and the Midrashic Literature* (2 vols., London, 1886–1903. Reprinted New York, 1950).

Kasowsky, Ch. J. and Kasowsky, B. (eds.), *Thesaurus Talmudis Concordantiae Verborum Quae in Talmude Babylonico Reperiuntur* (42 vols., Jerusalem, 1954–89).

Kiraz, G. A. (ed.), *Comparative Edition of the Syriac Gospels, Aligning the Sinaiticus, Curetonianus, Peshîṭtâ and Ḥarklean Versions* (4 vols., NTTS XXI. Leiden, 1996).

Klein, M. L., *Genizah Manuscripts of the Palestinian Targum to the Pentateuch* (2 vols., Cincinatti, 1986).

Kosovsky, M. (ed.), *Concordance to the Talmud Yerushalmi* (many vols., Jerusalem, 1979–).

Lagarde, P. de (ed.), *Hagiographa Chaldaice* (Leipzig, 1873. Reprinted Osnabruck, 1967).

Leloir, L. (ed.), *Saint Ephrem. Commentaire de l'evangile concordant. Texte Syriaque (Ms Chester Beatty 709)* (CBM 8. Dublin, 1963).

Levine, E. (ed.), *The Aramaic Version of Lamentations* (New York, 1976).

Levy, J., *Chaldäisches Wörterbuch über die Targumim und einem grossen Theil des rabbinischer Schriftthums* (2 vols., Leipzig, 1867–8; 3rd edn, 1881).

Neuhebräisches und Chaldäisches Wörterbuch über die Talmudim und Midraschim (4 vols., Leipzig, 1876–89. 2nd edn, Berlin and Vienna, 1924).

Lewis, A. S. and Gibson, M. D. (eds.), *The Palestinian Syriac Lectionary of the Gospels, Re-edited from Two Sinai MSS. and from P. de Lagarde's Edition of the 'Evangeliarium Hierosolymitanum'* (London, 1899).

Macuch, R., *Grammatik des Samaritanischen Aramäisch* (Berlin, 1982).

Mandelkern, S., קונקורדנציה לתנ"ך *Concordance on the Bible* (2 vols., Leipzig, 1896; revised by C. M. Brecher, New York, 1955).

Milik, J. T., *The Books of Enoch. Aramaic Fragments of Qumrân Cave 4* (Oxford, 1976).

Müller-Kessler, Ch., *Grammatik des Christlich-Palästinisch-Aramäischen*, part I: *Schriftlehre, Lautlehre, Formenlehre* (Hildesheim, 1991).

Müller-Kessler, Ch. and Sokoloff, M., *A Corpus of Christian Palestinian Aramaic* (5 vols. so far. Groningen, 1996–).

Muraoka, T. and Porten, B., *A Grammar of Egyptian Aramaic* (Leiden, 1998).

Patrologia Orientalis (many vols., Paris and Turnhout, 1907–).

Payne-Smith, R. et al. (eds.), *Thesaurus Syriacus* (2 vols., Oxford, 1868–1901).

Ploeg, J. P. M. van der and Woude, A. S. van der (eds.), *Le Targum de Job de la Grotte XI de Qumrân* (Leiden, 1971).

Porten, B. and Yardeni, A., *Textbook of Aramaic Documents from Ancient Egypt, Newly Copied, Edited and Translated into Hebrew and English* (4 vols., Jerusalem, 1986–).

Puech, E. (ed.), *Qumrân Grotte 4*, vol. XXII: *Textes Araméens première partie. 4Q529–549* (DJD XXXI. Oxford, 2001).

Rosenthal, F., *A Grammar of Biblical Aramaic* (2nd edn, Wiesbaden, 1963).

Schäfer, P. and Becker, H.-J., with Reeg, G. et al. (eds.), *Synopse zum Talmud Yerushalmi*. סינופסיס לתלמוד הירושלמי (7 vols., Tübingen, 1991–2000).

Schulthess, F., *Lexicon Syropalaestinum* (Berlin, 1903).
Grammatik des christlich-palästinischen Aramäisch (Tübingen, 1924).

Sokoloff, M., *The Targum to Job from Qumran Cave XI* (Ramat Gan, 1974).
A Dictionary of Jewish Palestinian Aramaic of the Byzantine Period (Ramat-Gan, 1990).

Sperber, A. (ed.), *The Bible in Aramaic* (5 vols., Leiden, 1959–73).

Strack, H. L. and Stemberger, L., *Introduction to the Talmud and Midrash* (1982. ET Edinburgh, 2nd edn, 1996).

Stuckenbruck, L. T., 'Revision of Aramaic–Greek and Greek–Aramaic Glossaries in *The Books of Enoch: Aramaic Fragments of Qumrân Cave 4*, by J. T. Milik', *JJS* 41, 1990, 13–48.
The Book of Giants from Qumran. Texts, Translation, and Commentary (TSAJ 63. Tübingen, 1997).

Tal, A., *A Dictionary of Samaritan Aramaic*/מילון הארמית של השומרונים (2 vols. Brill, 2000).

Tal, A. (ed.), התרגום השומרוני לתורה *The Samaritan Targum of the Pentateuch* (3 vols., Tel Aviv, 1980–3).

Secondary literature

Abrahams, I., *Studies in Pharisaism and the Gospels* (2nd series. Cambridge, 1924).

Aitken, W. E. M., 'Beelzebul', *JBL* 31, 1912, 34–53.

Alexander, L., 'Ancient Book Production and the Circulation of the Gospels', in R. Bauckham (ed.), *The Gospels for All Christians. Rethinking the Gospel Audiences* (Edinburgh, 1998), pp. 71–111.

Allison, D. C., 'Jesus and the Covenant: A Response to E. P. Sanders', *JSNT* 29, 1987, 57–78.

The Jesus Tradition in Q (Harrisburgh, 1997).

Arnal, W. E., 'Gendered Couplets in Q and Legal Formulations: From Rhetoric to Social History', *JBL* 116, 1997, 75–94.

Aune, D. E., 'Jesus and Cynics in First-Century Palestine: Some Critical Considerations', in J. H. Charlesworth and L. L. Johns (eds.), *Hillel and Jesus. Comparisons of Two Major Religious Leaders* (Minneapolis, 1997), pp. 176–92.

Baarda, T., ' "Chose" or "Collected": Concerning an Aramaism in Logion 8 of the Gospel of Thomas and the Question of Independence', *HThR* 84, 1991, 373–91.

' "The Cornerstone": An Aramaism in the Diatessaron and the Gospel of Thomas?', *NT* 37, 1995, 285–300.

Baillet, M., 'V. Grotte 8. I. Textes Bibliques. 3. Phylactère' with Milik J. T., 'III. Textes de la Grotte 5Q. I. Textes Bibliques. 8. Phylactère', in M. Baillet et al., *Les 'Petites Grottes' de Qumrân* (DJD III. Oxford, 1962), pp. 149–57, 178.

Banks, R., *Jesus and the Law in the Synoptic Tradition*, (SNTS.MS 28. Cambridge, 1975).

Barr, J., 'The Hebrew/Aramaic Background of "Hypocrisy" in the Gospels', in P. R. Davies and R. T. White (eds.), *A Tribute to Geza Vermes. Essays on Jewish and Christian Literature and History* (JSOT.S 100. Sheffield, 1990), pp. 307–26.

Barrett, C. K., 'Q: A Re-examination', *ExpT* 54, 1942–3, 320–3.

Beare, F. W., *The Gospel according to Matthew* (Oxford, 1981).

Beattie, D. R. G. and McNamara, M. J., *The Aramaic Bible. Targums in their Historical Context* (JSOT.S 166. Sheffield, 1994).

Beckwith, R., *The Old Testament Canon of the New Testament and Its Background in Early Judaism* (Grand Rapids, 1985).

Bellinzoni, A. J., *The Sayings of Jesus in the Writings of Justin Martyr* (NT.S 17. Leiden, 1967).

Bergemann, T., *Q auf dem Prüfstand. Die Zuordnung des Mt/Lk-Stoffes zu Q am Beispiel der Bergpredigt* (FRLANT 158. Göttingen, 1993).

Berkey, R. F., 'Ἐγγίζειν, φθάνειν and Realized Eschatology', JBL 82, 1963, 177–87.

Bertman, S., 'Tasseled Garments in the Ancient East Mediterranean', *BA* 24, 1961, 119–28.

Betz, H. D., 'Jesus and the Cynics: Survey and Analysis of a Hypothesis', *JR* 74, 1994, 453–75.

Birdsall, N., 'A Fresh Examination of the Fragments of the Gospel of St Luke in ms 0171 and an Attempted Reconstruction with Special Reference to the Recto', in R. Gryson (ed.), *PHILOLOGIA SACRA. Biblische und patristische Studien für Hermann J. Frede und Walter Thiele zu ihrem siebzigsten Geburtstag*, vol. I: *ALTES UND NEUES TESTAMENT* (Freiburg, 1993), pp. 212–27.

Bishop, E. F. F., 'Rue–πήγανον', *ET* 59, 1947–8, 81.

Black, M., *An Aramaic Approach to the Gospels and Acts* (Oxford, 1946; 2nd edn, 1954; 3rd edn, 1967).
  'Unsolved New Testament Problems. The Problem of the Aramaic Element in the Gospels', *ET* 59, 1947–8, 171–5.
  'The Recovery of the Language of Jesus', *NTS* 3, 1956–7, 305–13.
  'Aramaic Studies and the Language of Jesus', in M. Black and G. Fohrer (eds.), *In Memoriam Paul Kahle* (BZAW 103. Berlin, 1968), pp. 17–28, reprinted with corrections in S. E. Porter (ed.), *The Language of the New Testament. Classic Essays* (JSNT.S 60. Sheffield, 1991), pp. 112–25.
  'The Aramaic Dimension in Q with Notes on Luke 17.22 and Matthew 24.26 (Luke 17.23)', *JSNT* 40, 1990, 33–41.
Boring, M. E., 'How May We Identify Oracles of Christian Prophets in the Synoptic Tradition? Mark 3:28–29 as a Test Case', *JBL* 91, 1972, 501–21.
  'The Unforgivable Sin Logion Mark III 28–29/Matt XII 31–32/Luke XII 10: Formal Analysis and History of the Tradition', *NT* 18, 1976, 258–79.
Bowman, J. 'Phylacteries', in K. Aland et al. (eds.), *Studia Evangelica*, vol. I (TU 73. Berlin, 1959), 523–38.
Branham, R. B. and Goulet-Cazé, M.-O. (eds.), *The Cynics. The Cynic Movement in Antiquity and Its Legacy* (Berkeley, 1996).
Broadhead, E. K., 'On the (Mis)Definition of Q', *JSNT* 68, 1997, 3–12.
Brodie, T., 'Again Not Q: Luke 7:18–35 as an Acts-orientated Transformation of the Vindication of the Prophet Micaiah (1 Kings 22:1–18)', *Irish Biblical Studies* 16, 1994, 2–30.
Brown, J. P., 'Mark as Witness to an Edited Form of Q', *JBL* 80, 1961, 29–44.
  'The Form of "Q" Known to Matthew', *NTS* 8, 1961–2, 27–42.
Bultmann, R. K., *Die Geschichte der synoptischen Tradition* (FRLANT 29, NF 12. Göttingen, 1921); ET *The History of the Synoptic Tradition* (Oxford, 1963).
Burney, C. F., *The Poetry of Our Lord* (Oxford, 1925).
Bussby, F., 'Is Q an Aramaic Document?', *ET* 65, 1953–4, 272–5.
Bussmann, W., *Synoptische Studien*, vol. II: *Zur Redenquelle* (Halle, 1929).
Butler, B. C., *The Originality of St Matthew* (Cambridge, 1951).
Cameron, P. S., *Violence and the Kingdom: The Interpretation of Matthew 11:12* (ANTJ 5. Frankfurt am Main, 1984; 2nd edn, 1988).
Cameron, R., '"What Have You Come Out to See?" Characterizations of John and Jesus in the Gospels', *Semeia* 49, 1990, 35–69.
Casey, P. M., 'The Use of the Term "son of man" in the Similitudes of Enoch', *JSJ* VII, 1976, 11–29.
  Son of Man. The Interpretation and Influence of Daniel 7 (London, 1980).
  'The Jackals and the Son of Man (Matt. 8.20//Luke 9.58)', *JSNT* 23, 1985, 3–22.
  'General, Generic and Indefinite: The Use of the Term 'Son of Man' in Aramaic Sources and in the Teaching of Jesus', *JSNT* 29, 1987, 21–56.
  From Jewish Prophet to Gentile God. The Origins and Development of New Testament Christology (The Edward Cadbury Lectures at the University of Birmingham, 1985–6. Cambridge and Louisville, 1991).
  'Method in Our Madness, and Madness in Their Methods. Some Approaches to the Son of Man Problem in Recent Scholarship', *JSNT* 42, 1991, 17–43.
  'The Use of the Term (א)שׁנ(א) בר in the Aramaic Translations of the Hebrew Bible' *JSNT* 54, 1994, 87–118.

'Idiom and Translation. Some Aspects of the Son of Man Problem', *NTS* 41, 1995, 164–82.

Is John's Gospel True? (London, 1996).

'Culture and Historicity: The Cleansing of the Temple', *CBQ* 59, 1997, 306–32.

Aramaic Sources of Mark's Gospel (SNTS.MS 102. Cambridge, 1998).

Catchpole, D., *The Quest for Q* (Edinburgh, 1993).

Chancey, M., 'The Cultural Milieu of Ancient Sepphoris', *NTS* 47, 2001, 127–45.

Chilton, B. D., *GOD in STRENGTH. Jesus' Announcement of the Kingdom* (StNTU B1. Freistadt, 1978. Reprinted Sheffield, 1987).

'A Comparative Study of Synoptic Development: The Dispute between Cain and Abel in the Palestinian Targums and the Beelzebul controversy in the Gospels', *JBL* 101, 1982, 553–62.

The Glory of Israel. The Theology and Provenience of the Isaiah Targum (JSOT.S 23. Sheffield, 1983).

A Galilean Rabbi and His Bible. Jesus' Own Interpretation of Isaiah (London, 1984).

'Jesus and the Repentance of E. P. Sanders', *TynB* 39, 1988, 1–18.

Chilton, B. D. and Evans, C. A. (eds.), *Authenticating the Activities of Jesus* (NTTS 28.2. Leiden, 1999).

Authenticating the Words of Jesus (NTTS 28.1. Leiden, 1999).

Clark, K. W., 'Realized Eschatology', *JBL* 59, 1940, 367–83.

Collins, J. J., 'The Works of the Messiah', *DSD* 1, 1994, 98–112.

Cook, E. M., 'Our Translated Tobit', in K. J. Cathcart and M. Maher, *Targumic and Cognate Studies. Essays in Honour of Martin McNamara* (JSOT.S 230. Sheffield, 1996), pp. 153–62.

Correns, D., 'Die Verzehntung der Raute. Lk xi 42 and M Schebi ix 1', *NT* 6, 1963–4, 110–12.

Cotter, W., 'The Parable of the Children in the Market Place, Q (Luke) 7:31–35: An Examination of the Parable's Image and Significance', *NT* 29, 1987, 289–304.

Creed, J. M., *The Gospel According to St Luke* (London, 1930).

Crossan, J. D., 'Mark and the Relatives of Jesus', *NT* 15, 1973, 81–113.

Dalman, G. H., *Die Worte Jesu*, vol. I: *Einleitung und wichtige Begriffe* (Leipzig, 1898. There was no second volume. 2nd edn, 1930); ET *The Words of Jesus*, vol. I: *Introduction and Fundamental Ideas* (Edinburgh, 1902).

Jesus-Jeschua. Die drei Sprachen Jesu (Leipzig, 1922); ET *Jesus-Jeshua. Studies in the Gospels* (London, 1929).

Davies, S. L., *The Gospel of Thomas and Christian Wisdom* (New York, 1983).

Davies, W. D. and Allison, D. C., *A Critical and Exegetical Commentary on the Gospel according to Saint Matthew* (3 vols., ICC. Edinburgh, 1988–97).

Delobel, J. (ed.), *Logia: Les Paroles de Jésus – The Sayings of Jesus. Mémorial Joseph Coppens* (BEThL 59. Leuven, 1982).

Del Verme, M., 'I "Guai" di Matteo e Luca e le decime dei farisei (Mt 23,23; Lk 11,42)', *Rivista Biblica* 32, 1984, 273–314.

Derrett, J. D. M., *The Anastasis: The Resurrection of Jesus as an Historical Event*, (Shipston-on-Stour, 1982).

'Receptacles and Tombs (Mt 23 24–30)', *ZNW* 77, 1986, 255–66.

Dodd, C. H., ' "The Kingdom of God Has Come" ', *ET* 48, 1936–7, 138–42.

Downing, F. G., *Jesus and the Threat of Freedom* (London, 1987).

'The Social Contexts of Jesus the Teacher: Construction or Reconstruction', *NTS* 33, 1987, 439–51.

Christ and the Cynics: Jesus and other Radical Preachers in First-Century Tradition (Sheffield, 1988).

'Quite like Q: A Genre for "Q": The "Lives" of Cynic Philosophers', *Bib* 69, 1988, 196–225.

Cynics and Christian Origins (Edinburgh, 1992).

'A Genre for Q and a Socio-Cultural Context for Q: Comparing Sets of Similarities with Sets of Differences', *JSNT* 55, 1994, 3–26.

'Word-Processing in the Ancient World: The Social Production and Performance of Q', *JSNT* 64, 1996, 29–48.

'Deeper Reflections on the Jewish Cynic Jesus', *JBL* 117, 1998, 97–104.

Doing Things with Words in the First Christian Century (JSNT.S 200. Sheffield, 2000).

Dunn, J. D. G., 'Matthew 12:28/Luke 11:20 – A Word of Jesus?', in W. H. Gloer (ed.), *Eschatology and the New Testament: Essays in Honour of G. R. Beasley-Murray*, (Peabody, 1988), pp. 29–49.

'The Making of Christology – Evolution or Unfolding?', in J. B. Green and M. Turner (eds.), *Jesus of Nazareth: Lord and Christ: In Honour of Prof. I. H. Marshall* (Carlisle, 1994), pp. 437–52.

Easton, B. S., 'The Beezebul Sections', *JBL* 32, 1913, 57–73.

Ebner, M., *Jesus – Ein Weihseitslehrer?* (sic!) *Synoptische Weisheitslogien im Traditionsprozess* (Freiburg, Basel and Vienna, 1998).

Eddy, P. R., 'Jesus as Diogenes? Reflections on the Cynic Jesus Thesis', *JBL* 115, 1996, 449–69.

Edwards, R. A., *A Theology of Q. Eschatology, Prophecy, and Wisdom* (Philadelphia, 1976).

Ennulat, E., *Die 'Minor Agreements'. Untersuchungen zu einer offenen Frage des synoptischen Problems* (WUNT II.62. Tübingen, 1994).

Evans, C. A., *Jesus & His Contemporaries. Comparative Studies* (Leiden, 1995).

Fallon, F. T. and Cameron, R., 'The Gospel of Thomas: A Forschungsbericht and Analysis', *ANRW* II.25.6 (1988), pp. 4195–4251.

Farrer, A. M., 'On Dispensing with Q', in D. E. Nineham (ed.), *Studies in the Gospels. Essays in Memory of R. H. Lightfoot* (Oxford, 1957), pp. 57–88.

Fieger, M., *Das Thomasevangelium. Einleitung Kommentar und Systematik* (NTA NF 22. Münster, 1991).

Fitzmyer, J. A., 'The Languages of Palestine in the First Century A.D.', *CBQ* 32, 1970, 501–31, revised in *A Wandering Aramean* (SBL.MS 25. Missoula, 1979), pp. 29–56.

The Gospel according to Luke (2 vols., AB 28–28A. New York, 1981–5).

Fleddermann, H. T., *Mark and Q. A Study of the Overlap Texts* (BEThL 122. Leuven, 1995).

Fuchs, A., *Die Entwicklung der Beelzebulkontroverse bei den Synoptikern. Traditionsgeschichtliche und redaktionsgeschichtliche Untersuchung von Mk 3,22–27 und Parallelen, verbunden mit der Rückfrage nach Jesus* (StNTU B5. Linz, 1980).

'Die Sünde wider den Heiligen Geist Mk 3,28–30 par Mt 12,31–37 par Lk 12,10', *StNTSU* 19, 1994, 113–30.

Garland, D. E., *The Intention of Matthew 23* (NT.S 52, 1979).

Gaston, L., 'Beelzebul', *TZ* 18, 1962, 247–55.

Goodacre, M. S., *Goulder and the Gospels. An Examination of a New Paradigm* (JSNT.S 133. Sheffield, 1996).

Goulder, M. D., 'On Putting Q to the Test', *NTS* 24, 1978, 218–34.

    'A House Built on Sand', in A. E. Harvey (ed.), *Alternative Approaches to New Testament Study* (London, 1985), pp. 1–24.

    Luke. A New Paradigm (2 vols., JSNT.S 20. Sheffield, 1989).

    'Is Q a Juggernaut?', *JBL* 115, 1996, 667–81.

    'Self-Contradiction in the IQP', *JBL* 118, 1999, 506–17.

Green, J. B., *The Gospel of Luke* (NICNT. Grand Rapids, 1997).

Guenther, H. O., 'Greek: Home of Primitive Christianity', *Toronto Journal of Theology* 5, 1989, 247–79.

    'The Sayings Gospel Q and the Quest for Aramaic Sources: Rethinking Christian Origins', *Semeia* 55, 1991, 41–76.

Guillaumont, A., 'Les sémitismes dans l'évangile selon Thomas. Essai de classement', in R. van den Broek and M. J. Vermaseren (eds.), *Studies in Gnosticism and Hellenistic Religions presented to Gilles Quispel on the Occasion of his 65th Birthday* (Leiden, 1981), pp. 190–204.

Gundry, R. H., *Matthew. A Commentary on His Literary and Theological Art* (Grand Rapids, 1982).

Haenchen, E., 'Matthäus 23', *ZThK* 48, 1951, 38–63.

Häfner, G., 'Gewalt gegen die Basileia? Zum Problem der Auslegung des "Stürmerspruches" Mt 11,12', *ZNW* 83, 1992, 21–51.

    Der verheißene Vorläufer. Redaktionskritische Untersuchung zur Darstellung Johannes des Täufers im Matthäusevangelium (SBB 27. Stuttgart, 1994).

Hagner, D. A., *Matthew* (2 vols. WBC 33A-B. Dallas, 1993–5).

Harding, G. L., 'Minor Finds' with D. Barthélemy, 'I.13.Phylactère', in D. Barthélemy et al., *Qumrân Cave I* (DJD I. Oxford, 1955) pp. 7, 72–6.

Harnack, A. von, *Sprüche und Reden Jesu. Die Zweite Quelle des Matthäus und Lukas* (Leipzig, 1907); ET *New Testament Studies*, vol. II: *The Sayings of Jesus. The Second Source of St Matthew and St Luke* (London, 1908).

Harvey, A. E., *Jesus and the Constraints of History* (BaL 1980. London, 1982).

Held, M., 'The Root ZBL/SBL in Akkadian, Ugaritic and Biblical Hebrew', *JAOS* 88, 1968, 90–6.

Hengel, M., *Judaism and Hellenism. Studies in Their Encounter in Palestine during the Early Hellenistic Period* (2 vols., 1968. ET from 2nd edn. London, 1974).

    Jews, Greeks and Barbarians. Aspects of the Hellenisation of Judaism in the pre-Christian period (1976. ET London, 1980).

    The 'Hellenization' of Judaea in the First Century after Christ (ET London, 1989).

    The Four Gospels and the One Gospel of Jesus Christ (London, 2000).

Hoffmann, P., *Studien zur Theologie der Logienquelle* (NTA 8. Munster, 1972).

Hollenbach, P. W., 'Jesus, Demoniacs, and Public Authorities: A Socio-Historical Study', *JAAR* 49, 1981, 567–88.

Holtzmann, H. J., *Die synoptischen Evangelien: Ihr Ursprung und geschichtlicher Charakter* (Leipzig, 1863).

Horsley, R. A., 'Logoi Prophētōn?: Reflections on the Genre of Q', in B. Pearson (ed.), *The Future of Early Christianity: Essays in Honor of Helmut Koester* (Minneapolis, 1991), pp. 195–209.

Horsley, R. A. with Draper, J. A., *Whoever Hears You Hears Me. Prophets, Performance and Tradition in Q* (Harrisburg, 1999).

Hughes, J. H., 'John the Baptist: The Forerunner of God Himself', *NT* 14, 1972, 191–218.

Hultgren, A. J., *Jesus and His Adversaries. The Form and Function of the Conflict Stories in the Synoptic Tradition* (Minneapolis, 1979).

Jacobson, A. D., *The First Gospel. An Introduction to Q* (Sonoma, 1992).

Jeremias, J., *Heiligengräber in Jesus Umwelt (Mt.23,39; Lk.11,47): Eine Untersuchung zur Volksreligion der Zeit Jesu* (Göttingen, 1958).

　New Testament Theology, vol. I (London, 1971).

　Die Sprache des Lukasevangeliums: Redaktion und Tradition im Nicht-Markusstoff des dritten Evangeliums (Göttingen, 1980).

Kaufman, S. A., *The Akkadian Influences on Aramaic* (Assyriological Studies 19. Chicago, 1974).

Kee, H. C., ' "Becoming a Child" in the Gospel of Thomas', *JBL* 82, 1963, 307–14.

　'The Terminology of Mark's Exorcism Stories', *NTS* 14, 1967–8, 232–46.

　'Jesus: A Glutton and a Drunkard', *NTS* 42, 1996, pp. 374–93.

Kennard, J. S., 'The Lament over Jerusalem: A Restudy of the Zacharias Passage', *AThR* 29, 1947, 173–9.

Kennedy, J. M., 'The Root G'R in the Light of Semantic Analysis', *JBL* 106, 1987, 47–64.

Kilpatrick, G. D., 'Scribes, Lawyers and Lucan Origins', *JThS* 1, 1950, 56–60.

Kirk, A., *The Composition of the Sayings Source. Genre, Synchrony and Wisdom Redaction in Q* (NT.S 91. Leiden, 1998).

　'Upbraiding Wisdom: John's Speech and the Beginning of Q (Q 3:7–9, 16–17), *NT* 40, 1998, 1–16.

　'Crossing the Boundary: Liminality and Transformative Wisdom in Q', *NTS* 45, 1999, 1–18.

Kloppenborg, J. S., *The Formation of Q. Trajectories in Ancient Wisdom Collections* (Philadelphia, 1987).

　'Nomos and Ethos in Q', in J. E. Goehring, J. T. Sanders and C. W. Hedrick (eds.), *Gospel Origins and Christian Beginnings: In Honor of James M. Robinson* (Sonoma, CA, 1990), pp. 35–48.

　'The Sayings Gospel Q: Recent Opinion on the People behind the Document', *Currents in Research: Biblical Studies* 1, 1993, 9–34.

　'The Sayings Gospel Q and the Quest of the Historical Jesus', *HThR* 89, 1996, 307–44.

Kloppenborg, J. S. (ed.), *The Shape of Q. Signal Essays on the Sayings Gospel* (Minneapolis, 1994).

　Conflict and Invention: Literary, Rhetorical and Social Studies on the Sayings Gospel Q (Valley Forge, 1995).

Kloppenborg, J. S. and Vaage, L. E. (eds.), *Early Christianity, Q and Jesus (Semeia* 55. Atlanta, 1992).

Kloppenborg Verbin, J. S., *Excavating Q. The History and Setting of the Sayings Gospel* (Minneapolis and Edinburgh, 2000).

　'A Dog among the Pigeons: The "Cynic Hypothesis" as a Theological Problem', in J. M. Asgeirsson, K. de Troyer and M. W. Meyer (eds.), *From Quest to Q. Festschrift James M. Robinson* (BEThL 146. Leuven, 2000), pp. 73–117.

Koester, H., *Ancient Christian Gospels. Their History and Development* (London and Philadelphia, 1990).

'Q and Its Relatives', in J. E. Goehring, J. T. Sanders and C. W. Hedrick (eds.), *Gospel Origins and Christian Beginnings: In Honor of James M. Robinson* (Sonoma, CA, 1990), pp. 49–63.

Kosch, D., *Die eschatologische Tora des Menschensohnes. Untersuchungen zur Rezeption des Stellung Jesu zur Tora in Q* (NTOA 12. Freiburg and Göttingen, 1989).

'Q und Jesus', *BZ* 36, 1992, 30–58.

Kruse, H., 'Das Reich Satans', *Bib* 58, 1977, 29–61.

Kuhn, K. G., *Phylakterien aus Höhle 4 von Qumran* (AHAW.PH Heidelberg, 1957).

Kümmel, W. G., *Verheißung und Erfüllung* (AThANT 6. Basel, 1945. 2nd edn, Zurich, 1953); ET *Promise and Fulfilment* (SBT 23. London, 1957).

Jesu Antwort an Johannes den Täufer: Ein Beispiel zum Methodenproblem in der Jesusforschung (Wiesbaden, 1974).

Lachs, S. T., 'On Matthew 23:27–28', *HThR* 68, 1975, 385–8.

Lambrecht, J., 'The Relatives of Jesus in Mark', *NT* 16, 1974, 241–58.

Laufen, R., *Die Doppelüberlieferungen der Logienquelle und des Markusevangeliums* (BBB 54. Bonn, 1980).

Layton, B., *Nag Hammadi Codex II,2–7 together with XIII,2, Brit. Lib. Or. 4926(1), and P.Oxy.1, 654, 655*, vol. I (Nag Hammadi Studies 20. Leiden, 1989).

Leaney, A. R. C., 'ΝΟΜΙΚΟΣ in St Luke's Gospel', *JThS* 2, 1951, 166–7.

Légasse, S., 'L' "homme fort" de Luc xi 21–22', *NT* 5, 1962, 5–9.

Linton, O., 'The Q-Problem Reconsidered', in D. E. Aune (ed.), *Studies in New Testament and Early Christian Literature. Essays in Honor of A. P. Wikgren* (NT.S 33. Leiden, 1972), pp. 43–59.

'The Parable of the Children's Game', *NTS* 22, 1975–6, 159–79.

'Das *Dilemma* der synoptischen Forschung', *ThLZ* 101, 1976, 881–92.

Llewelyn, S., 'The *Traditionsgeschichte* of Matt. 11:12–13, par. Luke 16:16', *NT* 36, 1994, 330–49.

Loader, W. R. G., *Jesus' Attitude towards the Law* (WUNT II.97. Tübingen, 1997).

Lövestam, E., *Jesus and 'This Generation'. A New Testament Study* (CB.NT 25. Stockholm, 1995).

Löw, I., *Aramäische Pflanzennamen* (Leipzig, 1881).

Die Flora der Juden (4 vols., Berlin and Vienna, 1924–34).

Lührmann, D., *Die Redaktion der Logienquelle* (WMANT 33. Neukirchen-Vluyn, 1969).

'The Gospel of Mark and the Sayings Collection Q', *JBL* 108, 1989, 51–71.

Luz, U., *Das Evangelium nach Matthäus* (2 vols. so far, EKK 1,1–2. Zurich and Neukirchen-Vluyn, 1985–, 3rd edn, 1992–); ET of vol. I, *Matthew 1–7* (Minneapolis, 1989).

Maccoby, H., 'The Washing of Cups', *JSNT* 14, 1982, 3–15.

McCol, A. J. with Dungan, D. L. and Peabody, D. B. (eds.), *Beyond the Q Impasse. Luke's Use of Matthew* (Valley Forge, 1996).

Mack, B. L., *The Lost Gospel. The Book of Q and Christian Origins* (Rockport, 1993).

Mack, B. L. and Robbins, V. K., *Patterns of Persuasion in the Gospels* (Sonoma, 1989).

Maclauren, E. C. B., 'Beelzeboul', *NT* 20, 1978, 156–60.

McNeile, A. H., *The Gospel of Matthew* (London, 1915).

Malina, B. J. and Rohrbaugh, R. L., *Social-Science Commentary on the Synoptic Gospels* (Minneapolis, 1992).

Manson, T. W., *The Teaching of Jesus* (Cambridge, 1931; 2nd edn, 1935).

'Some Outstanding New Testament Problems. XII. The Problem of Aramaic Sources in the Gospels', *ET* 47, 1935–6, 7–11.

The Sayings of Jesus (1937, as Part II of *The Mission and Message of Jesus*, ed. H. D. A. Major et al. Reprinted separately, London, 1949).

Marshall, I. H., *The Gospel of Luke: A Commentary on the Greek Text* (NIGTC. Exeter, 1978).

Marshall, J. T., 'The Aramaic Gospel', *Expositor*, 4th series, 3, 1891, 1–17, 109–24, 275–91.

Mason, S., 'Pharisaic Dominance Before 70 CE and the Gospels' Hypocrisy Charge (Matt 23:2–3)', *HThR* 83, 1990, 363–83.

Mattila, S. L., 'A Problem Still Clouded: Yet Again – Statistics and "Q"', *NT* 36, 1994, 313–29.

'A Question Too Often Neglected', *NTS* 41, 1995, 199–217.

Meier, J. P., *A Marginal Jew. Rethinking the Historical Jesus* (2 vols. so far. ABRL. New York, 1991–4).

Metzger, B. M., *A Textual Commentary on the Greek New Testament* (3rd edn, Swindon, 1971).

Meyer, A., *Jesu Muttersprache. Das galiläische Aramäisch in seiner Bedeutung für die Erklärung der Reden Jesu und der Evangelien überhaupt* (Freiburg i.B. and Leipzig, 1896).

Meyer, M. W., 'Making Mary Male: The Categories "Male" and "Female" in the Gospel of Thomas', *NTS* 31, 1985, 554–70.

Milik, J. T., 'Introduction', and 'Phylactères A-U (**128–48**)', in R. de Vaux and J. T. Milik, *Qumrân Grotte 4.II* (DJD VI. Oxford, 1977), pp. 34–79.

Millard, A., *Reading and Writing in the Time of Jesus* (Sheffield, 2000).

Miller, R. J., 'The Inside Is (Not) the Outside. Q 11:39–41 and GThom 89', *Forum* 5, 1989, 92–105.

Moore, W. E., 'ΒΙΑΖω, ΆΡΠΑΖω and Cognates in Josephus', *NTS* 21, 1974–5, 519–43.

Mussner, F., 'Der nicht erkannte Kairos (Mt 11.16–19 = Lc 7.31–5)', *Bib* 40, 1959, 599–612.

Navia, L. E., *Classical Cynicism. A Critical Study* (Westport, CT, 1996).

Neirynck, F., 'Mt 12,25a/Lc 11,17a et la rédaction des évangiles', *EThL* 62, 1986, 122–33.

'ΤΙΣ ΕΣΤΙΝ Ο ΠΑΙΣΑΣ ΣΕ Mt 26,68/Lk 22,64 (diff. Mk 14,64)', *EThL* 63, 1987, 5–47.

Neusner, J., '"First Cleanse the Inside." The "Halakhic" Background of a Controversy-Saying', *NTS* 22, 1975–6, 486–95.

Newport, K. G. C., *The Sources and Sitz im Leben of Matthew 23* (JSNT.S 117. Sheffield, 1995).

Nolland, J., *Luke* (3 vols. WBC 35A-C. Dallas, 1989–93).

Oakman, D. E., 'Rulers' Houses, Thieves and Usurpers. The Beelzebul Pericope', *Forum* 4.3, 1988, 109–23.

O'Neill, J. C., 'The Unforgivable Sin', *JSNT* 19, 1983, 37–42.

Page, S. H. T., *Powers of Evil. A Biblical Study of Satan and Demons* (Leicester and Grand Rapids, 1995).

Painter, J., 'When Is a House Not Home? Disciples and Family in Mark 3.13–35', *NTS* 45, 1999, 498–513.

Patterson, S. J., 'The Gospel of Thomas and the Synoptic Tradition: A Forschungs-bericht and Critique', *Forum* 8, 1992, 45–98.

    The Gospel of Thomas and Jesus (Sonoma, 1993).

Penney, D. L. and Wise, M. O., 'By the Power of Beelzebub: An Aramaic Incan-tation Formula from Qumran (4Q560)', *JBL* 113, 1994, 627–50.

Petersen, W. L., *Tatian's Diatessaron. Its Creation, Dissemination, Significance and History in Scholarship* (*VigChr.S* XXV. Leiden, 1994).

    'Textual Evidence of Tatian's Dependence upon Justin's ΑΠΟΜΝΗΜΟΝΕΥ-ΜΑΤΑ', *NTS* 36, 1990, 512–34.

Petersen, W. L., Vos, J. S. and De Jonge, H. J., *Sayings of Jesus: Canonical and Non-Canonical. Essays in Honour of Tjitze Baarda* (NT.S 89. Leiden, 1997).

Petrie, S., ' "Q" Is Only What You Make It', *NT* 3, 1959, 28–33.

Piper, R. A., *Wisdom in the Q-Tradition. The Aphoristic Teaching of Jesus* (SNTS.MS 61. Cambridge, 1989).

Piper, R. A. (ed.), *The Gospel Behind the Gospels. Current Studies on Q* (NT.S 75. Leiden, 1995).

Polag, A., *Die Christologie der Logienquelle* (WMANT 45. Neukirchen-Vluyn, 1977).

Potterie, I. de la (ed.), *De Jésus aux évangiles. Tradition et rédaction dans les évangiles synoptiques* (BEThL 24. Gembloux and Paris, 1967).

Puech, E., 'Une Apocalypse messianique (4Q521)', *RQ* 15, 1992, 475–519.

Quispel, G., 'The Gospel of Thomas and the New Testament', *VigChr* 11, 1957, 189–207.

Rahmani, L. Y., 'Jewish Rock-Cut Tombs in Jerusalem', *'Atiqot* 3, 1961, 93–120.

Robbins, V. K., 'Beelzebul Controversy in Mark and Luke. Rhetorical and Social Analysis', *Forum* 7, 1991, 261–77.

Roberts, C. H. and Skeat, T. C., *The Birth of the Codex* (London, 1987).

Robinson, J. M., 'ΛΟΓΟΙ ΣΟΦΟΝ: Zur Gattung der Spruchquelle Q', in E. Dinkler (ed.), *Zeit und Geschichte. Dankesgabe an Rudolf Bultmann zum 80. Geburtstag* (Tübingen, 1964), pp. 77–96; revised ET '*LOGOI SOPHON*: On the Gattung of Q', in J. M. Robinson and H. Koester (eds.), *Trajecto-ries through Early Christianity* (Philadelphia, 1971), pp. 71–113, and in J. M. Robinson (ed.), *The Future of Our Religious Past: Essays in Honour of Rudolf Bultmann* (London, 1971), pp. 84–130.

    'On Bridging the Gulf from Q to the Gospel of Thomas (or vice versa)', in C. W. Hedrick and R. Hodgson Jr. (eds.), *Nag Hammadi, Gnosticism and Early Christianity* (Peabody MA, 1986), pp. 127–75.

Robinson, J. M., Hoffmann P. and Kloppenborg, J. S. (eds.), *Documenta Q. Reconstructions of Q through Two Centuries of Gospel Research Excerpted, Sorted and Evaluated. The Database of the International Q Project* (several vols. Leuven, 1996–).

The Critical Edition of Q. Synopsis, including the Gospels of Matthew and Luke, Mark and Thomas, with English, German and French Translations of Q and Thomas (Leuven, 2000).

Ross, J. M., 'Which Zechariah?', *IBS* 9, 1987, 70–3.

Sanday, W. (ed.), *Studies in the Synoptic Problem by Members of the University of Oxford* (Oxford, 1911).

Sanders, E. P., 'Jesus and the Sinners', *JSNT* 19, 1983, 5–36.

Jesus and Judaism (London, 1985).

Judaism: Practice and Belief 63 BCE–66CE (London and Philadelphia, 1992).

Sato, M., *Q und Prophetie. Studien zur Gattungs- und Traditionsgeschichte der Quelle Q* (WUNT II.29. Tübingen, 1988).

Schenk, W., 'Der Einfluß der Logienquelle auf das Markusevangelium', *ZNW* 70, 1979, 141–65.

Schnackenburg, R., *Gottes Herrschaft und Reich* (Herder, 1963); ET *God's Rule and Kingdom* (2nd end, London and New York, 1968).

Schrage, W., *Das Verhältnis des Thomas-Evangeliums zur synoptischen Tradition and zu den koptischen Evangelienübersetzungen* (BZNW 29. Berlin, 1964).

Schröter, J., *Erinnerung an Jesus Worte. Studien zur Rezeption der Logienüberlieferung in Markus, Q und Thomas* (WMANT 76. Neukirchen-Vluyn, 1997).

Schüling, J., *Studien zum Verhältnis von Logienquelle und Markusevangelium* (FB 65. Würzburg, 1991).

Schulz, S., *Q: Die Spruchquelle der Evangelisten* (Zurich, 1972).

Schürmann, H., *Das Lukasevangelium* (2 vols. so far, HTKNT 3/1–2. Freiburg/Basel/Wien, 1969–94).

'Die Redekomposition wider "dieses Geschlecht" und seine Führung in der Redenquelle (vgl. Mt 23,1–39 par Lk 11,37–54): Bestand-Akolouthie-Kompositionsformen', *StNTU* 11, 1986, 33–81.

Schwarz, G., '"Unkenntliche Gräber" (Lukas XI.44)', *NTS* 23, 1976–7, 345–6.

'Und Jesus sprach'. Untersuchungen zur aramäischen Urgestalt der Worte Jesu (BWANT 118 = VI,18. Stuttgart, 1985; 2nd edn, 1987).

Seeley, D., 'Jesus and the Cynics Revisited', *JBL* 116, 1997, 704–12.

Sevenich-Bax, E., *Israels Konfrontation mit den letzten Boten der Weisheit. Form, Funktion und Interdependenz der Weisheitselemente in der Logienquelle* (MThA 21. Altenberge, 1993).

Shirock, R., 'Whose Exorcists Are They?: The Referents of οἱ υἱοὶ ὑμῶν at Matthew 12.27/Luke 11.19', *JSNT* 46, 1992, 41–51.

Simons, E., *Hat der dritte Evangelist den kanonischen Matthäus benutzt?* (Bonn, 1880).

Steck, O. H., *Israel und das gewaltsame Geschick der Propheten* (WMANT 23. Neukirchen, 1967).

Steele, E. S., 'Luke 11:37–54 – A Modified Hellenistic Symposium', *JBL* 103, 1984, 379–94.

Stendahl, K., *The School of St Matthew and Its Use of the Old Testament* (Lund, 1954).

Streeter, B. H., 'On the Original Order of Q', in Sanday (ed.), *Studies in the Synoptic Problem* (1911), pp. 141–64.

'St Mark's Knowledge and Use of Q', in Sanday (ed.), *Studies*, pp. 165–83.

'The Original Extent of Q', in Sanday (ed.), *Studies*, pp. 185–208.

The Four Gospels. A Study of Origins (London, 1924).

Stuckenbruck, L. T., 'An Approach to the New Testament through Aramaic Sources: The Recent Methodological Dabate', *JSP* 8, 1994, 3–29.

Syx, R., 'Jesus and the Unclean Spirit. The Literary Relation between Mark and Q in the Beelzebul Controversy (Mark 3:20–30 Par)', *Louvain Studies* 17, 1992, 166–80.

Taylor, V., 'The Order of Q', *JThS* NS 4, 1953, 27–31.

'The Original Order of Q', in A. J. B. Higgins (ed.), *New Testament Essays: Studies in Memory of T. W. Manson* (Manchester, 1959), pp. 246–69.

Theissen, G., 'Wanderradikalismus: Literatursoziologische Aspekte der Überlieferung von Worten Jesu im Urchristentum', *ZThK* 70, 1973, 245–71.

The Gospels in Context. Social and Political History in the Synoptic Tradition (1991. ET Edinburgh, 1992).

Thompson, R. C., *A Dictionary of Assyrian Botany* (London, 1949).

Tigay, J. H., 'On the Term Phylacteries (Matt 23:5)', *HThR* 72, 1979, 45–52.

Tödt, H. E., *Der Menschensohn in der synoptischen Überlieferung* (Gütersloh, 1959); ET *The Son of Man in the Synoptic Tradition* (London, 1965).

Tristram, H. B., *The Natural History of the Bible* (London, 1867; 10th edn, 1911).

Tuckett, C. M., *The Revival of the Griesbach Hypothesis* (SNTS.MS 44. Cambridge, 1983).

Nag Hammadi and the Gospel Tradition. Synoptic Tradition in the Nag Hammadi Library (Edinburgh, 1986).

'Thomas and the Synoptics', *NT* 30, 1988, 132–57.

'A Cynic Q?', *Bib* 10, 1989, 349–76.

'Q and Thomas: Evidence of a Primitive "Wisdom Gospel"?', *EThL* 67, 1991, 346–60.

Q and the History of Early Christianity (Edinburgh, 1996).

Turner, J. D. and McGuire, A. (eds.), *The Nag Hammadi Library after Fifty Years. Proceedings of the 1995 Society of Biblical Literature Commemoration* (Leiden, 1997).

Twelftree, G. H., *Jesus the Exorcist* (WUNT II.54. Tübingen, 1993).

Uro, R. (ed.), *Symbols and Strata. Essays on the Sayings Gospel Q* (Publications of the Finnish Exegetical Society 65. Helsinki and Göttingen, 1996).

Vaage, L. E., *Galilean Upstarts. Jesus' First Followers According to Q* (Valley Forge, 1994).

Valantasis, R., *The Gospel of Thomas* (London, 1997).

Van der Loos, H. *The Miracles of Jesus* (NT.S 9. Leiden, 1965).

Vassiliadis, P., ΛΟΓΟΙ ΊΗΣΟΥ: *Studies in Q* (Atlanta, 1999).

'The Nature and Extent of the Q-Document', *NT* 20, 1978, 49–73.

Vermes, G., 'Pre-Mishnaic Jewish Worship and the Phylacteries from the Dead Sea', *VT* 9, 1959, 65–72.

'The Use of בר נש/בר נשא in Jewish Aramaic', App. E in Black, *Aramaic Approach* (3rd edn, 1967), pp. 310–28; reprinted in G. Vermes, *Post-Biblical Jewish Studies* (Leiden, 1975), pp. 147–65.

Jesus the Jew (London, 1973).

'The Present State of the "Son of Man" Debate', *JJS* 29, 1978, 123–34.

'The "Son of Man" Debate', *JSNT* 1, 1978, 19–32.

Verseput, D., *The Rejection of the Humble Messianic King. A Study of the Composition of Matthew 11–12* (Frankfurt am Main, 1986).

Walker, W. O., 'Jesus and the Tax Collectors', *JBL* 97, 1978, 221–38.

Wall, R. W., ' "The Finger of God": Deuteronomy 9.10 and Luke 11.20', *NTS* 33, 1987, 144–50.

Wansbrough, H., 'Mark iii.21 – Was Jesus Out of His Mind?', *NTS* 18, 1971–2, 233–5.

Weiß, J., 'Die Verteidigung Jesus gegen den Vorwurf des Bündnisses mit Beelzebul', *Theologische Studien und Kritiken* 63, 1890, 555–69.

Die Predigt Jesu vom Reiche Gottes (Göttingen, 1892; 2nd edn, 1897); ET *Jesus' Proclamation of the Kingdom of God* (with critical and historical introduction by R. H. Hiers and L. Holland. London and Philadelphia, 1971).

Wellhausen, J., *Das Evangelium Matthaei* (Berlin, 1904).

Einleitung in die drei ersten Evangelien (2nd edn, Berlin, 1911).

Wenham, D., 'The Meaning of Mark iii.21', *NTS* 21, 1974–5, 295–300.

Wernle, P., *Die synoptische Frage* (Freiburg i. B., Leipzig and Tübingen, 1899).

Williams, J. G., 'Parable and Chreia: from Q to Narrative Gospel', *Semeia* 43, 1988, 85–144.

Yadin, Y., *Tefillin from Qumran (X Q Phyl 1–4)* (Jerusalem, 1969).

Yadin, Y. (ed.), *Jerusalem Revealed: Archaeology in the Holy City 1968–74* (Jerusalem, 1975).

Yardeni, A., 'New Jewish Aramaic Ostraca', *IEJ* 40, 1990, 130–52.

Zeller, D., 'Die Bildlogik des Gleichnisses Mt 11:16f/Lk 7:31f', *ZNW* 68, 1977, 252–7.

Kommentar zur Logienquelle (Stuttgart, 1984).

Zimmermann, F., *The Aramaic Origin of the Four Gospels* (New York, 1979).

Zohary, M., *Plants of the Bible* (Cambridge, 1982).

INDEX OF PASSAGES DISCUSSED

The Hebrew bible

Genesis
4.10   100
Exodus
8.15   167
13.9   84
13.16   85–6
23.20   118–21
Leviticus
11.4   76
11.10   77
11.20   76
11.44   77
11.46   77
19.29   140
21.9   140
27.30   72
Numbers
15.37–9   84
Deuteronomy
6.8   84–6
11.18   84–6
14.19   76
14.22–6   79
14.23   72
21.20   136
22.6–7   74
22.12   84
23.17–18   140
1 Kings
8.13   159
2 Chronicles
24.20–2   100
Isaiah
8.14–15   114
29.18–19   112
35.5–6   112
61.1   112
63.15   159–60
Jeremiah

17.21–2   68, 69, 146
Malachi
3.1   118–21, 127, 129
3.23–4   118–21, 127, 129
Psalms
47.3   168
Daniel
4.31   168
7.13–14   13

Other Jewish sources

As. Mos. 7.3–10   78
Babylonian Talmud
 B. Qam. 69a   90
 Ḥag. 12b   159–60
 Shebu. 20b   73
Tefillin   85, 87
CD XII.11–13   76–7
1 En. 22.5–7   100
Exod. Rab. X.7   167
Gen. Rab. LXXIX.6   134
Josephus
 A.J.
  IV.213   86
  IX.168–9   100
  XVIII.116–19   108
 B.J.
  II.123   91
  IV.334–44   102
Jub. 50.6–13   67
Lev. Rab. 34.7   23
1 Macc. *2.29–41*   67, 68
Mishnah
 Dem.
  2.1   72
  2.3   94
 Kel. 25.6   77–8
 Maas.
  1.1   72–3
  4.5   72

Maas. Sh. 5.1   89–90
Sheq. 1.1   89
Shebu. 9.1   73
1QapGen XXI.13   134
1QM XII.1–2   159
1QM XIII.2   159
1QM XIII.10   159
4Q246   169
4Q405   169
4Q510   163
4Q521   113
Tg. Isa.
  41.10–13   126
  56.1–2   126
Tg. Lam. 2.20   101
Tosephta
  Men.
    13.21   78–9
    13.22   73

Canonical Gospels

Matthew
3.7–10   30–1
3.11–12   30–1, 108–9
4.12–17   108
5.46   11
6.2   58
6.3   59–60
6.12   55
6.19–20   11–12
6.33   30
8.5–10   16
8.19–20   31
8.20   61, 62
9.32–3   149, 156
9.34   156
10.25   159
10.32–3   179
10.39   25
11.2–3   107–11
11.2–19   105–45
11.4–6   111–14
11.7–9   39–40
11.7–10   115–21
11.11   121–3
11.12–13   125–8
11.14   125, 129
11.15   125, 129
11.16   18
11.16–19   129–44
11.21–4   102
12.22–4   158–61
12.22–32   146–84

12.25–6   161–2, 163–4
12.27   164–7, 169–70
12.28   167–73
12.29   173–6
12.30   176–7
12.31–2   177–82
12.32   20
21.31–2   140–1
21.32   95,
23.5–7   83–9
23.23   20–1, 24, 56–7, 72–6
23.23–4   39
23.23–36   64–104
23.24   76–7
23.25–6   77–83
23.26   10, 23, 38
23.27   89–92
23.28   92
23.29–31   92–8
23.32–3   92, 98
23.34–6   98–103
26.68   14–15, 16, 26–7
26.75   14–15, 16, 27–9
Mark
1.6   117
1.7–8   30–1, 108–10
1.14–15   108
1.23–7   146
1.24   152
[1.32   68, 146
1.34   146
1.40   152
2.16   132, 141–2
2.23–8   68, 95
3.1–6   68–9, 95
3.11–12   152
3.14–15   146, 152
3.20–1   150–5
3.20–30   146–84
3.22   158–61
3.23–6   161–4
3.27   173–5
3.28–30   177–82
3.31–5   151, 154, 155
5.22–4   112
5.35–43   112
6.1–6   152
6.7   146–7
6.13   146–7
6.18   109
7.3   59
9.11–13   95
9.29   175
9.38   147

9.40   176
10.35–45   96
11.18   96
11.27–33   95
11.31–2   109
12.1–12   96
14.36   54
14.65   14, 26–7
14.72   27–8
Luke
3.16–17   30–1, 108–10
6.32–3   11
7.18–19   107–11
7.18–35   105–45
7.20–1   111
7.22–3   111–15
7.24–6   39–40
7.24–7   115–21
7.28   121–4
7.29–30   124–5
7.31   18
7.31–4   129–44
9.57–8   31
9.58   14
10.12–15   102
10.18   147
11.14–15   155–8
11.14–23   146–84
11.16   158
11.17–18   161–2, 163–4
11.19   164–7, 169–70
11.20   167–23
11.21–2   173–6
11.23   176–7
11.37–8   71
11.39–40   37–8
11.39–41   77–83
11.39–51   64–104
11.41   10, 20, 23, 38, 46

11.42   24, 39, 46, 56–7, 72–6
11.43   83, 88–9
11.44   89, 92
11.45   71
11.47–8   92–8
11.49–51   18, 98–103
12.8–9   13–14
12.10   20
12.31   29–30
12.33   11–12
12.50   96
13.16   68
13.31-3   95
15.30   166
16.16   125–8
17.33   25
22.48   25–6, 189
22.62   14–15, 16, 27–9
22.64   14–15, 16, 26–7
24.19   184
John
1.1–14   59
5.2–18   69
6.50   58–9
8.17   166

Gospel of Thomas

9   36–7
35   176
44   181–2
46   123–4
53   35–6
77   34, 35
78   117–18
89   34, 35
90   33–4
114   34–5

INDEX OF NAMES AND SUBJECTS

Allison, C. Dale 44–5, 113
apocalyptic 13–14, 29–30
Aramaic *passim*, esp. 51–63

Barrett, C. K. 9, 12, 189
Betz, H. D. 38–9, 50
Black, M. 9–12, 21, 24, 36, 43, 49, 74
Burney, C. F. 6–8, 9, 58–9
Bussmann, W. 8

Catchpole, D. 44–5
Chilton, B. D. 60, 126
chreia 31, 43
Cynics 1, 32, 38–42, 49–50, 185

Davies, S. L. 32–5
devil 133, 136, 138, 147–63, 156–7,
    158–67, 172, 174–8, 182, 183–4,
    188
Draper, J. A. 47
Dunn, J. D. G. 69–70

Elijah 40, 95, 113, 118–21, 129, 145, 187
eschatology 13–14, 29–30, 44, 98–103,
    108–11, 112–13, 118–29, 145,
    167–73, 179, 186
exorcism 127, 136, 146–84

Farrer, A. M. 12, 21, 47
Fleddermann, H. T. 173–4

Galilee 41–2, 49, 56, 108, 117, 141
Gnosticism 32–5, 117–18, 123–4
Goulder, M. 21–2, 45–7
Guenther, H. O. 42–4

Harnack, A. von 4, 9
healing 67–9, 111–13, 127, 146, 152
    see also exorcism
Hebrew 24, 52–3, 74, 136, 138–9,
    159–61

Holtzmann, H. J. 2–3
Horsley, R. A. 47

Jeremias, J. 40, 42, 113, 131–2, 138, 142
Jesus of Nazareth *passim*
    family of 150–3, 188
    see also eschatology, exorcism, healing,
        kingdom of God, prophecy, sinners,
        Son of man
John the Baptist 8, 17, 18, 30–1, 96–8,
    102, 105–45, 187

kingdom of God 29–30, 34–5, 95, 102,
    113–14, 122–4, 125–8, 140, 161–72,
    187–8
Kloppenborg, J. S. 13, 15, 21, 22–32, 42,
    47, 49–50, 74
Koester, H. 37–8, 42

Law, *see* Torah
Lührmann, D. 17–19

Manson, T. W. 9–10, 91, 176
Meyer, A. 3, 10, 20, 42
Millard, A. 48–9

orthodoxy, Jewish 64–104, esp. 65–70,
    132, 136–8, 140, 141–2, 143, 157–8,
    160, 186–7, 190

Painter, J. 154–5
Pharisees 37–8, 53, 56–7, 64–104, 125,
    132, 136–8, 140, 141–2, 157–8, 160,
    177
phylacteries 83–7
prophecy 20, 29–30, 70, 92–103,
    105–45, 160, 184, 184, 186,
    187
prostitutes 95, 140–1
purity 23–4, 71, 76–83, 89–92, 137–42,
    186

Q *passim*
  language of *passim*
  model of 1–50, 103, 143–5, 147, 183,
    185, 186–90
  passion narrative 1, 14–15, 22, 25–9,
    31–2, 40–1, 45, 189
  see also apocalyptic, Cynics,
    eschatology, Galilee
Quispel, G. 36–7

redaction criticism 17–21, 154–5
Robinson, J. M. 15–17, 22, 35, 50

sabbath 66–9, 141, 146
Sanders, E. P. 137–42
Satan, *see* devil
Schulz, S. 17, 19–21
Schwarz, G. 42, 58, 59–60
sinners 137–42
Son of man 13–15, 22, 42, 43–4, 55, 60–1,
    62, 133–5, 142, 177–82
Streeter, B. H. 4–6, 9

tax-collectors 95, 136–7, 139–41
Taylor, V. 12–13, 189

tefillin 83–7
textual variants 11, 26–7, 28–9, 81,
    116–17, 123, 150, 154, 158, 164,
    176–7, 181
tithing 24, 39, 57, 72–6, 78–80, 186
Thomas, Gospel of 32–8
  see also Index of passages discussed
Tödt, H. E. 13–15
Torah 20–1, 30, 36, 38, 53, 64–104,
    136–42, 186–7
  see also orthodoxy, Pharisees, purity,
    sabbath, *tefillin*, tithing
Torrey, C. C. 59
translation *passim*
transliteration 141, 156, 158
Tuckett, C. M. 13, 17, 22, 38–9, 44–5, 50

Vaage, L. 38–41, 42, 50

Wellhausen, J. 3–4, 10, 20, 23–4, 36, 49,
    82, 142
wisdom 16–17, 29–30, 33–4, 98–9, 142–4

Zechariah 93, 100–2
Zimmerman, F. 43, 59